Mometrix
TEST PREPARATION

FTCE

Physics 6-12 Secrets Study Guide

Dear Future Exam Success Story

First of all, **THANK YOU** for purchasing Mometrix study materials!

Second, congratulations! You are one of the few determined test-takers who are committed to doing whatever it takes to excel on your exam. **You have come to the right place.** We developed these study materials with one goal in mind: to deliver you the information you need in a format that's concise and easy to use.

In addition to optimizing your guide for the content of the test, we've outlined our recommended steps for breaking down the preparation process into small, attainable goals so you can make sure you stay on track.

We've also analyzed the entire test-taking process, identifying the most common pitfalls and showing how you can overcome them and be ready for any curveball the test throws you.

Standardized testing is one of the biggest obstacles on your road to success, which only increases the importance of doing well in the high-pressure, high-stakes environment of test day. Your results on this test could have a significant impact on your future, and this guide provides the information and practical advice to help you achieve your full potential on test day.

Your success is our success

We would love to hear from you! If you would like to share the story of your exam success or if you have any questions or comments in regard to our products, please contact us at **800-673-8175** or **support@mometrix.com**.

Thanks again for your business and we wish you continued success!

Sincerely,
The Mometrix Test Preparation Team

TABLE OF CONTENTS

Introduction

Thank you for purchasing this resource! You have made the choice to prepare yourself for a test that could have a huge impact on your future, and this guide is designed to help you be fully ready for test day. Obviously, it's important to have a solid understanding of the test material, but you also need to be prepared for the unique environment and stressors of the test, so that you can perform to the best of your abilities.

For this purpose, the first section that appears in this guide is the **Secret Keys**. We've devoted countless hours to meticulously researching what works and what doesn't, and we've boiled down our findings to the five most impactful steps you can take to improve your performance on the test. We start at the beginning with study planning and move through the preparation process, all the way to the testing strategies that will help you get the most out of what you know when you're finally sitting in front of the test.

We recommend that you start preparing for your test as far in advance as possible. However, if you've bought this guide as a last-minute study resource and only have a few days before your test, we recommend that you skip over the first two Secret Keys since they address a long-term study plan.

If you struggle with **test anxiety**, we strongly encourage you to check out our recommendations for how you can overcome it. Test anxiety is a formidable foe, but it can be beaten, and we want to make sure you have the tools you need to defeat it.

Secret Key #1 – Plan Big, Study Small

There's a lot riding on your performance. If you want to ace this test, you're going to need to keep your skills sharp and the material fresh in your mind. You need a plan that lets you review everything you need to know while still fitting in your schedule. We'll break this strategy down into three categories.

Information Organization

Start with the information you already have: the official test outline. From this, you can make a complete list of all the concepts you need to cover before the test. Organize these concepts into groups that can be studied together, and create a list of any related vocabulary you need to learn so you can brush up on any difficult terms. You'll want to keep this vocabulary list handy once you actually start studying since you may need to add to it along the way.

Time Management

Once you have your set of study concepts, decide how to spread them out over the time you have left before the test. Break your study plan into small, clear goals so you have a manageable task for each day and know exactly what you're doing. Then just focus on one small step at a time. When you manage your time this way, you don't need to spend hours at a time studying. Studying a small block of content for a short period each day helps you retain information better and avoid stressing over how much you have left to do. You can relax knowing that you have a plan to cover everything in time. In order for this strategy to be effective though, you have to start studying early and stick to your schedule. Avoid the exhaustion and futility that comes from last-minute cramming!

Study Environment

The environment you study in has a big impact on your learning. Studying in a coffee shop, while probably more enjoyable, is not likely to be as fruitful as studying in a quiet room. It's important to keep distractions to a minimum. You're only planning to study for a short block of time, so make the most of it. Don't pause to check your phone or get up to find a snack. It's also important to **avoid multitasking**. Research has consistently shown that multitasking will make your studying dramatically less effective. Your study area should also be comfortable and well-lit so you don't have the distraction of straining your eyes or sitting on an uncomfortable chair.

The time of day you study is also important. You want to be rested and alert. Don't wait until just before bedtime. Study when you'll be most likely to comprehend and remember. Even better, if you know what time of day your test will be, set that time aside for study. That way your brain will be used to working on that subject at that specific time and you'll have a better chance of recalling information.

Finally, it can be helpful to team up with others who are studying for the same test. Your actual studying should be done in as isolated an environment as possible, but the work of organizing the information and setting up the study plan can be divided up. In between study sessions, you can discuss with your teammates the concepts that you're all studying and quiz each other on the details. Just be sure that your teammates are as serious about the test as you are. If you find that your study time is being replaced with social time, you might need to find a new team.

Secret Key #2 – Make Your Studying Count

You're devoting a lot of time and effort to preparing for this test, so you want to be absolutely certain it will pay off. This means doing more than just reading the content and hoping you can remember it on test day. It's important to make every minute of study count. There are two main areas you can focus on to make your studying count.

Retention

It doesn't matter how much time you study if you can't remember the material. You need to make sure you are retaining the concepts. To check your retention of the information you're learning, try recalling it at later times with minimal prompting. Try carrying around flashcards and glance at one or two from time to time or ask a friend who's also studying for the test to quiz you.

To enhance your retention, look for ways to put the information into practice so that you can apply it rather than simply recalling it. If you're using the information in practical ways, it will be much easier to remember. Similarly, it helps to solidify a concept in your mind if you're not only reading it to yourself but also explaining it to someone else. Ask a friend to let you teach them about a concept you're a little shaky on (or speak aloud to an imaginary audience if necessary). As you try to summarize, define, give examples, and answer your friend's questions, you'll understand the concepts better and they will stay with you longer. Finally, step back for a big picture view and ask yourself how each piece of information fits with the whole subject. When you link the different concepts together and see them working together as a whole, it's easier to remember the individual components.

Finally, practice showing your work on any multi-step problems, even if you're just studying. Writing out each step you take to solve a problem will help solidify the process in your mind, and you'll be more likely to remember it during the test.

Modality

Modality simply refers to the means or method by which you study. Choosing a study modality that fits your own individual learning style is crucial. No two people learn best in exactly the same way, so it's important to know your strengths and use them to your advantage.

For example, if you learn best by visualization, focus on visualizing a concept in your mind and draw an image or a diagram. Try color-coding your notes, illustrating them, or creating symbols that will trigger your mind to recall a learned concept. If you learn best by hearing or discussing information, find a study partner who learns the same way or read aloud to yourself. Think about how to put the information in your own words. Imagine that you are giving a lecture on the topic and record yourself so you can listen to it later.

For any learning style, flashcards can be helpful. Organize the information so you can take advantage of spare moments to review. Underline key words or phrases. Use different colors for different categories. Mnemonic devices (such as creating a short list in which every item starts with the same letter) can also help with retention. Find what works best for you and use it to store the information in your mind most effectively and easily.

Secret Key #3 – Practice the Right Way

Your success on test day depends not only on how many hours you put into preparing, but also on whether you prepared the right way. It's good to check along the way to see if your studying is paying off. One of the most effective ways to do this is by taking practice tests to evaluate your progress. Practice tests are useful because they show exactly where you need to improve. Every time you take a practice test, pay special attention to these three groups of questions:

- The questions you got wrong
- The questions you had to guess on, even if you guessed right
- The questions you found difficult or slow to work through

This will show you exactly what your weak areas are, and where you need to devote more study time. Ask yourself why each of these questions gave you trouble. Was it because you didn't understand the material? Was it because you didn't remember the vocabulary? Do you need more repetitions on this type of question to build speed and confidence? Dig into those questions and figure out how you can strengthen your weak areas as you go back to review the material.

Additionally, many practice tests have a section explaining the answer choices. It can be tempting to read the explanation and think that you now have a good understanding of the concept. However, an explanation likely only covers part of the question's broader context. Even if the explanation makes perfect sense, **go back and investigate** every concept related to the question until you're positive you have a thorough understanding.

As you go along, keep in mind that the practice test is just that: practice. Memorizing these questions and answers will not be very helpful on the actual test because it is unlikely to have any of the same exact questions. If you only know the right answers to the sample questions, you won't be prepared for the real thing. **Study the concepts** until you understand them fully, and then you'll be able to answer any question that shows up on the test.

It's important to wait on the practice tests until you're ready. If you take a test on your first day of study, you may be overwhelmed by the amount of material covered and how much you need to learn. Work up to it gradually.

On test day, you'll need to be prepared for answering questions, managing your time, and using the test-taking strategies you've learned. It's a lot to balance, like a mental marathon that will have a big impact on your future. Like training for a marathon, you'll need to start slowly and work your way up. When test day arrives, you'll be ready.

Start with the strategies you've read in the first two Secret Keys—plan your course and study in the way that works best for you. If you have time, consider using multiple study resources to get different approaches to the same concepts. It can be helpful to see difficult concepts from more than one angle. Then find a good source for practice tests. Many times, the test website will suggest potential study resources or provide sample tests.

Practice Test Strategy

If you're able to find at least three practice tests, we recommend this strategy:

Untimed and Open-Book Practice

Take the first test with no time constraints and with your notes and study guide handy. Take your time and focus on applying the strategies you've learned.

Timed and Open-Book Practice

Take the second practice test open-book as well, but set a timer and practice pacing yourself to finish in time.

Timed and Closed-Book Practice

Take any other practice tests as if it were test day. Set a timer and put away your study materials. Sit at a table or desk in a quiet room, imagine yourself at the testing center, and answer questions as quickly and accurately as possible.

Keep repeating timed and closed-book tests on a regular basis until you run out of practice tests or it's time for the actual test. Your mind will be ready for the schedule and stress of test day, and you'll be able to focus on recalling the material you've learned.

Secret Key #4 – Pace Yourself

Once you're fully prepared for the material on the test, your biggest challenge on test day will be managing your time. Just knowing that the clock is ticking can make you panic even if you have plenty of time left. Work on pacing yourself so you can build confidence against the time constraints of the exam. Pacing is a difficult skill to master, especially in a high-pressure environment, so **practice is vital**.

Set time expectations for your pace based on how much time is available. For example, if a section has 60 questions and the time limit is 30 minutes, you know you have to average 30 seconds or less per question in order to answer them all. Although 30 seconds is the hard limit, set 25 seconds per question as your goal, so you reserve extra time to spend on harder questions. When you budget extra time for the harder questions, you no longer have any reason to stress when those questions take longer to answer.

Don't let this time expectation distract you from working through the test at a calm, steady pace, but keep it in mind so you don't spend too much time on any one question. Recognize that taking extra time on one question you don't understand may keep you from answering two that you do understand later in the test. If your time limit for a question is up and you're still not sure of the answer, mark it and move on, and come back to it later if the time and the test format allow. If the testing format doesn't allow you to return to earlier questions, just make an educated guess; then put it out of your mind and move on.

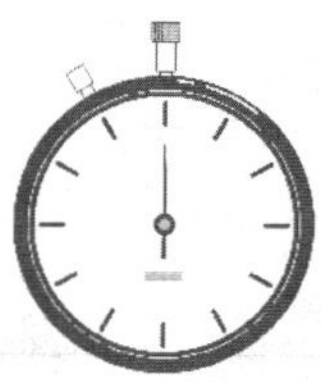

On the easier questions, be careful not to rush. It may seem wise to hurry through them so you have more time for the challenging ones, but it's not worth missing one if you know the concept and just didn't take the time to read the question fully. Work efficiently but make sure you understand the question and have looked at all of the answer choices, since more than one may seem right at first.

Even if you're paying attention to the time, you may find yourself a little behind at some point. You should speed up to get back on track, but do so wisely. Don't panic; just take a few seconds less on each question until you're caught up. Don't guess without thinking, but do look through the answer choices and eliminate any you know are wrong. If you can get down to two choices, it is often worthwhile to guess from those. Once you've chosen an answer, move on and don't dwell on any that you skipped or had to hurry through. If a question was taking too long, chances are it was one of the harder ones, so you weren't as likely to get it right anyway.

On the other hand, if you find yourself getting ahead of schedule, it may be beneficial to slow down a little. The more quickly you work, the more likely you are to make a careless mistake that will affect your score. You've budgeted time for each question, so don't be afraid to spend that time. Practice an efficient but careful pace to get the most out of the time you have.

Secret Key #5 – Have a Plan for Guessing

When you're taking the test, you may find yourself stuck on a question. Some of the answer choices seem better than others, but you don't see the one answer choice that is obviously correct. What do you do?

The scenario described above is very common, yet most test takers have not effectively prepared for it. Developing and practicing a plan for guessing may be one of the single most effective uses of your time as you get ready for the exam.

In developing your plan for guessing, there are three questions to address:

- When should you start the guessing process?
- How should you narrow down the choices?
- Which answer should you choose?

When to Start the Guessing Process

Unless your plan for guessing is to select C every time (which, despite its merits, is not what we recommend), you need to leave yourself enough time to apply your answer elimination strategies. Since you have a limited amount of time for each question, that means that if you're going to give yourself the best shot at guessing correctly, you have to decide quickly whether or not you will guess.

Of course, the best-case scenario is that you don't have to guess at all, so first, see if you can answer the question based on your knowledge of the subject and basic reasoning skills. Focus on the key words in the question and try to jog your memory of related topics. Give yourself a chance to bring the knowledge to mind, but once you realize that you don't have (or you can't access) the knowledge you need to answer the question, it's time to start the guessing process.

It's almost always better to start the guessing process too early than too late. It only takes a few seconds to remember something and answer the question from knowledge. Carefully eliminating wrong answer choices takes longer. Plus, going through the process of eliminating answer choices can actually help jog your memory.

Summary: Start the guessing process as soon as you decide that you can't answer the question based on your knowledge.

How to Narrow Down the Choices

The next chapter in this book (**Test-Taking Strategies**) includes a wide range of strategies for how to approach questions and how to look for answer choices to eliminate. You will definitely want to read those carefully, practice them, and figure out which ones work best for you. Here though, we're going to address a mindset rather than a particular strategy.

Your odds of guessing an answer correctly depend on how many options you are choosing from.

Number of options left	5	4	3	2	1
Odds of guessing correctly	20%	25%	33%	50%	100%

You can see from this chart just how valuable it is to be able to eliminate incorrect answers and make an educated guess, but there are two things that many test takers do that cause them to miss out on the benefits of guessing:

- Accidentally eliminating the correct answer
- Selecting an answer based on an impression

We'll look at the first one here, and the second one in the next section.

To avoid accidentally eliminating the correct answer, we recommend a thought exercise called **the $5 challenge**. In this challenge, you only eliminate an answer choice from contention if you are willing to bet $5 on it being wrong. Why $5? Five dollars is a small but not insignificant amount of money. It's an amount you could afford to lose but wouldn't want to throw away. And while losing $5 once might not hurt too much, doing it twenty times will set you back $100. In the same way, each small decision you make—eliminating a choice here, guessing on a question there—won't by itself impact your score very much, but when you put them all together, they can make a big difference. By holding each answer choice elimination decision to a higher standard, you can reduce the risk of accidentally eliminating the correct answer.

The $5 challenge can also be applied in a positive sense: If you are willing to bet $5 that an answer choice *is* correct, go ahead and mark it as correct.

Summary: Only eliminate an answer choice if you are willing to bet $5 that it is wrong.

Which Answer to Choose

You're taking the test. You've run into a hard question and decided you'll have to guess. You've eliminated all the answer choices you're willing to bet $5 on. Now you have to pick an answer. Why do we even need to talk about this? Why can't you just pick whichever one you feel like when the time comes?

The answer to these questions is that if you don't come into the test with a plan, you'll rely on your impression to select an answer choice, and if you do that, you risk falling into a trap. The test writers know that everyone who takes their test will be guessing on some of the questions, so they intentionally write wrong answer choices to seem plausible. You still have to pick an answer though, and if the wrong answer choices are designed to look right, how can you ever be sure that you're not falling for their trap? The best solution we've found to this dilemma is to take the decision out of your hands entirely. Here is the process we recommend:

Once you've eliminated any choices that you are confident (willing to bet $5) are wrong, select the first remaining choice as your answer.

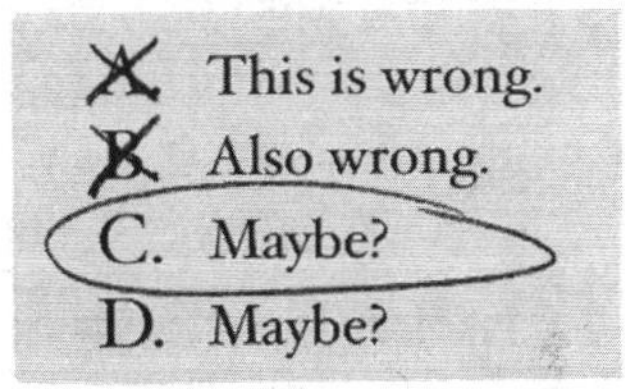

Whether you choose to select the first remaining choice, the second, or the last, the important thing is that you use some preselected standard. Using this approach guarantees that you will not be enticed into selecting an answer choice that looks right, because you are not basing your decision on how the answer choices look.

This is not meant to make you question your knowledge. Instead, it is to help you recognize the difference between your knowledge and your impressions. There's a huge difference between thinking an answer is right because of what you know, and thinking an answer is right because it looks or sounds like it should be right.

Summary: To ensure that your selection is appropriately random, make a predetermined selection from among all answer choices you have not eliminated.

Test-Taking Strategies

This section contains a list of test-taking strategies that you may find helpful as you work through the test. By taking what you know and applying logical thought, you can maximize your chances of answering any question correctly!

It is very important to realize that every question is different and every person is different: no single strategy will work on every question, and no single strategy will work for every person. That's why we've included all of them here, so you can try them out and determine which ones work best for different types of questions and which ones work best for you.

Question Strategies

✓ Read Carefully

Read the question and the answer choices carefully. Don't miss the question because you misread the terms. You have plenty of time to read each question thoroughly and make sure you understand what is being asked. Yet a happy medium must be attained, so don't waste too much time. You must read carefully and efficiently.

✓ Contextual Clues

Look for contextual clues. If the question includes a word you are not familiar with, look at the immediate context for some indication of what the word might mean. Contextual clues can often give you all the information you need to decipher the meaning of an unfamiliar word. Even if you can't determine the meaning, you may be able to narrow down the possibilities enough to make a solid guess at the answer to the question.

✓ Prefixes

If you're having trouble with a word in the question or answer choices, try dissecting it. Take advantage of every clue that the word might include. Prefixes can be a huge help. Usually, they allow you to determine a basic meaning. *Pre-* means before, *post-* means after, *pro-* is positive, *de-* is negative. From prefixes, you can get an idea of the general meaning of the word and try to put it into context.

✓ Hedge Words

Watch out for critical hedge words, such as *likely, may, can, often, almost, mostly, usually, generally, rarely*, and *sometimes*. Question writers insert these hedge phrases to cover every possibility. Often an answer choice will be wrong simply because it leaves no room for exception. Be on guard for answer choices that have definitive words such as *exactly* and *always*.

✓ Switchback Words

Stay alert for *switchbacks*. These are the words and phrases frequently used to alert you to shifts in thought. The most common switchback words are *but, although*, and *however*. Others include *nevertheless, on the other hand, even though, while, in spite of, despite*, and *regardless of*. Switchback words are important to catch because they can change the direction of the question or an answer choice.

✓ Face Value

When in doubt, use common sense. Accept the situation in the problem at face value. Don't read too much into it. These problems will not require you to make wild assumptions. If you have to go beyond creativity and warp time or space in order to have an answer choice fit the question, then you should move on and consider the other answer choices. These are normal problems rooted in reality. The applicable relationship or explanation may not be readily apparent, but it is there for you to figure out. Use your common sense to interpret anything that isn't clear.

Answer Choice Strategies

⊘ Answer Selection

The most thorough way to pick an answer choice is to identify and eliminate wrong answers until only one is left, then confirm it is the correct answer. Sometimes an answer choice may immediately seem right, but be careful. The test writers will usually put more than one reasonable answer choice on each question, so take a second to read all of them and make sure that the other choices are not equally obvious. As long as you have time left, it is better to read every answer choice than to pick the first one that looks right without checking the others.

⊘ Answer Choice Families

An answer choice family consists of two (in rare cases, three) answer choices that are very similar in construction and cannot all be true at the same time. If you see two answer choices that are direct opposites or parallels, one of them is usually the correct answer. For instance, if one answer choice says that quantity *x* increases and another either says that quantity *x* decreases (opposite) or says that quantity *y* increases (parallel), then those answer choices would fall into the same family. An answer choice that doesn't match the construction of the answer choice family is more likely to be incorrect. Most questions will not have answer choice families, but when they do appear, you should be prepared to recognize them.

⊘ Eliminate Answers

Eliminate answer choices as soon as you realize they are wrong, but make sure you consider all possibilities. If you are eliminating answer choices and realize that the last one you are left with is also wrong, don't panic. Start over and consider each choice again. There may be something you missed the first time that you will realize on the second pass.

⊘ Avoid Fact Traps

Don't be distracted by an answer choice that is factually true but doesn't answer the question. You are looking for the choice that answers the question. Stay focused on what the question is asking for so you don't accidentally pick an answer that is true but incorrect. Always go back to the question and make sure the answer choice you've selected actually answers the question and is not merely a true statement.

⊘ Extreme Statements

In general, you should avoid answers that put forth extreme actions as standard practice or proclaim controversial ideas as established fact. An answer choice that states the "process should be used in certain situations, if…" is much more likely to be correct than one that states the "process should be discontinued completely." The first is a calm rational statement and doesn't even make a definitive, uncompromising stance, using a hedge word *if* to provide wiggle room, whereas the second choice is far more extreme.

⊘ Benchmark

As you read through the answer choices and you come across one that seems to answer the question well, mentally select that answer choice. This is not your final answer, but it's the one that will help you evaluate the other answer choices. The one that you selected is your benchmark or standard for judging each of the other answer choices. Every other answer choice must be compared to your benchmark. That choice is correct until proven otherwise by another answer choice beating it. If you find a better answer, then that one becomes your new benchmark. Once you've decided that no other choice answers the question as well as your benchmark, you have your final answer.

✓ Predict the Answer

Before you even start looking at the answer choices, it is often best to try to predict the answer. When you come up with the answer on your own, it is easier to avoid distractions and traps because you will know exactly what to look for. The right answer choice is unlikely to be word-for-word what you came up with, but it should be a close match. Even if you are confident that you have the right answer, you should still take the time to read each option before moving on.

General Strategies

✓ Tough Questions

If you are stumped on a problem or it appears too hard or too difficult, don't waste time. Move on! Remember though, if you can quickly check for obviously incorrect answer choices, your chances of guessing correctly are greatly improved. Before you completely give up, at least try to knock out a couple of possible answers. Eliminate what you can and then guess at the remaining answer choices before moving on.

✓ Check Your Work

Since you will probably not know every term listed and the answer to every question, it is important that you get credit for the ones that you do know. Don't miss any questions through careless mistakes. If at all possible, try to take a second to look back over your answer selection and make sure you've selected the correct answer choice and haven't made a costly careless mistake (such as marking an answer choice that you didn't mean to mark). This quick double check should more than pay for itself in caught mistakes for the time it costs.

✓ Pace Yourself

It's easy to be overwhelmed when you're looking at a page full of questions; your mind is confused and full of random thoughts, and the clock is ticking down faster than you would like. Calm down and maintain the pace that you have set for yourself. Especially as you get down to the last few minutes of the test, don't let the small numbers on the clock make you panic. As long as you are on track by monitoring your pace, you are guaranteed to have time for each question.

✓ Don't Rush

It is very easy to make errors when you are in a hurry. Maintaining a fast pace in answering questions is pointless if it makes you miss questions that you would have gotten right otherwise. Test writers like to include distracting information and wrong answers that seem right. Taking a little extra time to avoid careless mistakes can make all the difference in your test score. Find a pace that allows you to be confident in the answers that you select.

✓ Keep Moving

Panicking will not help you pass the test, so do your best to stay calm and keep moving. Taking deep breaths and going through the answer elimination steps you practiced can help to break through a stress barrier and keep your pace.

Final Notes

The combination of a solid foundation of content knowledge and the confidence that comes from practicing your plan for applying that knowledge is the key to maximizing your performance on test day. As your foundation of content knowledge is built up and strengthened, you'll find that the strategies included in this chapter become more and more effective in helping you quickly sift through the distractions and traps of the test to isolate the correct answer.

Now that you're preparing to move forward into the test content chapters of this book, be sure to keep your goal in mind. As you read, think about how you will be able to apply this information on the test. If you've already seen sample questions for the test and you have an idea of the question format and style, try to come up with questions of your own that you can answer based on what you're reading. This will give you valuable practice applying your knowledge in the same ways you can expect to on test day.

Good luck and good studying!

Nature of Scientific Investigation and Instruction in Physics

Safety and Equipment

Laboratory Accidents

Any spills or accidents should be **reported** to the teacher so that the teacher can determine the safest clean-up method. The student should start to wash off a **chemical** spilled on the skin while reporting the incident. Some spills may require removal of contaminated clothing and use of the **safety shower**. Broken glass should be disposed of in a designated container. If someone's clothing catches fire they should walk to the safety shower and use it to extinguish the flames. A fire blanket may be used to smother a **lab fire**. A fire extinguisher, phone, spill neutralizers, and a first aid box are other types of **safety equipment** found in the lab. Students should be familiar with **routes** out of the room and the building in case of fire. Students should use the **eye wash station** if a chemical gets in the eyes.

Safety Procedures

Students should wear a **lab apron** and **safety goggles**. Loose or dangling clothing and jewelry, necklaces, and earrings should not be worn. Those with long hair should tie it back. Care should always be taken not to splash chemicals. Open-toed shoes such as sandals and flip-flops should not be worn, nor should wrist watches. Glasses are preferable to contact lenses since the latter carry a risk of chemicals getting caught between the lens and the eye. Students should always be supervised. The area where the experiment is taking place and the surrounding floor should be free of clutter. Only the lab book and the items necessary for the experiment should be present. Smoking, eating, and chewing gum are not permitted in the lab. Cords should not be allowed to dangle from work stations. There should be no rough-housing in the lab. Hands should be washed after the lab is complete.

Fume Hoods

Because of the potential safety hazards associated with chemistry lab experiments, such as fire from vapors and the inhalation of toxic fumes, a **fume hood** should be used in many instances. A fume hood carries away vapors from reagents or reactions. Equipment or reactions are placed as far back in the hood as practical to help enhance the collection of the fumes. The **glass safety shield** automatically closes to the appropriate height, and it should be low enough to protect the face and body. The safety shield should only be raised to move equipment in and out of the hood. One should not climb inside a hood or stick one's head inside. All spills should be wiped up immediately, and the glass should be cleaned if a splash occurs.

Common Safety Hazards

Some specific safety hazards possible in a chemistry lab include:

- **Fire**: Fire can be caused by volatile solvents such as ether, acetone, or benzene being kept in an open beaker or Erlenmeyer flask. Vapors can creep along the table and ignite if they reach a flame or spark. Solvents should be heated in a hood with a steam bath, not on a hot plate.
- **Explosion**: Heating or creating a reaction in a closed system can cause an explosion, resulting in flying glass and chemical splashes. The system should be vented to prevent this.
- **Chemical and thermal burns**: Many chemicals are corrosive to the skin and eyes.
- **Inhalation of toxic fumes**: Some compounds severely irritate membranes in the eyes, nose, throat, and lungs.
- **Absorption** of toxic chemicals such as dimethyl sulfoxide (DMSO) and nitrobenzene through the skin.
- **Ingestion** of toxic chemicals.

SAFETY GLOVES

There are many types of **gloves** available to help protect the skin from cuts, burns, and chemical splashes. There are many considerations when choosing a glove. For example, gloves that are highly protective may limit dexterity. Some gloves may not offer appropriate protection against a specific chemical. Other considerations include degradation rating, which indicates how effective a glove is when exposed to chemicals; breakthrough time, which indicates how quickly a chemical can break through the surface of the glove; and permeation rate, which indicates how quickly chemicals seep through after the initial breakthrough. Disposable latex, vinyl, or nitrile gloves are usually appropriate for most circumstances, and offer protection from incidental splashes and contact. Other types of gloves include butyl, neoprene, PVC, PVA, Viton, Silver Shield, and natural rubber. Each offers its own type of protection but may have drawbacks as well.

PROPER HANDLING AND STORAGE OF CHEMICALS

Students should take care when **carrying chemicals** from one place to another. Chemicals should never be taken from the room, tasted, or touched with bare hands. **Safety gloves** should be worn when appropriate and glove/chemical interactions and glove deterioration should be considered. Hands should always be **washed** thoroughly after a lab. Potentially hazardous materials intended for use in chemistry, biology, or other science labs should be secured in a safe area where relevant **Safety Data Sheets (SDS)** can be accessed. Chemicals and solutions should be used as directed and labels should be read before handling solutions and chemicals. Extra chemicals should not be returned to their original containers, but should be disposed of as directed by the school district's rules or local ordinances. Local municipalities often have hazardous waste disposal programs. Acids should be stored separately from other chemicals. Flammable liquids should be stored away from acids, bases, and oxidizers.

BUNSEN BURNERS

When using a **Bunsen burner**, loose clothing should be tucked in, long hair should be tied back, and safety goggles and aprons should be worn. Students should know what to do in case of a fire or accident. When lighting the burner, strikers should always be used instead of matches. Do not touch the hot barrel. Tongs (never fingers) should be used to hold the material in the flame. To heat liquid, a flask may be set upon wire gauze on a tripod and secured with an iron ring or clamp on a stand. The flame is extinguished by turning off the gas at the source.

SAFETY PROCEDURES RELATED TO ANIMALS

Animals to be used for **dissections** should be obtained from a company that provides animals for this purpose. Road kill or decaying animals that a student brings in should not be used. It is possible that such an animal may have a pathogen or a virus, such as rabies, which can be transmitted via the saliva of even a dead animal. Students should use gloves and should not participate if they have open sores or moral objections to dissections. It is generally accepted that biological experiments may be performed on lower-order life forms and invertebrates, but not on mammalian vertebrates and birds. No animals should be harmed physiologically. Experimental animals should be kept, cared for, and handled in a safe manner and with compassion. Pathogenic (anything able to cause a disease) substances should not be used in lab experiments.

LAB NOTEBOOKS

A **lab notebook** is a record of all pre-lab work and lab work. It differs from a lab report, which is prepared after lab work is completed. A lab notebook is a formal record of lab preparations and what was done. **Observational recordings** should not be altered, erased, or whited-out to make corrections. Drawing a single line through an entry is sufficient to make changes. Pages should be numbered and should not be torn out. Entries should be made neatly, but don't necessarily have to be complete sentences. **Entries** should provide detailed information and be recorded in such a way that another person could use them to replicate the experiment. **Quantitative data** may be recorded in tabular form, and may include calculations made during an experiment. Lab book entries can also include references and research performed before the experiment.

Entries may also consist of information about a lab experiment, including the objective or purpose, the procedures, data collected, and the results.

Lab Reports

A **lab report** is an item developed after an experiment that is intended to present the results of a lab experiment. Generally, it should be prepared using a word processor, not hand-written or recorded in a notebook. A lab report should be formally presented. It is intended to persuade others to accept or reject a hypothesis. It should include a brief but descriptive **title** and an **abstract**. The abstract is a summary of the report. It should include a purpose that states the problem that was explored or the question that was answered. It should also include a **hypothesis** that describes the anticipated results of the experiment. The experiment should include a **control** and one **variable** to ensure that the results can be interpreted correctly. Observations and results can be presented using written narratives, tables, graphs, and illustrations. The report should also include a **summation** or **conclusion** explaining whether the results supported the hypothesis.

Types of Laboratory Glassware

Two types of flasks are Erlenmeyer flasks and volumetric flasks. **Volumetric flasks** are used to accurately prepare a specific volume and concentration of a solution. **Erlenmeyer flasks** can be used for mixing, transporting, and reacting, but are not appropriate for accurate measurements.

A **pipette** can be used to accurately measure small amounts of liquid. Liquid is drawn into the pipette through a bulb. The liquid measurement is read at the **meniscus**. There are also plastic disposable pipettes. A **repipette** is a hand-operated pump that dispenses solutions.

Beakers can be used to measure mass or dissolve a solvent into a solute. They do not measure volume as accurately as a volumetric flask, pipette, graduated cylinder, or burette.

Graduated cylinders are used for precise measurements and are considered more accurate than Erlenmeyer flasks or beakers. To read a graduated cylinder, it should be placed on a flat surface and read at eye level. The surface of a liquid in a graduated cylinder forms a lens-shaped curve. The measurement should be taken from the bottom of the curve. A ring may be placed at the top of tall, narrow cylinders to help avoid breakage if they are tipped over.

A **burette**, or buret, is a piece of lab glassware used to accurately dispense liquid. It looks similar to a narrow graduated cylinder, but it includes a stopcock and tip. It may be filled with a funnel or pipette.

Microscopes

There are different kinds of microscopes, but **optical** or **light microscopes** are the most commonly used in lab settings. Light and lenses are used to magnify and view samples. A specimen or sample is placed on a slide, and the slide is placed on a stage with a hole in it. Light passes through the hole and illuminates the sample. The sample is magnified by lenses and viewed through the eyepiece. A simple microscope has one lens, while a typical compound microscope has three lenses. The light source can be room light redirected by a mirror, or the microscope can have its own independent light source that passes through a condenser. In this case, there are diaphragms and filters to allow light intensity to be controlled. Optical microscopes also have coarse and fine adjustment knobs.

Other types of microscopes include **digital microscopes**, which use a camera and a monitor to allow viewing of the sample. **Scanning electron microscopes (SEMs)** provide greater detail in terms of a sample's surface topography and can produce magnifications much greater than those possible with optical microscopes. The technology of an SEM is quite different from an optical microscope in that it does not rely on lenses to magnify objects, but uses samples placed in a chamber. In one type of SEM, a beam of electrons from an electron gun scans and actually interacts with the sample to produce an image.

Wet mount slides designed for use with a light microscope typically require a thin portion of the specimen to be placed on a standard glass slide. A drop of water is added, and a cover slip or cover glass is placed on top. Air bubbles and fingerprints can make viewing difficult. Placing the cover slip at a 45-degree angle and allowing it to drop into place can help avoid the problem of air bubbles. A **cover slip** should always be used when viewing wet mount slides. The viewer should start with the objective in its lowest position and then fine-focus. The microscope should be carried with two hands and stored with the low-power objective in the down position. **Lenses** should be cleaned with lens paper only. A **graticule slide** is marked with a grid line, and is useful for counting or estimating a quantity.

Balances

Balances such as triple-beam balances, spring balances, and electronic balances measure mass and force. An **electronic balance** is the most accurate, followed by a **triple-beam balance** and then a **spring balance**. One part of a **triple-beam balance** is the plate, which is where the item to be weighed is placed. There are also three beams, which have hash marks indicating amounts and which hold the weights that rest in the notches. The front beam measures weights between 0 and 10 grams, the middle beam measures weights in 100-gram increments, and the far beam measures weights in 10-gram increments. The sum of the weight of each beam is the total weight of the object. A triple beam balance also includes a set screw to calibrate the equipment, as well as a mark indicating that the object and counterweights are in balance.

Chromatography

Chromatography refers to a set of laboratory techniques used to separate or analyze **mixtures**. Mixtures are dissolved in their mobile phases. In the stationary or bonded phase, the desired component is separated from other molecules in the mixture. In chromatography, the analyte is the substance to be separated. **Preparative chromatography** refers to the type of chromatography that involves purifying a substance for further use rather than further analysis. **Analytical chromatography** involves analyzing the isolated substance. Other types of chromatography include column, planar, paper, thin layer, displacement, supercritical fluid, affinity, ion exchange, and size exclusion chromatography. Reversed phase, two-dimensional, simulated moving bed, pyrolysis, fast protein, counter current, and chiral are also types of chromatography. **Gas chromatography** refers to the separation technique in which the mobile phase of a substance is in gas form.

Review Video: Paper Chromatography
Visit mometrix.com/academy and enter code: 543963

Reagents and Reactants

A **reagent** or **reactant** is a chemical agent for use in chemical reactions. When preparing for a lab, it should be confirmed that glassware and other equipment have been cleaned and/or sterilized. There should be enough materials, reagents, or other solutions needed for the lab for every group of students completing the experiment. Distilled water should be used instead of tap water when performing lab experiments because distilled water has most of its impurities removed. Other needed apparatus such as funnels, filter paper, balances, Bunsen burners, ring stands, and/or microscopes should also be set up. After the lab, it should be confirmed that sinks, workstations, and any equipment used have been cleaned. If chemicals or specimens need to be kept at a certain temperature by refrigerating them or using another storage method, the temperature should be checked periodically to ensure the sample does not spoil.

Diluting Acids

When preparing a solution of **dilute acid**, always add the concentrated acid solution to water, not water to concentrated acid. Start by adding approximately $\frac{2}{3}$ of the total volume of water to the graduated cylinder or volumetric flask. Next, add the concentrated acid to the water. Add additional water to the diluted acid to bring the solution to the final desired volume.

Cleaning After Acid Spills

In the event of an **acid spill**, any clothes that have come into contact with the acid should be removed and any skin contacted with acid must be rinsed with clean water. To the extent a window can be opened or a fume hood can be turned on, do so. Do not try to force air circulation, such as by adding a fan, as acid fumes can be harmful if spread.

Next, pour one of the following over the spill area: sodium bicarbonate, baking soda, soda ash, or cat litter. Start from the outside of the spill and then move towards the center, in order to prevent splashing. When the clumps have thoroughly dried, sweep up the clumps and dispose of them as chemical waste.

Centrifuges

A centrifuge is used to separate the components of a heterogeneous mixture (consisting of two or more compounds) by spinning it. The solid precipitate settles in the bottom of the container, and the liquid component of the solution, called the **centrifugate**, is at the top. A well-known application of this process is using a centrifuge to separate blood cells and plasma. The heavier cells settle on the bottom of the test tube, and the lighter plasma stays on top. Another example is using a salad spinner to help dry lettuce.

Electrophoresis, Calorimetry, and Titration

- **Electrophoresis** is the separation of molecules based on electrical charge. This is possible because particles dispersed in a fluid usually carry electric charges on their surfaces. Molecules are pulled through the fluid toward the positive end if the molecules have a negative charge and are pulled through the fluid toward the negative end if the molecules have a positive charge.
- **Calorimetry** is used to determine the heat released or absorbed in a chemical reaction.
- **Titration** helps determine the precise endpoint of a reaction. With this information, the precise quantity of reactant in the titration flask can be determined. A burette is used to deliver the second reactant to the flask and an indicator or pH meter is used to detect the endpoint of the reaction.

Field Studies and Research Projects

Field studies may facilitate scientific inquiry in a manner similar to indoor lab experiments. Field studies can be interdisciplinary in nature and can help students learn and apply scientific concepts and processes. **Research projects** can be conducted in any number of locations, including school campuses, local parks, national parks, beaches, or mountains. Students can practice the general techniques of observation, data collection, collaborative planning, and analysis of experiments. Field studies give students the chance to learn through hands-on applications of scientific processes, such as map making in geography, observation of stratification in geology, observation of life cycles of plants and animals, and analysis of water quality.

Students should watch out for obvious outdoor **hazards**. These include poisonous flora and fauna such as poison ivy, poison oak, and sumac. Depending on the region of the United States in which the field study is being conducted, hazards may also include rattlesnakes and black widow or brown recluse spiders. Students should also be made aware of potentially hazardous situations specific to **geographic locales** and the possibility of coming into contact with **pathogens**.

Field studies allow for great flexibility in the use of traditional and technological methods for **making observations** and **collecting data**. For example, a nature study could consist of a simple survey of bird species within a given area. Information could be recorded using still photography or a video camera. This type of activity gives students the chance to use technologies other than computers. Computers could still be used to create a slide show of transferred images or a digital lab report. If a quantitative study of birds was being performed, the simple technique of using a pencil and paper to tabulate the number of birds counted in the field could also be used. Other techniques used during field studies could include collecting specimens for lab study, observing coastal ecosystems and tides, and collecting weather data such as temperature, precipitation amounts, and air pressure in a particular locale.

Scientific Concepts Related to Physical Science

Basic Safety Equipment

All labs should contain the following items:

- Bucket of sand for absorption of spills and smothering of alkali fires
- Fire blanket
- First-aid kit, containing bandages and antiseptic
- One GFCI within two feet of all water supplies
- Exit signs
- Emergency shower
- Emergency eyewash station
- Splashproof eye protection for all parties, and a means to sanitize it
- Face shields
- Emergency exhaust fans that vent to the outside of the building
- Fire blanket
- Gloves, both rubber and nitrile
- Master cutoff switches for gas, electricity, and compressed air
- ABC fire extinguisher
- Storage cabinets for flammable items
- Chemical spill-control kit
- Fume hood with a spark-proof motor
- Flame-retardant lab aprons
- Mercury clean-up kit
- Neutralizing agents, including acetic acid and sodium bicarbonate
- Signs drawing attention to potential hazards
- Segregated, clearly labeled containers for storing broken glassware, flammable items, solid chemicals, corrosive items, and waste.

Major Energy Issues

Since the Industrial Revolution, energy for industrialized human needs has come from **fossil fuels**, particularly coal and petroleum, but increased use means that this source of fuel is quickly being depleted, in addition to causing pollution. The search for alternative, safe sources of energy for an increasingly industrialized world population is therefore increasingly important to scientists.

An ideal source of energy would be **efficient, renewable, and sustainable**. Various sources of alternative energy have been proposed, including wind, water, solar, nuclear, geothermal, and biomass, but thus far none have been made practically available on a large scale. Some, such as wind and water, blight the landscape, while the conversion methods for other sources, such as solar and biomass, are still relatively inefficient. The scientific community is still unclear on the best way to harness the power of photosynthesis and biomass for energy needs in a way that would allow a large-scale energy industry to use it. Scientists remain at work studying the long-term solutions to an increasingly urgent problem for humanity.

Effects of Improvements in Scientific and Technological Knowledge

Since the Industrial Revolution, technological **improvements to agricultural production** have made agriculture productive on an industrial scale, while advances in medical knowledge have brought about the **cures for many diseases**. People in many parts of the world live longer and enjoy a higher standard of living than ever before.

However, this progress does not come without a price. The **effects on the environment** of industrialization are almost exclusively negative. Monoculture farming practices resulting from industrialization mean that

farming no longer exists as a closed ecosystem; the chemical fertilizers that create record crop yields have changed the nutrient environment, and the waste products of industrial agriculture pollute the water rather than fertilizing the soil. Increased travel creates dangerous carbon dioxide emissions and depletes the earth's limited store of fossil fuels. **Water pollution** means limited access to potable water, and **deforestation** has begun to change the makeup of ecosystems and cause the extinction of many species. However, through the increased contact made available by improved technology, humans are collaborating on solutions to these new problems.

Increased Production of Consumer Goods

Electric-based, industrial production of manufactured goods has led to an increase in the standard of living for many, especially those in the industrialized world. Consumer goods are produced more cheaply than ever before, since the means of production is not as dependent on the physical abilities of human beings. Scientific advancements have led to a huge number of new synthetic materials from which goods can be made, including plastics and nylon.

However, this increased production damages the environment. Waste products are now created of which humans can make no use, which constitutes a new phenomenon. Trash created from these new products is buried in landfills, where it has no access to the air, water, and sunlight that are a necessary part of biodegradation; trash made from some synthetic materials does not biodegrade at all. While some waste products can be recycled, many byproducts of industrial manufacturing are hazardous, with no safe way to dispose of them. The long-term sustainability of the environment as a result of massively increased consumer production is an issue of increasing urgency for scientists.

Nuclear Power Controversy

Nuclear fission power, while sustainable, has a host of attendant controversial problems. Among them is the **incredibly dangerous transportation and long-term storage of its radioactive waste** products, for which there is still no safe permanent solution. The effects on environments and creatures that come in contact with nuclear waste are still largely unknown. In addition, nuclear materials can be used in weaponry, and accidents at nuclear power plants like the one at Chernobyl can be devastating for thousands of years.

Scientists continue their study of the process of nuclear fusion, hoping that if humans can learn to harness the energy produced by smashing atoms (nuclear fusion) rather than splitting them (nuclear fission), the attendant problems of nuclear waste storage will be minimized.

Management of Non-Renewable Resources

Non-renewable resources include minerals, which are created naturally over millions of years. The industrialized world extracts minerals for fuel as well as for use in electronic equipment and medicine. Increased human extraction of **non-renewable resources** has endangered their availability, and over-mining has created other ecological problems, including runoff and water pollution. The use of fossil fuels for energy and transportation causes air pollution and is unsustainable. Fossil fuels cannot be replaced once depleted, and they are being depleted at an increasing rate. The need to find a sustainable alternative to the use of non-renewable fossil fuels is imperative.

Management of Renewable Resources

Natural resources can be divided into two types, renewable and non-renewable. **Renewable** resources include plants and animals, along with water, air, and soil.

A **pre-industrial earth** was a self-sustaining system, maintaining a natural balance among plants, animals, and non-living elements in which waste products from one natural process were the fuel for another. Modern humans have intervened in this process in a way that upsets the natural balance of life. Humans have introduced non-native species from one part of the world to another, resulting in the devastation of local populations. Industrial-scale buildings can create disasters for local ecosystems, ruining habitats for animal populations.

Humans remove an increasing amount of the world's resources for industrial use, too quickly for nature to recover from easily. Renewable resources must be carefully managed to maintain a balanced ecosystem; over-harvesting of forests or over-hunting of animal populations can be devastating. Pollution of the air and water with chemical pollutants has far-reaching effects on the ecosystems of the earth, including the depletion of the ozone layer that protects earth life from ultraviolet rays, as does the removal of forests that produce the earth's oxygen.

Social Impacts of Science and Technology

Recent developments in science and technology have had both positive and negative effects on human society. The issue of **sustainable growth** is an increasingly important one, as humans realize that the resources they use are not unlimited. Genetic research into diseases, stem cell research, and cloning technology have created great controversies as they have been introduced, and an increasing number of people reject the morality of scientific practices like animal testing in the pursuit of scientific advancement. In addition, an increasingly technology-based world has produced a new social inequality based on access to computers and Internet technology.

These issues are beginning to be debated at all levels of human government, from city councils to the United Nations. Does science provide the authoritative answer to all human problems, or do ethics carry weight in scientific debates as well? Ultimately, humans must weigh the competing needs of facilitating scientific pursuits and maintaining an ethical society as they face new technological questions.

Recent Applications of Science and Technology

Scientific and technological developments have led to the widespread availability of technologies heretofore unheard of, including cellular phones, satellite-based applications, and a worldwide network of connected computers. Some of the notable recent applications include:

- **Health care:** Antibiotics, genetic screening for diseases, the sequencing of the human genome. Issues include problems with health care distribution on an increasingly industrialized planet.
- **The environment**: Computerized models of climate change and pollution monitoring. Issues include increased pollution of the water, air, and soil, and the over-harvesting of natural resources with mechanized equipment.
- **Agriculture**: Genetic improvements in agricultural practices, including increased output on the same amount of arable land. Issues include unknown environmental effects of hybrid species, cross-pollination with organic species, and pollution caused by synthetic chemical fertilizers.
- **Information technology**: New Internet-based industries, increased worldwide collaboration, and access to information. Issues include the depletion of natural resources for electronics production.

Contributing Individuals to Physics

Archimedes (Ancient Greece)

Archimedes designed the **compound pulley**, articulated the principles of the lever, and made important contributions to engineering and geometry, calculating the area of a sphere and an ellipse and approximating the value of **pi**. Archimedes' Law of the Lever states that when objects are set at distances reciprocally proportional to their respective weights, they are in equilibrium.

Amedeo Avogadro (Italian, 18th Century)

Avogadro established the principles of **molarity**, clarified the relationship between atoms and molecules, and formalized what became known as Avogadro's principle: that equal volumes of gases held at the same pressure and temperature will contain an equal number of molecules, and that their masses will be proportionate to their respective molecular weights. **Avogadro's constant** is the number of particles present in 1 mole of any substance.

Review Video: Avogadro's Hypothesis
Visit mometrix.com/academy and enter code: 968309

Robert Boyle (Irish, 17th Century)

Though regarded as the first modern chemist, Boyle also distinguished himself in physics and contributed to **experimental design**. Boyle's Law is a mathematical expression of the relationship between volume and pressure within an **ideal gas**.

Sir Isaac Newton (English, 17th/18th Century)

Newton, one of the most important scientists of all time, made critical breakthroughs in the understanding of **scientific methods, motion, and optics**. Newton described **universal gravitation**, observed that white light contains the entire spectrum of colors, and discovered the calculus independently of Leibniz (who is credited with it). The three Newtonian laws of motion are:

- An object in motion (or at rest) remains in motion (or at rest) unless acted upon by an external force.
- Force equals mass times acceleration.
- For every action, there is an equal and opposite reaction.

Galileo Galilei (Italian, 17th Century)

Galileo determined that all bodies, regardless of mass, fall at the same rate. He argued that motion is continuous, changed only when an external force is applied to it (later incorporated in Newton's laws of motion). His work in astronomy was important in confirming **Copernicus' heliocentric model of the solar system**. His principle of relativity states that the laws of physics are constant within a constantly moving system, a theory that became central to Einstein's work on relativity.

Marie Curie (Polish/French, 19th Century)

Curie was the foremost pioneer of **radioactivity**. She isolated the radioactive elements polonium and radium, and established that radioactivity was a property of an atom itself rather than of the relationship between multiple molecules.

Michael Faraday (English, 18th/19th Century)

Faraday's most important work was in the fields of **electromagnetism** and **electrochemistry**. His work led directly to some of the most important breakthroughs in electrical technology of the twentieth century. Faraday introduced the concept of fields to the study of magnetism and electricity. He discovered what would become known as the Faraday Effect, the effect of a strong magnetic field on the behavior of light rays. The Farad (the SI unit of capacitance) and the Faraday constant (the amount of charge on one mole of electrons) are both named for him.

Wilhelm Ostwald (Latvian, 19th/20th Century)

One of the founders of classical physical chemistry, Ostwald did important work on the **properties of atomic particles**, and defined a **mole** as the molecular weight, in grams, of a given substance.

Albert Einstein (German, 20th Century)

Einstein, the most famous twentieth-century scientist, was a theoretical physicist **whose special theory of relativity** describes the relationship of **time** and **space**, and **mass** and **gravity**. In it, he declared that gravity is a consequence of the properties of space-time and that the speed of light is constant. He hypothesized that electromagnetic energy can be absorbed or expelled by matter in quanta, and he discovered the photoelectric effect.

Stephen Hawking (English, 20th/21st Century)

Hawking's principal fields of research were theoretical cosmology and quantum gravity. Expanding on Einstein's work, he hypothesized about the physical properties of black holes, described conditions necessary for a singularity, and made important contributions in string theory, in an attempt to generalize Einstein's special theory of relativity.

J. Robert Oppenheimer (American, 20th Century)

Oppenheimer's scientific contributions were in astrophysics, nuclear physics, and quantum field theory. He served as scientific director of the Manhattan Project, which constructed the first atomic bomb.

Linus Pauling (American, 20th Century)

Pauling applied new discoveries in **quantum mechanics** to the field of chemistry, pioneering the study of **molecular medicine**. He researched the biochemical origins of genetic diseases like sickle-cell anemia.

Enrico Fermi (Italian/American, 20th Century)

Fermi discovered the process of making **elements artificially radioactive** by bombarding them with neutrons. He divided elements into the two groups of **fermions** and **bosons**. His work on nuclear reactions led him to participate in the **Manhattan Project**.

Niels Bohr (Danish, 20th Century)

Bohr established that the number of electrons determined the **atom's chemical properties**. He articulated the organization of electrons, in discrete orbits around an atom's nucleus, and that electrons could move orbits, thereby emitting radiation—the **basis for quantum theory**. Bohr worked on the Manhattan Project along with Oppenheimer and Fermi.

Scientific Inquiry and Reasoning

Scientific Inquiry

The concept of **scientific inquiry** refers to the idea of how one thinks and asks questions in a logical way to gain trustworthy information. The underlying motivation of science is to try to understand the natural world. Much of human thought is based on assumptions about how things work that may or may not be true. The goal of scientific inquiry is to test those assumptions to gain a greater understanding of the world with good questions and objective tests, and then re-use what was learned to ask better questions. The more we understand about the natural world, the better the questions we can ask, and that is the general idea behind scientific inquiry. The applied practice of scientific inquiry is to ask questions in a systematic method, called the scientific method.

Scientific Knowledge

Scientific knowledge refers to any topic that is studied **empirically**, meaning that it is based on observation of a **phenomenon** in an objective way. The body of **scientific knowledge** is often broken down into several domains including biology, ecology, Earth science, space science, physics, and chemistry. These each have further subdomains and are overlapping in many ways. For instance, ecology is the study of ecosystems, which are made up of biological factors and geological factors, so it contains elements of both biology and Earth science. Each of these domains is subject to the concepts of scientific inquiry, such as the scientific method, scientific facts, hypotheses, and scientific laws.

Important Terminology

- A **phenomenon** is an event or effect that is observed.
- A **scientific fact** is considered an objective and verifiable observation. Usually, a fact can be repeated or demonstrated to others.
- A **scientific theory** is a proposition explaining why or how something happens and is built on scientific facts and laws. Scientific theories can be tested, but are not fully proven. If new evidence is found that disproves the theory, it is no longer considered true.
- A **hypothesis** is an educated guess that is not yet proven. It is used to predict the outcome of an experiment in an attempt to solve a problem or answer a question.
- A **law** is an explanation of events that always leads to the same outcome. It is a fact that an object falls. The law of gravity explains why an object falls. The theory of relativity, although generally accepted, has been neither proven nor disproved.
- A **model** is used to explain something on a smaller scale or in simpler terms to provide an example. It is a representation of an idea that can be used to explain events or applied to new situations to predict outcomes or determine results.

History of Scientific Knowledge

When one examines the history of **scientific knowledge**, it is clear that it is constantly **evolving**. The body of facts, models, theories, and laws grows and changes over time. In other words, one scientific discovery leads to the next. Some advances in science and technology have important and long-lasting effects on science and society. Some discoveries were so alien to the accepted beliefs of the time that not only were they rejected as wrong, but were also considered outright blasphemy. Today, however, many beliefs once considered incorrect have become an ingrained part of scientific knowledge, and have also been the basis of new advances. Examples of advances include: Copernicus's heliocentric view of the universe, Newton's laws of motion and planetary orbits, relativity, geologic time scale, plate tectonics, atomic theory, nuclear physics, biological evolution, germ theory, industrial revolution, molecular biology, information and communication, quantum theory, galactic universe, and medical and health technology.

Scientific Inquiry and Scientific Method

Scientists use a number of generally accepted techniques collectively known as the **scientific method**. The scientific method generally involves carrying out the following steps:

- Identifying a problem or posing a question
- Formulating a hypothesis or an educated guess
- Conducting experiments or tests that will provide a basis to solve the problem or answer the question
- Observing the results of the test
- Drawing conclusions

An important part of the scientific method is using acceptable experimental techniques. Objectivity is also important if valid results are to be obtained. Another important part of the scientific method is peer review. It is essential that experiments be performed and data be recorded in such a way that experiments can be reproduced to verify results. Historically, the scientific method has been taught with a more linear approach, but it is important to recognize that the scientific method should be a cyclical or **recursive process**. This means that as hypotheses are tested and more is learned, the questions should continue to change to reflect the changing body of knowledge. One cycle of experimentation is not enough.

Review Video: The Scientific Method
Visit mometrix.com/academy and enter code: 191386

Metric and International System of Units

The **metric system** is the accepted standard of measurement in the scientific community. The **International System of Units (SI)** is a set of measurements (including the metric system) that is almost globally accepted. The United States, Liberia, and Myanmar have not accepted this system. **Standardization** is important because it allows the results of experiments to be compared and reproduced without the need to laboriously convert measurements. The SI is based partially on the **meter-kilogram-second (MKS) system** rather than the **centimeter-gram-second (CGS) system**. The MKS system considers meters, kilograms, and seconds to be the basic units of measurement, while the CGS system considers centimeters, grams, and seconds to be the basic units of measurement. Under the MKS system, the length of an object would be expressed as 1 meter instead of 100 centimeters, which is how it would be described under the CGS system.

Review Video: Metric System Conversions
Visit mometrix.com/academy and enter code: 163709

Basic Units of Measurement

Using the **metric system** is generally accepted as the preferred method for taking measurements. Having a **universal standard** allows individuals to interpret measurements more easily, regardless of where they are located. The basic units of measurement are: the **meter**, which measures length; the **liter**, which measures volume; and the **gram**, which measures mass. The metric system starts with a base unit and increases or decreases in units of 10. The prefix and the base unit combined are used to indicate an amount. For example, deka- is 10 times the base unit. A dekameter is 10 meters; a dekaliter is 10 liters; and a dekagram is 10 grams. The prefix hecto- refers to 100 times the base amount; kilo- is 1,000 times the base amount. The prefixes that indicate a fraction of the base unit are deci-, which is $\frac{1}{10}$ of the base unit; centi-, which is $\frac{1}{100}$ of the base unit; and milli-, which is $\frac{1}{1,000}$ of the base unit.

Common Prefixes

The prefixes for multiples are as follows:

Deka	(da)	$\mathbf{10^1}$ (deka is the American spelling, but deca is also used)
Hecto	(h)	10^2
Kilo	(k)	10^3
Mega	(M)	10^6
Giga	(G)	10^9
Tera	(T)	10^{12}

The prefixes for subdivisions are as follows:

Deci	(d)	$\mathbf{10^{-1}}$
Centi	(c)	10^{-2}
Milli	(m)	10^{-3}
Micro	(μ)	10^{-6}
Nano	(n)	10^{-9}
Pico	(p)	10^{-12}

The rule of thumb is that prefixes greater than 10^3 are capitalized when abbreviating. Abbreviations do not need a period after them. A decimeter (dm) is a tenth of a meter, a deciliter (dL) is a tenth of a liter, and a decigram (dg) is a tenth of a gram. Pluralization is understood. For example, when referring to 5 mL of water, no "s" needs to be added to the abbreviation.

Basic SI Units of Measurement

SI uses **second(s)** to measure time. Fractions of seconds are usually measured in metric terms using prefixes such as millisecond ($\frac{1}{1,000}$ of a second) or nanosecond ($\frac{1}{1,000,000,000}$ of a second). Increments of time larger than a second are measured in **minutes** and **hours**, which are multiples of 60 and 24. An example of this is a swimmer's time in the 800-meter freestyle being described as 7:32.67, meaning 7 minutes, 32 seconds, and 67 one-hundredths of a second. One second is equal to $\frac{1}{60}$ of a minute, $\frac{1}{3,600}$ of an hour, and $\frac{1}{86,400}$ of a day. Other SI base units are the **ampere** (A) (used to measure electric current), the **kelvin** (K) (used to measure thermodynamic temperature), the **candela** (cd) (used to measure luminous intensity), and the **mole** (mol) (used to measure the amount of a substance at a molecular level). **Meter** (m) is used to measure length and **kilogram** (kg) is used to measure mass.

Significant Figures

The mathematical concept of **significant figures** or **significant digits** is often used to determine the accuracy of measurements or the level of confidence one has in a specific measurement. The significant figures of a measurement include all the digits known with certainty plus one estimated or uncertain digit. There are a number of rules for determining which digits are considered "important" or "interesting." They are:

- All non-zero digits are *significant*.
- Zeros between digits are *significant*.
- Leading and trailing zeros are *not significant* unless they appear to the right of the non-zero digits in a decimal.

For example, in 0.01230, the significant digits are 1230, and this number would be said to be accurate to the hundred-thousandths place. The zero indicates that the amount has actually been measured as 0. Other zeros are considered placeholders and are not important. A decimal point may be placed after zeros to indicate their importance (in "100." for example).

Graphs and Charts

Graphs and charts are effective ways to present scientific data such as observations, statistical analyses, and comparisons between dependent variables and independent variables. On a line chart, the **independent variable** (the one that is being manipulated for the experiment) is represented on the horizontal axis (the x-axis). Any **dependent variables** (the ones that may change as the independent variable changes) are represented on the y-axis. An **XY** or **scatter plot** is often used to plot many points. A "best fit" line is drawn, which allows outliers to be identified more easily. Charts and their axes should have titles. The x and y interval units should be evenly spaced and labeled. Other types of charts are **bar charts** and **histograms**, which can be used to compare differences between the data collected for two variables. A **pie chart** can graphically show the relation of parts to a whole.

Review Video: Identifying Variables
Visit mometrix.com/academy and enter code: 627181

Review Video: Data Interpretation of Graphs
Visit mometrix.com/academy and enter code: 200439

Data Presentation

Data collected during a science lab can be organized and **presented** in any number of ways. While **straight narrative** is a suitable method for presenting some lab results, it is not a suitable way to present numbers and quantitative measurements. These types of observations can often be better presented with **tables** and **graphs**. Data that is presented in tables and organized in rows and columns may also be used to make graphs quite easily. Other methods of presenting data include illustrations, photographs, video, and even audio formats. In a **formal report**, tables and figures are labeled and referred to by their labels. For example, a picture of a bubbly solution might be labeled Figure 1, Bubbly Solution. It would be referred to in the text in the following way: "The reaction created bubbles 10 mm in size, as shown in Figure 1, Bubbly Solution." Graphs are also labeled as figures. Tables are labeled in a different way. Examples include: Table 1, Results of Statistical Analysis, or Table 2, Data from Lab 2.

Statistical Precision and Errors

Errors that occur during an experiment can be classified into two categories: random errors and systematic errors. **Random errors** can result in collected data that is wildly different from the rest of the data, or they may result in data that is indistinguishable from the rest. Random errors are not consistent across the data set. In large data sets, random errors may contribute to the variability of data, but they will not affect the average. Random errors are sometimes referred to as noise. They may be caused by a student's inability to take the same measurement in exactly the same way or by outside factors that are not considered variables, but influence the data. A **systematic error** will show up consistently across a sample or data set, and may be the result of a flaw in the experimental design. This type of error affects the average, and is also known as bias.

Scientific Notation

Scientific notation is used because values in science can be very large or very small, which makes them unwieldy. A number in **decimal notation** is 93,000,000. In **scientific notation**, it is 9.3×10^7. The first number, 9.3, is the **coefficient**. It is always greater than or equal to 1 and less than 10. This number is followed by a multiplication sign. The base is always 10 in scientific notation. If the number is greater than ten, the exponent is positive. If the number is between zero and one, the exponent is negative. The first digit of the number is followed by a decimal point and then the rest of the number. In this case, the number is 9.3, and the decimal point was moved seven places to the right from the end of the number to get 93,000,000. The number of places moved, seven, is the exponent.

Statistical Terminology

- **Mean**—The average, found by taking the sum of a set of numbers and dividing by the number of numbers in the set.
- **Median**—The middle number in a set of numbers sorted from least to greatest. If the set has an even number of entries, the median is the average of the two in the middle.
- **Mode**—The value that appears most frequently in a data set. There may be more than one mode. If no value appears more than once, there is no mode.
- **Range**—The difference between the highest and lowest numbers in a data set.
- **Standard deviation**—Measures the dispersion of a data set, or how far from the mean a single data point is likely to be.
- **Regression analysis**—A method of analyzing sets of data and sets of variables. It involves studying how the typical value of the dependent variable changes when any one of the independent variables is varied and the other independent variables remain fixed.

Review Video: Mean, Median, and Mode
Visit mometrix.com/academy and enter code: 286207

Review Video: Standard Deviation
Visit mometrix.com/academy and enter code: 419469

History and Impact of Science

Greenhouse Effect

The **greenhouse effect** refers to a naturally occurring and necessary process. **Greenhouse gases**, which are ozone, carbon dioxide, water vapor, and methane, trap infrared radiation that is reflected toward the atmosphere. Without the greenhouse effect, it is estimated that the temperature on Earth would be 30 degrees less on average. The problem occurs because human activity generates more greenhouse gases than necessary. Practices that increase the amount of greenhouse gases include the burning of natural gas and oil, farming practices that result in the release of methane and nitrous oxide, factory operations that produce gases, and deforestation practices that decrease the amount of oxygen available to offset greenhouse gases. Population growth also increases the volume of gases released. Excess greenhouse gases cause more infrared radiation to become trapped, which increases the temperature at the Earth's surface.

Ozone Depletion

Ultraviolet light breaks O_2 into two very reactive oxygen atoms with unpaired electrons, which are known as **free radicals**. A free radical of oxygen pairs with another oxygen molecule to form **ozone** (O_3). Ultraviolet light also breaks ozone (O_3) into O_2 and a free radical of oxygen. This process usually acts as an ultraviolet light filter for the planet. Other free radical catalysts are produced by natural phenomena such as volcanic eruptions and by human activities. When these enter the atmosphere, they disrupt the normal cycle by breaking down ozone so it cannot absorb more ultraviolet radiation. One such catalyst is the chlorine in chlorofluorocarbons (CFCs). CFCs were used as aerosols and refrigerants. When a CFC like CF_2Cl_2 is broken down in the atmosphere, chlorine free radicals are produced. These act as catalysts to break down ozone. Whether a chlorine free radical reacts with an ozone or oxygen molecule, it is able to react again.

Human Impacts on Ecosystems

Human impacts on **ecosystems** take many forms and have many causes. They include widespread disruptions and specific niche disturbances. Humans practice many forms of **environmental manipulation** that affect plants and animals in many biomes and ecosystems. Many human practices involve the consumption of natural resources for food and energy production, the changing of the environment to produce food and energy, and the intrusion on ecosystems to provide shelter. These general behaviors include a multitude of specific behaviors, including the use and overuse of pesticides, the encroachment upon habitat, over hunting and over fishing, the introduction of plant and animal species into non-native ecosystems, and the introduction of hazardous wastes and chemical byproducts into the environment. These behaviors have led to a number of consequences, such as acid rain, ozone depletion, deforestation, urbanization, accelerated species loss, genetic abnormalities, endocrine disruption in populations, and harm to individual animals.

Global Warming

Global warming may cause the permanent loss of glaciers and permafrost. There might also be increases in air pollution and acid rain. Rising temperatures may lead to an increase in sea levels as polar ice melts, lower amounts of available fresh water as coastal areas flood, species extinction because of changes in habitat, increases in certain diseases, and a decreased standard of living for humans. Less fresh water and losses of habitat for humans and other species can also lead to decreased agricultural production and food supply shortages. Increased desertification leads to habitat loss for humans and other species. There may be more moisture in the atmosphere due to evaporation.

Acid Rain and Eutrophication

Acid rain is made up water droplets for which the pH has been lowered due atmospheric pollution. The common sources of this pollution are **sulfur** and **nitrogen** that have been released through the burning of fossil fuels. This can lead to a lowering of the pH of lakes and ponds, thereby destroying aquatic life, or damaging the leaves and bark of trees. It can also destroy buildings, monuments, and statues made of rock.

Eutrophication is the depletion of oxygen in a body of water. It may be caused by an increase in the amount of nutrients, particularly **phosphates**, which leads to an increase in plant and algae life that use up the oxygen. The result is a decrease in water quality and death of aquatic life. Sources of excess phosphates may be detergents, industrial run-off, or fertilizers that are washed into lakes or streams.

Waste Disposal Methods

- Landfills – **Methane** (CH_4) is a greenhouse gas emitted from landfills. Some is used to generate electricity and some gets into the atmosphere. CO_2 is also emitted, and landfill gas can contain nitrogen, oxygen, water vapor, sulfur, mercury, and radioactive contaminants such as tritium. **Landfill leachate** contains acids from car batteries, solvents, heavy metals, pesticides, motor oil, paint, household cleaning supplies, plastics, and many other potentially harmful substances. Some of these are dangerous when they get into the ecosystem.
- Incinerators – These contribute to air pollution in that they can release nitric and sulfuric oxides, which cause **acid rain**.
- Sewage – When dumped in raw form into oceans, sewage can introduce **fecal contaminants** and **pathogenic organisms**, which can harm ocean life and cause disease in humans.

Effects of Consumerism

Economic growth and quality of living are associated with a wasteful cycle of production. Goods are produced as cheaply as possible with little or no regard for the **ecological effects**. The ultimate goal is profitability. The production process is wasteful, and often introduces **hazardous byproducts** into the environment. Furthermore, byproducts may be dumped into a landfill instead of recycled. When consumer products get dumped in landfills, they can leach **contamination** into groundwater. Landfills can also leach gases. These are or have been dumping grounds for illegal substances, business and government waste, construction industry waste, and medical waste. These items also get dumped at illegal dump sites in urban and remote areas.

Ethical and Moral Concerns

Ethical and moral concerns related to genetic engineering arise in the scientific community and in smaller communities within society. Religious and moral beliefs can conflict with the economic interests of businesses, and with research methods used by the scientific community. For example, the United States government allows genes to be patented. A company has patented the gene for breast and ovarian cancer and will only make it available to researchers for a fee. This leads to a decrease in research, a decrease in medical solutions, and possibly an increase in the occurrence of breast and ovarian cancers. The possibility of lateral or incidental discoveries as a result of research is also limited. For example, a researcher working on a genetic solution to treat breast cancer might accidentally discover a cure for prostate cancer. This, however, would not occur if the researcher could not use the patented gene in the first place.

Energy Production

- **Coal-fired power plants**: These generate electricity fairly cheaply, but are the largest source of **greenhouse gases**.
- **Gasoline**: Gasoline is cheap, generates less CO_2 than coal, and requires less water than coal. But it nevertheless releases a substantial amount of CO_2 in the aggregate and is a limited resource. The burning of gas and other fossil fuels releases carbon dioxide (a greenhouse gas) into the atmosphere.
- **Nuclear power plants**: A small nuclear power plant can cheaply produce a large amount of electricity. But the waste is potentially harmful and a substantial amount of **water** is required to generate electricity. The cost of storing and transporting the **radioactive waste** is also very large.
- **Hydropower**: Hydropower is sustainable and environmentally benign once established. A disadvantage is that the building of a dam and the re-routing of a river can be very **environmentally disruptive**.

- **Wind power**: Wind power is sustainable, non-polluting, and requires little to no cooling water. But it will not produce power in the absence of **wind** and requires a large area over which the turbines can be laid out.
- **Solar power**: Solar power is sustainable, can be used for a single house or building, and generates peak energy during times of peak usage. But production is limited to when the sun is shining, the panels themselves are expensive to make, and making the panels generates harmful **toxins**.
- **Geothermal power:** Geothermal power is sustainable, relatively cheap, and non-polluting. Disadvantages are that it can only be utilized in areas with specific **volcanic activity**.

Remote Sensing

Remote sensing refers to the gathering of data about an object or phenomenon without physical or intimate contact with the object being studied. The data can be viewed or recorded and stored in many forms (visually with a camera, audibly, or in the form of data). Gathering weather data from a ship, satellite, or buoy might be thought of as remote sensing. The monitoring of a fetus through the use of ultrasound technology provides a remote image. Listening to the heartbeat of a fetus is another example of remote sensing. Methods for remote sensing can be grouped as radiometric, geodetic, or acoustic. Examples of **radiometric remote sensing** include radar, laser altimeters, light detection and ranging (LIDAR) used to determine the concentration of chemicals in the air, and radiometers used to detect various frequencies of radiation. **Geodetic remote sensing** involves measuring the small fluctuations in Earth's gravitational field. Examples of **acoustic remote sensing** include underwater sonar and seismographs.

Cell Phones and GPS

A **cell phone** uses **radio waves** to communicate information. When speaking into a cell phone, the user's voice is converted into an electrical signal which is transmitted via radio waves to a cell tower, then to a satellite, then to a cell tower near the recipient, and then to the recipient's cell phone. The recipient's cell phone converts the digital signal back into an electrical signal.

A similar process occurs when data is transmitted over the **Internet** via a wireless network. The cell phone will convert any outgoing communication into a radio wave that will be sent to a wireless router. The router is "wireless" in the sense that the router is not wired to the phone. But the router is connected to the Internet via a cable. The router converts the radio signal into digital form and sends the communication through the Internet. The same basic process also occurs when a cell phone receives information from the Internet.

Wireless networks use radio frequencies of 2.4 GHz or 5 GHz.

Global Positioning System (GPS) is a system of **satellites** that orbit the Earth and communicate with mobile devices to pinpoint the mobile device's **position**. This is accomplished by determining the distance between the mobile device and at least three satellites. A mobile device might calculate a distance of 400 miles between it and the first satellite. The possible locations that are 400 miles from the first satellite and the mobile device will fall along a circle. The possible locations on Earth relative to the other two satellites will fall somewhere along different circles. The point on Earth at which these three circles intersect is the location of the mobile device. The process of determining position based on distance measurements from three satellites is called **trilateration**.

The Role of Pedagogy and Scientific Inquiry in Science Education

Developing Scientific Understanding

Scientific understanding involves not merely the knowledge of scientific theories and equations, but a comprehension of how science is done, how we come to know these theories (and how confident we are in them), and how the different domains of science fit together. Students are unlikely to develop a good scientific understanding merely by being presented with isolated facts. Rather, research suggests that a scientific understanding is best fostered by **inquiry** and by **problem-based learning** approaches, which help students develop their own critical thinking and reasoning skills. In these methods, students are not just provided with facts and theories to memorize but are led to "discover" principles on their own, through experimentation and analogy. The instructor must still provide guidance in the process; if students are completely left to their own devices they may be confused or arrive at incorrect conclusions that may do more harm than good. Furthermore, assessments used in the classroom should promote **higher-order learning**, focusing not just on repetition of facts but on reasoning and evaluation of claims. It is critical that students understand that science is a process and a way of knowing, not a collection of facts.

Prior Knowledge

Students vary in their prior knowledge and capabilities, and science instruction is not a one-size-fits-all process. Sometimes prior knowledge helps student, in that they already have some knowledge about the subject in question, but sometimes prior knowledge may seem to conflict with the new information being taught—a dilemma sometimes called the "**paradox of continuity**." Learning therefore can require a **conceptual change**, in a way that allows the students to reformulate their understanding to fit new information.

Students' experience and developmental characteristics can also affect their science learning. Some students learn more effectively through different **learning styles**, or modalities: some learn best from what they see (**visual learners**), others from what they hear (**auditory learners**), still others from handling objects (**tactile learners**), and others from active participation (**kinesthetic learners**). **Abstract thinking** develops during adolescence and may develop more rapidly in some students than others; students who have not fully developed this capability may benefit from more structured teaching methods. Adolescents tend to be at a stage in their social development in which they learn well in cooperative group activities.

Planning Activities

Instructors should be aware of and sensitive to students' different preferred styles of learning and prepare lessons that engage all these styles. The instructor should also try to tie lessons to students' individual interests in order to promote active engagement. A **positive learning environment** is one that adapts to students' individual needs and that often involves students working cooperatively.

In science in particular it's important for instructors not to exclude women and minorities, since they have been excluded so much in the past that it's easy to do so unconsciously. The instructor should make an effort to mention scientists of different ethnicities and genders and make it clear that women and minorities can be and are capable scientists.

Students currently learning English have their own needs that must be addressed. The instructor can help English learners, for instance, by speaking slowly and clearly, by writing down and providing definitions of key terms, by using visual aids and graphic organizers (which also may help visual learners who are not English language learners), and by giving access to translating devices if necessary. English learners can also benefit from working in groups with capable English speakers who can help explain instructions and procedures they don't understand.

Motivation and Engagement

Regardless of how clearly and accurately an instructor explains the topic, the students may not learn if they're unengaged and not paying attention. Therefore, it's important for the teacher to engage the students' interest and keep their attention. One of the advantages of inquiry-based learning is that it actively involves the students and keeps them more engaged by relating the topic to their interests and goals and finding ways to tie the topics in to the students' own experiences, prior knowledge, and daily lives. This requires the teacher to get to know the students and their interests, but this has other benefits as well: the students are also more engaged when there is a good relationship between the teachers and students.

Students also tend to be more engaged by collaborative group activities than by working on their own. Adolescents are at a stage in their social development in which they are increasingly driven to form social attachments with their peers. They are comfortable working in groups and benefit from collaborative learning environments.

Texts Used in the Classroom

Science instruction often involves the students acquiring information from textbooks and handouts, but not all students may be able to effectively use these texts without guidance. Most textbooks have various features designed to make it easier to locate information: an **index**, a **table of contents**, and often a **glossary** and/or a list of important variables and formulas. An instructor can explain how to use these features at the beginning of the year and perhaps even assign an activity that involves making use of them.

It may also be helpful to teach **active reading** techniques. One such technique is **pre-reading**—skimming and reading the headings before reading the text in depth, making predictions and building background knowledge. The instructor can also encourage active reading techniques through providing graphic organizers or techniques like **SQ3R**—a method that involves the student first Surveying the chapter, then formulating Questions about each section, then Reading the section, Reciting the main ideas (putting them in their own words), and Reviewing the material.

In the modern classroom, textbooks aren't the only kind of text that students can take advantage of. An effective teacher can also show students how to find information online, through web searches and reference sites.

Total School Program

While the science teachers plan the curriculum for their classes, they must also be aware of the **total school program**—the overall objectives for the students' learning in all subjects. The science teacher must be aware of school-wide objectives, and make sure that they are being adequately met in his or her class. The science instructor may also have a role in *setting* those objectives, in conjunction with other teachers and administrators; the science instructor in this case should work cooperatively with the rest of the team and ensure that any issues unique or important to the science classroom are properly addressed and incorporated into the objectives.

The science teacher must also be mindful of the statewide objectives. State standards lay out the curriculum requirements for the course and specify topics that must be covered. Students must master these topics to be ready not only for standardized exams, but to ensure that no gaps in understanding exist prior to advancing to the next grade-level.

Supportive Learning Environment

Creating a learning environment that supports student inquiries involves both setting certain procedures and expectations in the class and providing resources that lend themselves to inquiry-based learning. To encourage inquiry-based learning, the instructor should encourage students to ask questions, but try to guide them toward finding answers for themselves rather than giving direct answers to their questions. The instructor should pose questions that require higher-order thinking rather than rote recall or yes or no answers and include a time for reflection in each lesson. Lessons in inquiry-based classrooms are centered around projects and experiments rather than lectures—in fact, one increasingly popular technique is to "**flip the classroom**," having the students read the lesson or watch video lectures you provide as their homework and freeing up class time for discussion and analysis.

An inquiry-centered classroom environment should put a priority on student collaboration. The instructor should give the students assignments that involve their working together as much as practical. It is helpful to have some online resources that facilitate collaboration and sharing of information, such as a class website, and perhaps a class blog and wiki. Many online resources allow students to share documents and work on them together.

Participation in Scientific Investigation

Scientific investigations are an important part of science teaching, and it is vital that all students are given the opportunity to participate. Ideally, there will be enough space and equipment for the students to work in small groups on an experiment, but in practice this may not be possible. In this case, one solution is to have rotating stations in the classroom, where for one day or for part of the period one group works on one experiment, while another group works on a different activity that uses different equipment; as they rotate through the different stations, all the students will have the opportunity to do every activity, just not in the same order.

Another important part of making it possible for all students to participate in scientific investigations is to ensure that they all have the means to understand and carry out the instructions. Going over the procedure in a lecture may not be enough; it may be better to have a written handout and/or a screencast that the students can watch and refer back to as needed. Students with special needs must also be accommodated; for instance, English language learners can be given definitions of key terms.

Active Learning, Inquiry, and Reflection

Active learning and inquiry-based learning are two related pedagogical techniques that have been shown by research to be effective in teaching science. **Active learning** refers to teaching by making the student an active participant in the learning process. A class in which the instructor lectures, the students take notes, and the students later demonstrate their learning of the topic by taking a written exam is *not* engaged in active learning, and is not likely to be as effective. Active learning can include experiments that the students perform, interactive online simulations of processes that they can't physically experience in the classroom, and having the students create presentations and projects rather than have exams and worksheets as the main assessments.

Inquiry-based learning is a form of teaching by asking questions, having discussions, and helping students do their own research rather than just presenting them with lists of facts and formulas to be learned. Inquiry-based learning is effective not only because it involves the students directly, but because allowing them to formulate their own questions engages their curiosity and critical thinking. **Reflection** is also an important part of inquiry-based learning, having students think back on what they learned and how they learned it.

Modeling Scientific Thought

Modeling, in a pedagogical context, refers to *showing* the students what they should do, rather than telling them. This doesn't mean just demonstrating an activity at the front of the classroom while the students watch passively; effective modeling also involves the students as active participants. The important thing is that the teacher sets an example of the principles he or she wants to convey.

To model scientific attitudes, therefore, means to demonstrate and embody those attitudes. To instill curiosity and skepticism in students, the teacher should display those attributes. If the teacher doesn't know the answer to a question, the teacher should not be afraid to say "I don't know"—but should follow that by trying to find the answer, by looking it up online or by performing an experiment. When discussing a topic and coming up with questions about it, the instructor should come up with questions as well—ideally questions the instructor honestly doesn't know the answer to. On the other hand, the instructor should not be too quick to accept answers—not, for instance, immediately latching onto the first answer found online, but looking for multiple sources of information and analyzing their credibility.

Inquiry-Based Scientific Investigation

An **inquiry-based scientific investigation** is one that follows the **scientific method**. While the scientific method is often formalized in different ways, there are some essential aspects. The investigator formulates a specific **question** that the investigation will answer. Usually this question is based on an **observation** that the investigation is intended to explain. The investigator then does some background **research**, reviewing previously published information on the subject in question. For a professional scientist, this will usually involve reading articles in scientific journals; in a classroom setting, a web search may suffice. The investigator may formulate a **hypothesis**—a proposed possible answer to the question.

The investigator decides how to **gather evidence** to find an answer to the question and prove or disprove the hypothesis, designing an **experiment** that will test the hypothesis, and selecting the proper tools to carry it out. The investigator makes **predictions** as to what will happen in the experiment if the hypothesis is true or if it is not. The investigator then carries out the experiment, gathers data, and analyzes the results, drawing **conclusions** based on the data.

There remain other important steps: **communication** of the results to others, defending the results, and possibly formulating further questions.

Formulating Scientific Questions

Formulating scientific questions is an important part of an inquiry-based investigation; an investigation starts with a specific question, and then an experiment is designed to answer that question. The question usually is based on an observation: the student observes a phenomenon and then formulates a question about what was observed. The question should be as concrete, objective, quantitative, and measurable as possible. "Why did this object move?" is a vague and abstract question that cannot be easily answered. "Did this object move because of this force?" is more concrete. "What is the relationship between this force and the motion of this object?" is a good quantitative question that can potentially be answered by experiment.

To help the student to formulate a question, the instructor can first guide students through an observation, encouraging the students to think of anything about the observation they're curious about or that they don't understand. The instructor can then help the students come up with questions addressing the subject of their curiosity, and then gradually guide the students into making the questions more specific and measurable.

Hypotheses

The **hypothesis** is an educated guess as to the answer to the central question of a scientific investigation. It is an important part of the investigation because it helps guide the inquiry and suggest specific lines of investigation that can prove or disprove the hypothesis: the experiment at the heart of the investigation should be designed such that it will have different results depending on whether or not the hypothesis is correct.

It is important that the hypothesis is an *educated* guess; the student may not know the answer to the question, but there should be some basis for choosing the hypothesis—by extrapolation from known cases, or by analogy with similar scenarios. If the student has trouble coming up with a hypothesis, the instructor might prompt the student to think of similar situations the student understands better, or to research such situations that have been investigated before, and then to consider what those situations imply about the present question. Even a very loose analogy can be enough to make a hypothesis—for the purposes of the investigation, it doesn't matter that the student chooses a hypothesis that turns out to be *right*, only that it relates to the question.

Scientific Results

There are many methods that can be used to analyze and evaluate scientific results. Often **graphs** help investigators and readers visualize data better. If one variable is plotted against another and the points seem to form a straight line, that is evidence that a linear relationship may exist between these variables; if they form a parabola, they may have a quadratic relationship; and so on. In more advanced classes, **statistical methods** may be useful, from methods as simple as taking the **mean** of multiple measurements and comparing the means of sets of data rather than the individual points, to methods as complex as calculating **standard deviations** and **correlation coefficients**. All of these methods help show the relationships between quantities and can help to evaluate possible explanations of a result.

Error analysis is another important part of evaluating results. Students should have an idea of what possible sources of error exist in the experiment, and whether they are **random** or **systematic**. Random error can be identified by taking repeated measurements and seeing how close they are; identifying systematic error involves a more thoughtful consideration of what could lead results to be off in one direction or the other.

Higher-Level Thinking Skills

Students should be encouraged to engage in not just rote memorization and learning of procedures, but in higher-order thinking as well that involves putting together what they've learned in constructive ways. The most commonly used model of different levels of thinking in education is **Bloom's taxonomy**, which divides cognitive processes into six categories or levels. The lowest level, **Remember**, involves simple recall of data. The next, **Understand**, requires students to be able to explain or discuss concepts in their own words. Then come **Apply**, using the concepts in practice; **Analyze**, drawing connections and comparisons between ideas; **Evaluate**, judging and justifying ideas; and **Create**, synthesizing something new from the concepts.

It's easy to design activities that utilize the lower levels of Bloom's Taxonomy. Engaging the higher orders of thinking is more difficult, but it is important for developing a more thorough understanding of a topic. Some verbs commonly associated with each level of Bloom's Taxonomy give clues as to how to promote them. "Create", for example, is associated with the verbs "construct," "plan," and "design" (among others)—certainly designing an experiment to answer a specific question fits here. "Evaluate" is associated with "appraise," "argue," and "justify"—students could be asked to assess a scientific claim and argue for or against it.

Systematic Observations and Measurements

In a scientific investigation, observations are not haphazard; there are certain systematic principles that must be followed for useful observations. As far as possible, the observations should be **quantitative**; there should be some measured value recorded, and not simply a qualitative observation such as "it is longer". Measurements should be taken by a consistent method and recorded with proper units—and with an estimate of their **uncertainty**. A measurement taken with a meter stick with markings every millimeter, for instance, has an uncertainty of ±0.5 mm.

It is also important when making observations to vary only one quantity at a time. If you want to measure how a plant's growth is affected by temperature and by amount of light, it isn't useful to change both factors for each measurement—that would make it impossible to see how much of the effect was produced by each change. Rather, it is better to do at least one set of measurements in which the temperature is held constant and the amount of light is changed, and another where the reverse is true, so that the effects of each factor can be isolated. In many cases, an **experimental control** is also desirable.

Students' Prior Knowledge

Prior knowledge refers to the knowledge the student has about the subject matter before it's covered in class. This may come from previous classes, from books and television, from peers or parents, from experience, or from other sources. It's useful to know what prior knowledge students possess before the lesson begins, and there are a number of ways of finding out. One way is through **formative assessments**, assessments that are designed not to test what the student has learned but to test what the students already know in order to guide lesson planning. Another popular way of testing prior knowledge is a **K-W-L chart**, in which students write down what they *know* about the topic, what they *want* to know, and, after the lesson, what they *learned.*

The instructor can use the students' prior knowledge as a starting point for the lesson; having the students share what they already know can help introduce the topic. Prior knowledge may also guide the instructor's approach to the topic, since it may carry some assumptions or preconceptions that will affect the way the student might react to different presentations. In some cases, prior knowledge may even lead to misconceptions that must be overcome.

Performance in Inquiry-Based Investigations

The stereotypical classroom assessment may be a multiple-choice quiz, but this is not generally the most effective way of assessing student learning in an inquiry-based classroom. There may be a place for written exams as summative assessments, but more effective assessment methods will engage students' higher-order thinking processes and may involve collaboration and active participation.

For example, in a science class, a lab report can be a useful assessment; after performing an experiment, students may be asked to turn in a written account of the procedure and results. Along similar lines, a laboratory journal that students keep during an experiment can also be used for assessment, or a field journal for longer-term projects. The instructor may require students to compile all their work in a portfolio, to be turned in at the end of the semester or at shorter intervals; this can serve as a summative assessment in lieu of or in addition to a traditional exam. To assess the student's participation in a classroom activity as objectively as possible, rather than make a subjective judgment call the instructor can use checklists or a detailed rubric prepared ahead of time.

Assessment and Instruction

An **assessment** is an activity designed to measure students' knowledge, learning, or abilities, such as an exam. Assessments are not limited to testing how much the student has learned after a lesson; there are also formative assessments used before or during a lesson to test the student's prior knowledge and how well they are learning the topic.

There are important relationships between assessment and instruction, and the two must be designed together. Formative assessments guide instruction, since the instructor should take into account students' prior knowledge in planning a lesson, and if a formative assessment shows that students are not learning what the instructor expects, the instructor should use that information to try a different pedagogical approach. As for summative assessments, they should be designed to match the learning objectives; the instructor should make sure that the summative assessment is designed to test that the students have met the specific instructional goals of the lessons.

Ongoing Assessment

Ongoing assessment is vital in science instruction for several reasons. For one thing, formative assessments are important so that the instructor can be informed of the students' prior knowledge and plan the lesson accordingly. If the instructor learns from a formative assessment that the students lack some prior knowledge necessary to the lesson, then the instructor will have to be sure to cover that first; if the instructor learns that the students have a significant misconception about the topic, then the instructor may have to plan for a conceptual change. During the lesson, further formative assessments can monitor students' learning and inform the instructor whether the students are absorbing the information and methodologies that the instructor intends them to absorb, or whether the pace of the lesson should be changed or different pedagogical methods adopted.

Ongoing assessments can also benefit the students by reinforcing the subject matter. The assessments give the students another opportunity to put what they have learned to use, and may help them better retain it. They also give the students an idea of how well they are learning, and what topics they might need to review or about which they should ask more questions.

TYPES OF ASSESSMENTS

Assessments are divided into two main categories: **summative assessments** that measure how well students have learned the subject matter at the end of a unit, and **formative assessments** that are used before or during a lesson to test the student's prior knowledge and how well they are learning the topic. Both these types of assessment are important, and both can be carried out in a number of ways. Assessments can also be **formal**—data-driven, standardized assessments the results of which can be compared against preset benchmarks—or **informal**—less structured assessments based around performance and content. An effective science classroom utilizes a variety of different assessment methods.

For example, a **performance assessment** is an assessment that requires the student to demonstrate skills by completing a task, rather than by selecting a pre-set answer or filling in a blank. A **self-assessment** is an activity in which the student assesses his or her own work, perhaps using a rubric provided by the instructor; these are often not graded and serve to inform the student of his or her own learning. A **peer assessment** is an activity in which the student's work is assessed not by the instructor, but by a fellow student.

Review Video: Formative and Summative Assessments
Visit mometrix.com/academy and enter code: 804991

COMBATTING MISCONCEPTIONS

One of the reasons it's important to gauge students' prior knowledge of a topic is because some of that prior knowledge may be incorrect or misleading, and the student may have misconceptions about the topic that must be overcome. Simply telling the students that their prior beliefs were incorrect is unlikely to be effective, and it may in fact be counterproductive, leading to their misconceptions being reinforced instead of removed. Rather, a better goal is to bring about a **conceptual change**, a gradual revision and rearrangement of prior knowledge to accommodate new ideas, in which the student is an active participant.

There are several research-based methods of bringing about conceptual change. One method is to promote **cognitive conflict**: presenting data or demonstrations that contradict the students' prior conceptions, and guiding the students into finding a resolution to the conflict. Another is the use of **refutational texts** that discuss and refute various views on the topic. Other methods include **collaborative argumentation**, in which students are encouraged to discuss, defend, and evaluate their positions; and **persuasive pedagogy**, applying methods of persuasion such as response shaping and reinforcing.

RELIABILITY AND VALIDITY

Two measurements of the soundness of an assessment are reliability and validity. An assessment is **reliable** if it yields consistent results; students' scores on the assessment should not depend on external circumstances and should be similar for different questions that test the same skill. An assessment is **valid** if it measures what it is meant to measure. These two qualities can vary independently; it is possible for an exam to have a high reliability but a low validity, or vice versa.

The reliability of an assessment can be affected by many factors. Longer tests tend to be more reliable; tests with a short time limit so that many students cannot complete all the questions, or must rush to do so, tend to be less reliable. Reliability is also affected by difficulty; a test is most reliable when the questions are not so easy that almost every student answers the questions correctly, but not so hard that almost none do. It requires finding a suitable middle ground of difficulty. An assessment will tend to be more valid if it is designed to cover all the material that it is supposed to cover, but only that material. It will be less valid if it has hidden biases against certain categories of student.

ASSESSMENT AS A LEARNING EXPERIENCE

Though an obvious purpose of assessments is to allow the instructor to assign students a grade in the class, the assessments themselves can provide learning experiences. For one thing, as the students see what questions on the assessment they are unable to answer, or do not answer correctly, this helps them see what topics they have not fully learned and may need to further review. On the other hand, the questions that the students got right will help build their confidence and perhaps help them better remember in the future what they learned about those topics. Assessments also give students further practice with the methods and concepts they are testing, which may further work to reinforce them. They may also help students to learn new problem-solving strategies; as students go over the assessment after the fact and discuss how they were supposed to solve a particular problem, the answer might give them information about a strategy they were previously unaware of or underutilizing.

Equitable Use of Assessments

One important consideration that must be kept in mind in designing assessments is that they must be **equitable**—they must not be biased toward or against any part of the student population. Every student must have an adequate opportunity to demonstrate his or her skills and knowledge. There are many biases that may carelessly enter into assessments: cultural biases, language biases, biases against students with special needs.

There are a number of steps that instructors can take to ensure that assessments are equitable. Questions should not rely on "common knowledge" that may not be common to students of different cultures. Students with special needs must be provided with adequate accommodations. English language learners should be given definitions or paraphrases of difficult words and sentences. Other steps that can be taken toward making assessments more equitable include clearly laying out learning outcomes and grading rubrics, using many different methods of assessment that allow students to show their accomplishments in different ways, and ensuring that the subject matter covered in assessments is closely matched to what the instructor teaches in class.

Sharing Criteria and Results

It's important to share the evaluation criteria of assessments with students so that the students will know what to expect from the assessments and prepare accordingly, and so that during the assessment they will know where to best focus their time and attention. If the students have no idea how an assessment will be graded, then the assessment is not fair or equitable; students will not know what aspects of the assessment they should focus on the most and doing well on the assessment may be largely a matter of luck. Sharing the rubric for the assessment ahead of time makes the instructor's expectations clear and ensures that the students know what specifically they will be tested on and can prepare accordingly.

It is also important to share the results of assessments with the students. If the students know the results of their assessments, they can gauge their own progress and learning, and decide where they need to focus in the future and what topics they may need to revisit. Knowing their assessment results may also help students evaluate their study strategies and judge whether or not they are working and how or if they might need to be revised.

Scientific Inquiry Skills for Elementary Students

The six abilities that **grades K-4 students** should acquire are as follows:

- They should be able to ask questions about objects, organisms, and events in the environment.
- They should be able to devise a simple investigation to answer a question.
- They should be able to use tools such as magnifying glasses, rulers, and balances to gather data and make observations.
- They should be able to use the gathered data and observations to provide an explanation.
- They should be able to talk about, draw pictures, or use another method to communicate the results of an investigation and what they learned.
- With respect to the nature of scientific inquiry and scientists, students should understand that investigations involve formulating questions and answers, using different methods of discovering and disclosing answers, using basic tools, observing, sharing answers, and looking at and understanding others' work.

SCIENTIFIC INQUIRY SKILLS FOR MIDDLE GRADE STUDENTS

The five abilities that **grades 5–8 students** should acquire are as follows:

- They should be able to reformulate and clarify questions until they can be answered through scientific investigation.
- They should be able to create and carry out a scientific investigation, interpret the data to provide explanations, and use further data to revise explanations.
- They should be able to identify the tools necessary to gather and analyze data. They should be able to use computer hardware and software to store, organize, and gather data.
- They should be able to provide descriptions and explanations, create models, and make predictions based on the body of knowledge they possess.
- They should be able to explain cause and effect relationships using explanations and data from experiments.

SCIENTIFIC INQUIRY SKILLS FOR OLDER STUDENTS

The six abilities that **grades 9–12 students** should acquire are as follows:

- They should be able to identify questions and concepts that guide scientific investigation. In other words, they should be able to create a hypothesis and an appropriate experiment to test that hypothesis.
- They should be able to design and conduct a scientific investigation from start to finish. This includes being able to guide the inquiry by choosing the proper technologies and methods, determining variables, selecting an appropriate method for presenting data, and conducting peer review.
- They should be able to use technology and mathematics in investigations.
- They should be able to formulate and revise scientific explanations and models.
- They should be able to recognize and analyze alternative explanations. In other words, they should be able to devise other possibilities based on the current body of knowledge.
- They should be able to communicate and defend a scientific argument in both written and oral form.

Chapter Quiz

Ready to see how well you retained what you just read? Scan the QR code to go directly to the chapter quiz interface for this study guide. If you're using a computer, simply visit the online resources page at **mometrix.com/resources719/ftcephysics** and click the Chapter Quizzes link.

Mathematics of Physics

Rounding and Estimation

Rounding is reducing the digits in a number while still trying to keep the value similar. The result will be less accurate but in a simpler form and easier to use. Whole numbers can be rounded to the nearest ten, hundred, or thousand, for instance.

To round a number, we make it a little smaller (rounding down) or a little larger (rounding up) to get a number that ends in zeros. We specify the number of zeros by naming the last place that we will not "zero out." For example, to round 8,327 to the nearest hundred, we round down to 8,300, zeroing out every digit to the right of the hundreds place. To round 4,728 to the nearest thousand, we round up to 5,000, increasing the thousands digit by one (to make the number larger) and zeroing out every digit to the right of the thousands place.

We decide whether to round down or up by looking at the first digit we are going to zero out. If it is less than 5 (namely, 0, 1, 2, 3, or 4) we round down. If it is greater than or equal to 5 (namely, 5, 6, 7, 8, or 9) we round up by adding 1 to the place we are rounding to. So, rounding 8,327 to the nearest hundred, we round down to 8,300 because the tens digit, 2, is less than 5. And rounding 4,728 to the nearest thousand, we round up to 5,000, increasing the thousands digit by 1, because the hundreds digit, 7, is greater than or equal to 5.

This even works with decimals. For example, rounding 39.7426 to the nearest tenth, we round down to 39.7000 (or simply 39.7) because the hundredths digit, 4, is less than 5. And rounding 0.019823 to the nearest thousandth, we round up to 0.020000 (or simply 0.02) by increasing the thousandths digit by 1, because the ten-thousandths digit, 8, is greater than or equal to 5.

When you are asked to estimate the solution to a problem, you will need to provide only an approximate figure or **estimation** for your answer. In this situation, you will need to round each number in the calculation to the level indicated (nearest hundred, nearest thousand, etc.) or to a level that makes sense for the numbers involved. When estimating a sum **all numbers must be rounded to the same level**. You cannot round one number to the nearest thousand while rounding another to the nearest hundred.

For instance, suppose you are considering buying four pieces of equipment for your home office. Their prices are \$485, \$1,217, \$750, and \$643. To estimate their total cost, you might round each price to the nearest hundred and add the rounded figures, getting an estimate of \$500 + \$1,200 + \$800 + \$600 = \$3,100. By estimating instead of making an exact calculation, you give up a little accuracy to get a simpler calculation.

Review Video: Rounding and Estimation
Visit mometrix.com/academy and enter code: 126243

Scientific Notation

Scientific notation is a way of writing large numbers in a shorter form. The form $a \times 10^n$ is used in scientific notation, where a is greater than or equal to 1 but less than 10, and n is the number of places the decimal must move to get from the original number to a. Example: The number 230,400,000 is cumbersome to write. To write the value in scientific notation, place a decimal point between the first and second numbers, and include all digits through the last non-zero digit ($a = 2.304$). To find the appropriate power of 10, count the number of places the decimal point had to move ($n = 8$). The number is positive if the decimal moved to the left, and negative if it moved to the right. We can then write 230,400,000 as 2.304×10^8. If we look instead at the number 0.00002304, we have the same value for a, but this time the decimal moved 5 places to the right ($n = -5$). Thus, 0.00002304 can be written as 2.304×10^{-5}. Using this notation makes it simple to compare very large or very small numbers. By comparing exponents, it is easy to see that 3.28×10^4 is smaller than 1.51×10^5, because 4 is less than 5.

Review Video: Scientific Notation
Visit mometrix.com/academy and enter code: 976454

Metric and Customary Measurements

Metric Measurement Prefixes

Giga-	One billion	1 *giga*watt is one billion watts
Mega-	One million	1 *mega*hertz is one million hertz
Kilo-	One thousand	1 *kilo*gram is one thousand grams
Deci-	One-tenth	1 *deci*meter is one-tenth of a meter
Centi-	One-hundredth	1 *centi*meter is one-hundredth of a meter
Milli-	One-thousandth	1 *milli*liter is one-thousandth of a liter
Micro-	One-millionth	1 *micro*gram is one-millionth of a gram

Review Video: How the Metric System Works
Visit mometrix.com/academy and enter code: 163709

Measurement Conversion

When converting between units, the goal is to maintain the same meaning but change the way it is displayed. In order to go from a larger unit to a smaller unit, multiply the number of the known amount by the equivalent amount. When going from a smaller unit to a larger unit, divide the number of the known amount by the equivalent amount.

For complicated conversions, it may be helpful to set up conversion fractions. In these fractions, one fraction is the **conversion factor**. The other fraction has the unknown amount in the numerator. So, the known value is placed in the denominator. Sometimes, the second fraction has the known value from the problem in the numerator and the unknown in the denominator. Multiply the two fractions to get the converted measurement. Note that since the numerator and the denominator of the factor are equivalent, the value of the fraction is 1. That is why we can say that the result in the new units is equal to the result in the old units even though they have different numbers.

It can often be necessary to chain known conversion factors together. As an example, consider converting 512 square inches to square meters. We know that there are 2.54 centimeters in an inch and 100 centimeters in a meter, and we know we will need to square each of these factors to achieve the conversion we are looking for.

$$\frac{512\text{ in}^2}{1} \times \left(\frac{2.54\text{ cm}}{1\text{ in}}\right)^2 \times \left(\frac{1\text{ m}}{100\text{ cm}}\right)^2 = \frac{512\cancel{\text{in}^2}}{1} \times \left(\frac{6.4516\cancel{\text{cm}^2}}{1\cancel{\text{in}^2}}\right) \times \left(\frac{1\text{ m}^2}{10{,}000\cancel{\text{cm}^2}}\right) = 0.330\text{ m}^2$$

Review Video: Measurement Conversions
Visit mometrix.com/academy and enter code: 316703

Review Video: Converting Kilograms to Pounds
Visit mometrix.com/academy and enter code: 241463

Common Units and Equivalents

Metric Equivalents

1000 μg (microgram)	1 mg
1000 mg (milligram)	1 g
1000 g (gram)	1 kg
1000 kg (kilogram)	1 metric ton
1000 mL (milliliter)	1 L
1000 μm (micrometer)	1 mm
1000 mm (millimeter)	1 m
100 cm (centimeter)	1 m
1000 m (meter)	1 km

Distance and Area Measurement

Unit	Abbreviation	US equivalent	Metric equivalent
Inch	in	1 inch	2.54 centimeters
Foot	ft	12 inches	0.305 meters
Yard	yd	3 feet	0.914 meters
Mile	mi	5280 feet	1.609 kilometers
Acre	ac	4840 square yards	0.405 hectares
Square Mile	sq. mi. or mi.^{2}	640 acres	2.590 square kilometers

Capacity Measurements

Unit	Abbreviation	US equivalent	Metric equivalent
Fluid Ounce	fl oz	8 fluid drams	29.573 milliliters
Cup	c	8 fluid ounces	0.237 liter
Pint	pt.	16 fluid ounces	0.473 liter
Quart	qt.	2 pints	0.946 liter
Gallon	gal.	4 quarts	3.785 liters
Teaspoon	t or tsp.	1 fluid dram	5 milliliters
Tablespoon	T or tbsp.	4 fluid drams	15 or 16 milliliters
Cubic Centimeter	cc or cm^3	0.271 drams	1 milliliter

Weight Measurements

Unit	Abbreviation	US equivalent	Metric equivalent
Ounce	oz	16 drams	28.35 grams
Pound	lb	16 ounces	453.6 grams
Ton	tn.	2,000 pounds	907.2 kilograms

Volume and Weight Measurement Clarifications

Always be careful when using ounces and fluid ounces. They are not equivalent.

1 pint = 16 fluid ounces	1 fluid ounce ≠ 1 ounce
1 pound = 16 ounces	1 pint ≠ 1 pound

Having one pint of something does not mean you have one pound of it. In the same way, just because something weighs one pound does not mean that its volume is one pint.

In the United States, the word "ton" by itself refers to a short ton or a net ton. Do not confuse this with a long ton (also called a gross ton) or a metric ton (also spelled *tonne*), which have different measurement equivalents.

$$1 \text{ US ton} = 2000 \text{ pounds} \quad \neq \quad 1 \text{ metric ton} = 1000 \text{ kilograms}$$

Precision, Accuracy, and Error

Measurements of physical quantities (e.g., length, area, volume, weight, mass, and time) in the real world are never perfect. Measurements miss the true value, and repeated measurements produce different values. For this reason, fields that depend on good measurement have technical terms, precision and accuracy, that describe how particular ways of measuring a quantity produce good or bad results. Note that these terms apply not to single measurements but to repeated measurements of the same quantity using the same procedure.

Precision describes the consistency of measurements. Measurements that cluster closely together, with little variation from one measurement to the next, have high precision. Measurements that vary a great deal from one measurement to the next have low precision.

Accuracy describes the closeness of measurements to the true value of the quantity being measured or, more technically, the tendency of measurements to cluster around the true value (though we do not usually know the true value; otherwise, we would not bother to measure it).

An analogy from archery may help. An outstanding archer aiming at the center of the target (the true value) produces a tight cluster of arrows around the center (high accuracy, high precision). Under the same circumstances a modestly good archer produces a loose cluster around the center (high accuracy, low precision). If, however, there is a strong crosswind and the archers do nothing to compensate for it, the outstanding archer's shots will cluster tightly around a point away from the center (low accuracy, high precision); and the modestly good archer's shots will cluster loosely around a point away from the center (low accuracy, low precision).

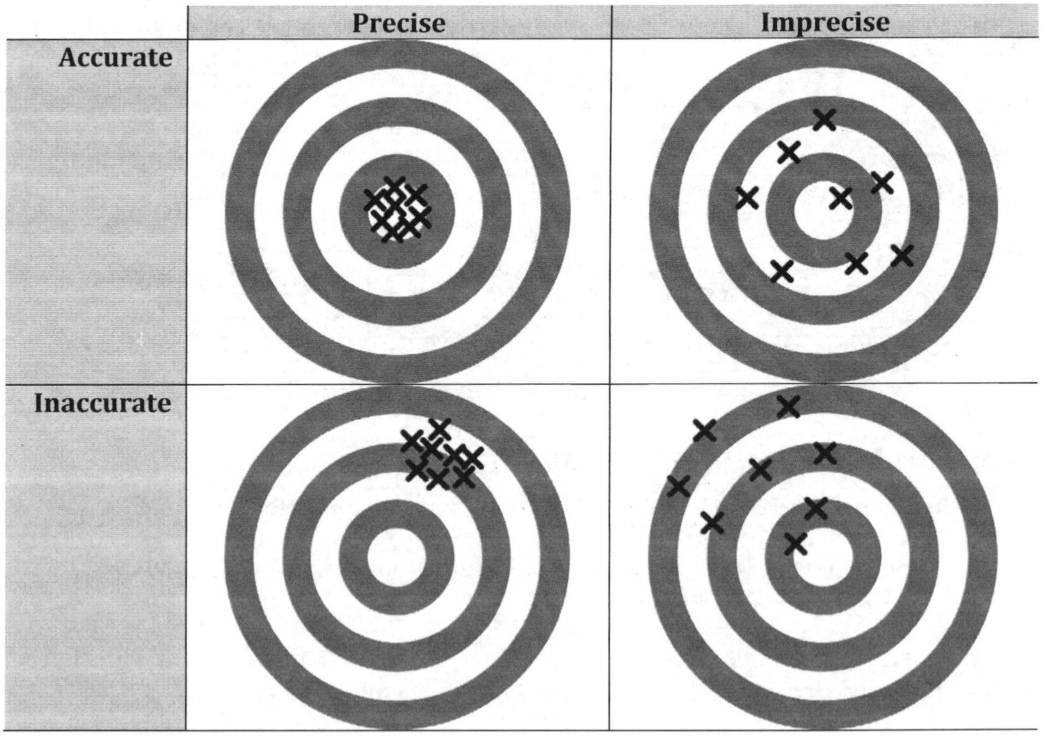

Error in measurement is not a mistake but simply the difference between the true value and the measured value. Since we seldom know the true value, we seldom know the exact error; but sometimes we know a limit on how big the error can be (an error bound), in which case we can use the plus-or-minus sign, $\pm$, to indicate how far the true value might lie from the measured value. For instance, if we measure the length of a metal bar as 25.6 cm and we know the error in our measurement is no more than 0.03 cm (some sources call this **approximate error**), then we might report the length of the bar as 25.6 ± 0.03 cm, which means it lies between 25.57 cm and 25.63 cm.

A particularly important application of this comes from the necessity of rounding whenever we make a measurement. For instance, if we measure the length of a pencil using a ruler marked off in whole inches (no fractions), then we must round our measurement to the nearest inch. Thus, if we report the length as 8 inches, it means that the actual value lies somewhere between 7.5 inches and 8.5 inches, which is to say 8 ± 0.5 inches. This built-in error bound due to rounding is called the **maximum possible error**, and it is always half the magnitude of the smallest unit used in the measurement. Determining the smallest unit can be somewhat subtle, involving the rules for significant figures commonly used in physics, chemistry, and other fields.

Review Video: Precision, Accuracy, and Error
Visit mometrix.com/academy and enter code: 520377

Points, Lines, and Planes

Points and Lines

A **point** is a fixed location in space, has no size or dimensions, and is commonly represented by a dot. A **line** is a set of points that extends infinitely in two opposite directions. It has length, but no width or depth. A line can be defined by any two distinct points that it contains. A **line segment** is a portion of a line that has definite endpoints. A **ray** is a portion of a line that extends from a single point on that line in one direction along the line. It has a definite beginning, but no ending.

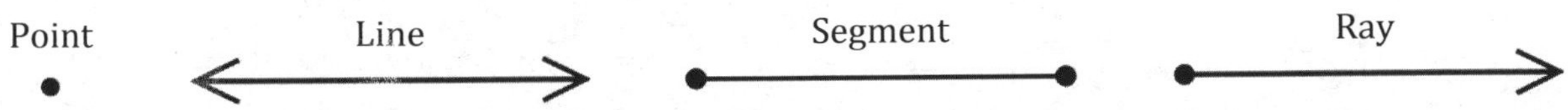

Points are **collinear** if there is a single line that passes through all of them. Otherwise, they are noncollinear. Two points are always collinear since two points define a line. Three points may be noncollinear. For example, the three vertices of a triangle are noncollinear since there is no line that goes through all three of them.

Interactions Between Lines

Intersecting lines are lines that have exactly one point in common. **Concurrent lines** are multiple lines that intersect at a single point. **Perpendicular lines** are lines that intersect at right angles. They are represented by the symbol ⊥. The shortest distance from a line to a point not on the line is a perpendicular segment from the point to the line. **Parallel lines** are lines in the same plane that have no points in common and never meet. Two distinct lines in a given plane are always either intersecting or parallel. **Skew lines** are two distinct lines in a three dimensional space that do not intersect and may also not be parallel because there is no single plane that contains them both.

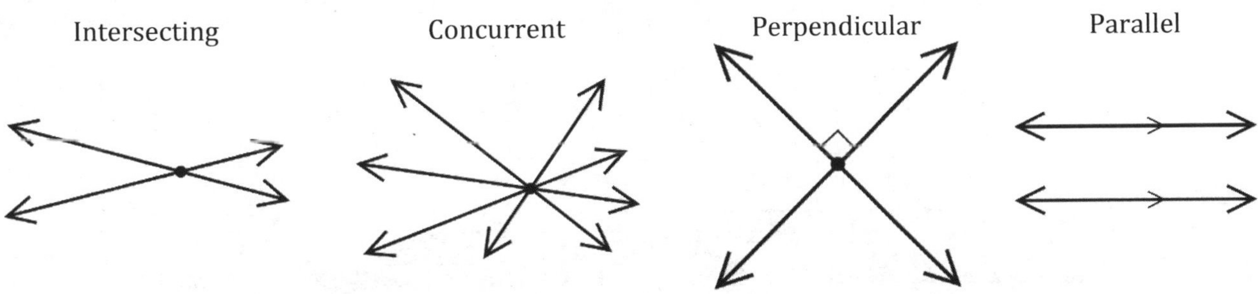

Review Video: Parallel and Perpendicular Lines
Visit mometrix.com/academy and enter code: 815923

A **transversal** is a line that intersects at least two other lines, which may or may not be parallel to one another. A transversal that intersects parallel lines is a common occurrence in geometry. A **bisector** is a line or line segment that divides another line segment into two equal lengths. A **perpendicular bisector** of a line segment is composed of points that are equidistant from the endpoints of the segment it is dividing.

Transversal

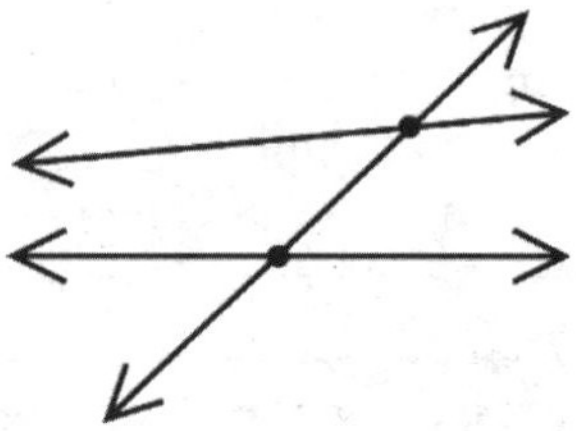

Bisector

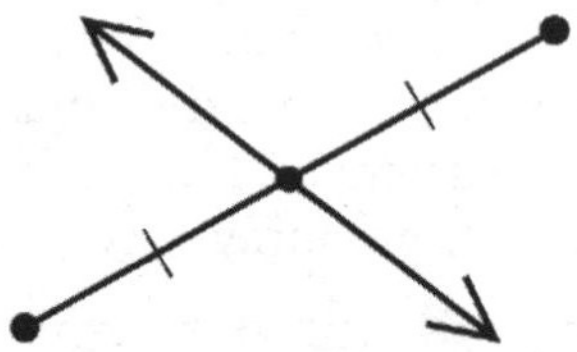

Perpendicular bisector

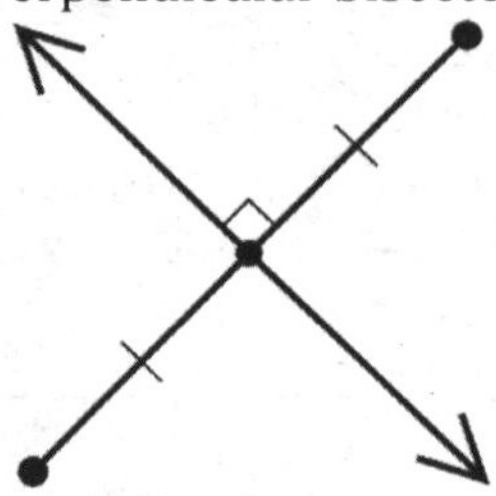

The **projection of a point on a line** is the point at which a perpendicular line drawn from the given point to the given line intersects the line. This is also the shortest distance from the given point to the line. The **projection of a segment on a line** is a segment whose endpoints are the points formed when perpendicular lines are drawn from the endpoints of the given segment to the given line. This is similar to the length a diagonal line appears to be when viewed from above.

Projection of a point on a line

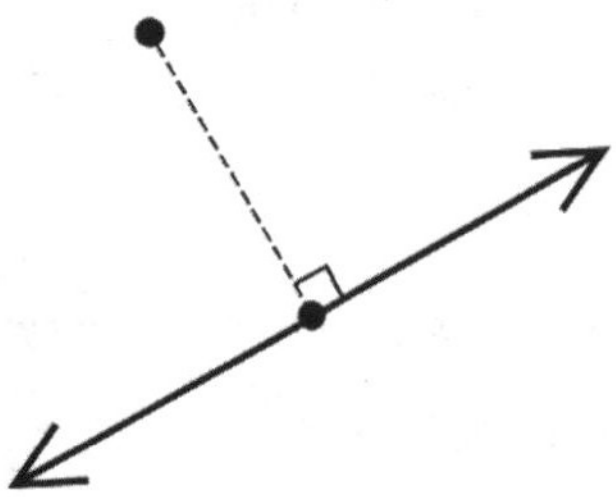

Projection of a segment on a line

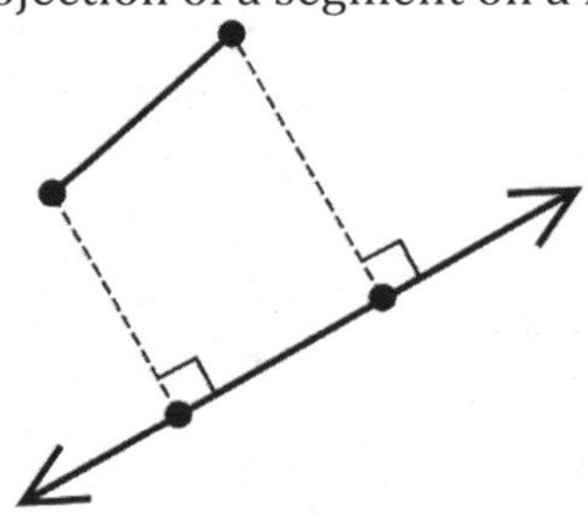

PLANES

A **plane** is a two-dimensional flat surface defined by three non-collinear points. A plane extends an infinite distance in all directions in those two dimensions. It contains an infinite number of points, parallel lines and segments, intersecting lines and segments, as well as parallel or intersecting rays. A plane will never contain a three-dimensional figure or skew lines. Two given planes are either parallel or they intersect at a line. A plane may intersect a circular conic surface to form **conic sections**, such as a parabola, hyperbola, circle or ellipse.

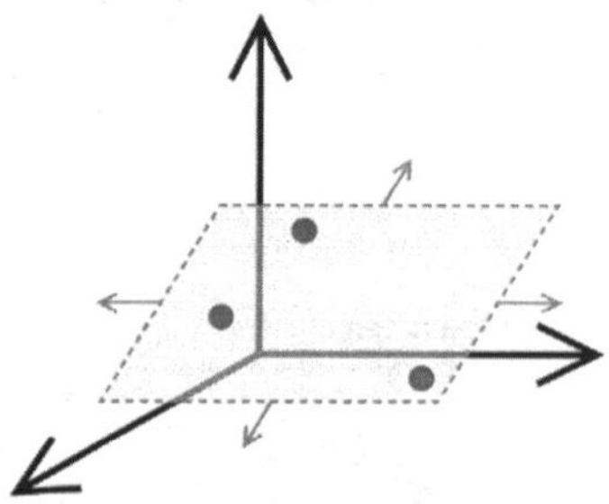

Review Video: Lines and Planes
Visit mometrix.com/academy and enter code: 554267

Pythagorean Theorem

The side of a triangle opposite the right angle is called the **hypotenuse.** The other two sides are called the legs. The Pythagorean theorem states a relationship among the legs and hypotenuse of a right triangle: $(a^2 + b^2 = c^2)$, where a and b are the lengths of the legs of a right triangle, and c is the length of the hypotenuse. Note that this formula will only work with right triangles.

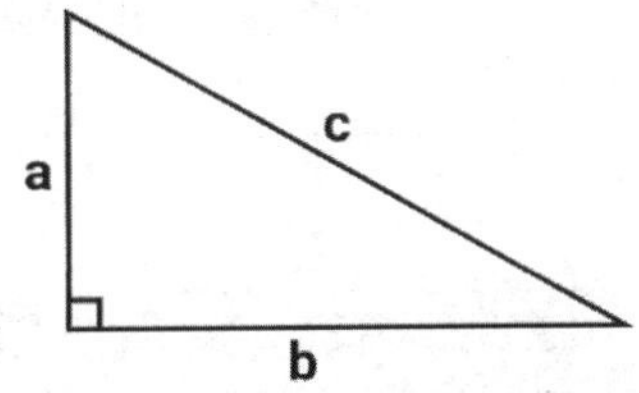

Review Video: Pythagorean Theorem
Visit mometrix.com/academy and enter code: 906576

Trigonometric Formulas

In the diagram below, angle C is the right angle, and side c is the hypotenuse. Side a is the side opposite to angle A and side b is the side opposite to angle B. Using ratios of side lengths as a means to calculate the sine, cosine, and tangent of an acute angle only works for right triangles.

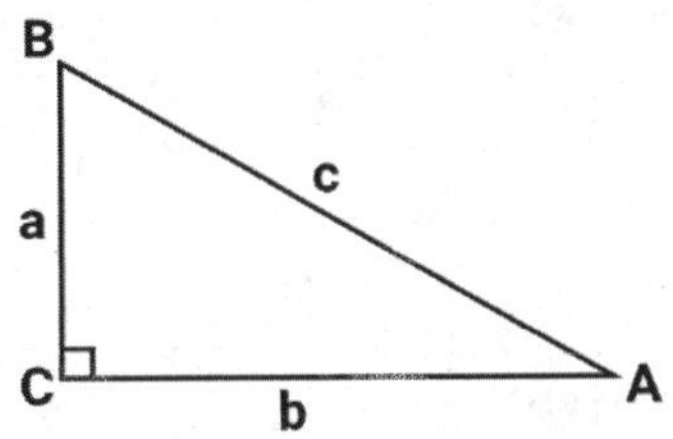

$$\sin A = \frac{\text{opposite side}}{\text{hypotenuse}} = \frac{a}{c} \qquad \csc A = \frac{1}{\sin A} = \frac{\text{hypotenuse}}{\text{opposite side}} = \frac{c}{a}$$

$$\cos A = \frac{\text{adjacent side}}{\text{hypotenuse}} = \frac{b}{c} \qquad \sec A = \frac{1}{\cos A} = \frac{\text{hypotenuse}}{\text{adjacent side}} = \frac{c}{b}$$

$$\tan A = \frac{\text{opposite side}}{\text{adjacent side}} = \frac{a}{b} \qquad \cot A = \frac{1}{\tan A} = \frac{\text{adjacent side}}{\text{opposite side}} = \frac{b}{a}$$

Laws of Sines and Cosines

The **law of sines** states that $\frac{\sin A}{a} = \frac{\sin B}{b} = \frac{\sin C}{c}$, where A, B, and C are the angles of a triangle, and a, b, and c are the sides opposite their respective angles. This formula will work with all triangles, not just right triangles.

The **law of cosines** is given by the formula $c^2 = a^2 + b^2 - 2ab(\cos C)$, where a, b, and c are the sides of a triangle, and C is the angle opposite side c. This is a generalized form of the Pythagorean theorem that can be used on any triangle.

Review Video: Law of Sines
Visit mometrix.com/academy and enter code: 206844

Review Video: Law of Cosines
Visit mometrix.com/academy and enter code: 158911

Data Analysis

Dispersion

A **measure of dispersion** is a single value that helps to "interpret" the measure of central tendency by providing more information about how the data values in the set are distributed about the measure of central tendency. The measure of dispersion helps to eliminate or reduce the disadvantages of using the mean, median, or mode as a single measure of central tendency, and give a more accurate picture of the dataset as a whole. To have a measure of dispersion, you must know or calculate the range, standard deviation, or variance of the data set.

Range

The **range** of a set of data is the difference between the greatest and lowest values of the data in the set. To calculate the range, you must first make sure the units for all data values are the same, and then identify the greatest and lowest values. If there are multiple data values that are equal for the highest or lowest, just use one of the values in the formula. Write the answer with the same units as the data values you used to do the calculations.

Review Video: Statistical Range
Visit mometrix.com/academy and enter code: 778541

Sample Standard Deviation

Standard deviation is a measure of dispersion that compares all the data values in the set to the mean of the set to give a more accurate picture. To find the **standard deviation of a sample**, use the formula

$$s = \sqrt{\frac{\sum_{i=1}^{n}(x_i - \bar{x})^2}{n-1}}$$

Note that s is the standard deviation of a sample, x_i represents the individual values in the data set, $\bar{x}$ is the mean of the data values in the set, and n is the number of data values in the set. The higher the value of the standard deviation is, the greater the variance of the data values from the mean. The units associated with the standard deviation are the same as the units of the data values.

Review Video: Standard Deviation
Visit mometrix.com/academy and enter code: 419469

Sample Variance

The **variance of a sample** is the square of the sample standard deviation (denoted s^2). While the mean of a set of data gives the average of the set and gives information about where a specific data value lies in relation to the average, the variance of the sample gives information about the degree to which the data values are spread out and tells you how close an individual value is to the average compared to the other values. The units associated with variance are the same as the units of the data values squared.

Percentile

Percentiles and quartiles are other methods of describing data within a set. **Percentiles** tell what percentage of the data in the set fall below a specific point. For example, achievement test scores are often given in percentiles. A score at the 80th percentile is one which is equal to or higher than 80 percent of the scores in the set. In other words, 80 percent of the scores were lower than that score.

Quartiles are percentile groups that make up quarter sections of the data set. The first quartile is the 25th percentile. The second quartile is the 50th percentile; this is also the median of the dataset. The third quartile is the 75th percentile.

Skewness

Skewness is a way to describe the symmetry or asymmetry of the distribution of values in a dataset. If the distribution of values is symmetrical, there is no skew. In general the closer the mean of a data set is to the median of the data set, the less skew there is. Generally, if the mean is to the right of the median, the data set is *positively skewed*, or right-skewed, and if the mean is to the left of the median, the data set is *negatively skewed*, or left-skewed. However, this rule of thumb is not infallible. When the data values are graphed on a curve, a set with no skew will be a perfect bell curve.

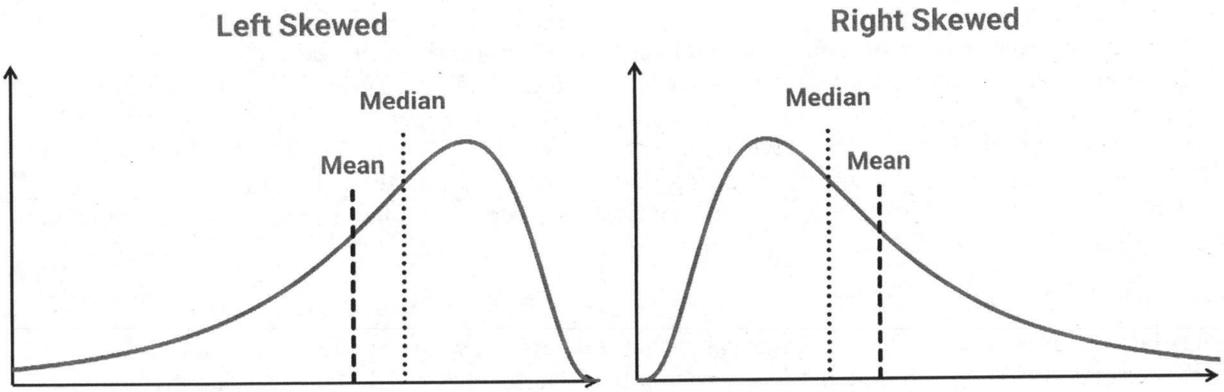

To estimate skew, use the formula:

$$\text{skew} = \frac{\sqrt{n(n-1)}}{n-2}\left(\frac{\frac{1}{n}\sum_{i=1}^{n}(x_i-\bar{x})^3}{\left(\frac{1}{n}\sum_{i=1}^{n}(x_i-\bar{x})^2\right)^{\frac{3}{2}}}\right)$$

Note that n is the datapoints in the set, x_i is the ith value in the set, and $\bar{x}$ is the mean of the set.

Review Video: Skew
Visit mometrix.com/academy and enter code: 661486

Unimodal vs. Bimodal

If a distribution has a single peak, it would be considered **unimodal**. If it has two discernible peaks it would be considered **bimodal**. Bimodal distributions may be an indication that the set of data being considered is actually the combination of two sets of data with significant differences. A **uniform distribution** is a distribution in which there is *no distinct peak or variation* in the data. No values or ranges are particularly more common than any other values or ranges.

Outlier

An outlier is an extremely high or extremely low value in the data set. It may be the result of measurement error, in which case, the outlier is not a valid member of the data set. However, it may also be a valid member of the distribution. Unless a measurement error is identified, the experimenter cannot know for certain if an outlier is or is not a member of the distribution. There are arbitrary methods that can be employed to designate an extreme value as an outlier. One method designates an outlier (or possible outlier) to be any value less than $Q_1 - 1.5(IQR)$ or any value greater than $Q_3 + 1.5(IQR)$.

Data Analysis

Simple Regression

In statistics, **simple regression** is using an equation to represent a relation between independent and dependent variables. The independent variable is also referred to as the explanatory variable or the predictor and is generally represented by the variable x in the equation. The dependent variable, usually represented by the variable y, is also referred to as the response variable. The equation may be any type of function – linear, quadratic, exponential, etc. The best way to handle this task is to use the regression feature of your graphing calculator. This will easily give you the curve of best fit and provide you with the coefficients and other information you need to derive an equation.

LINE OF BEST FIT

In a scatter plot, the **line of best fit** is the line that best shows the trends of the data. The line of best fit is given by the equation $\hat{y} = ax + b$, where a and b are the regression coefficients. The regression coefficient a is also the slope of the line of best fit, and b is also the y-coordinate of the point at which the line of best fit crosses the y-axis. Not every point on the scatter plot will be on the line of best fit. The differences between the y-values of the points in the scatter plot and the corresponding y-values according to the equation of the line of best fit are the residuals. The line of best fit is also called the least-squares regression line because it is also the line that has the lowest sum of the squares of the residuals.

CORRELATION COEFFICIENT

The **correlation coefficient** is the numerical value that indicates how strong the relationship is between the two variables of a linear regression equation. A correlation coefficient of −1 is a perfect negative correlation. A correlation coefficient of +1 is a perfect positive correlation. Correlation coefficients close to −1 or +1 are very strong correlations. A correlation coefficient equal to zero indicates there is no correlation between the two variables. This test is a good indicator of whether or not the equation for the line of best fit is accurate. The formula for the correlation coefficient is

$$r = \frac{\sum_{i=1}^{n}(x_i - \bar{x})(y_i - \bar{y})}{\sqrt{\sum_{i=1}^{n}(x_i - \bar{x})^2}\sqrt{\sum_{i=1}^{n}(y_i - \bar{y})^2}}$$

where r is the correlation coefficient, n is the number of data values in the set, (x_i, y_i) is a point in the set, and $\bar{x}$ and $\bar{y}$ are the means.

Z-SCORE

A **z-score** is an indication of how many standard deviations a given value falls from the sample mean. To calculate a z-score, use the formula:

$$\frac{x - \bar{x}}{\sigma}$$

In this formula x is the data value, $\bar{x}$ is the mean of the sample data, and σ is the standard deviation of the population. If the z-score is positive, the data value lies above the mean. If the z-score is negative, the data value falls below the mean. These scores are useful in interpreting data such as standardized test scores, where every piece of data in the set has been counted, rather than just a small random sample. In cases where standard deviations are calculated from a random sample of the set, the z-scores will not be as accurate.

CENTRAL LIMIT THEOREM

According to the **central limit theorem**, regardless of what the original distribution of a sample is, the distribution of the means tends to get closer and closer to a normal distribution as the sample size gets larger and larger (this is necessary because the sample is becoming more all-encompassing of the elements of the population). As the sample size gets larger, the distribution of the sample mean will approach a normal distribution with a mean of the population mean and a variance of the population variance divided by the sample size.

Measures of Central Tendency

A **measure of central tendency** is a statistical value that gives a reasonable estimate for the center of a group of data. There are several different ways of describing the measure of central tendency. Each one has a unique way it is calculated, and each one gives a slightly different perspective on the data set. Whenever you give a measure of central tendency, always make sure the units are the same. If the data has different units, such as hours, minutes, and seconds, convert all the data to the same unit, and use the same unit in the measure of central tendency. If no units are given in the data, do not give units for the measure of central tendency.

MEAN

The **statistical mean** of a group of data is the same as the arithmetic average of that group. To find the mean of a set of data, first convert each value to the same units, if necessary. Then find the sum of all the values, and count the total number of data values, making sure you take into consideration each individual value. If a value appears more than once, count it more than once. Divide the sum of the values by the total number of values and apply the units, if any. Note that the mean does not have to be one of the data values in the set, and may not divide evenly.

$$\text{mean} = \frac{\text{sum of the data values}}{\text{quantity of data values}}$$

For instance, the mean of the data set {88, 72, 61, 90, 97, 68, 88, 79, 86, 93, 97, 71, 80, 84, 89} would be the sum of the fifteen numbers divided by 15:

$$\frac{88 + 72 + 61 + 90 + 97 + 68 + 88 + 79 + 86 + 93 + 97 + 71 + 80 + 84 + 89}{15} = \frac{1242}{15} = 82.8$$

While the mean is relatively easy to calculate and averages are understood by most people, the mean can be very misleading if it is used as the sole measure of central tendency. If the data set has outliers (data values that are unusually high or unusually low compared to the rest of the data values), the mean can be very distorted, especially if the data set has a small number of values. If unusually high values are countered with unusually low values, the mean is not affected as much. For example, if five of twenty students in a class get a 100 on a test, but the other 15 students have an average of 60 on the same test, the class average would appear as 70. Whenever the mean is skewed by outliers, it is always a good idea to include the median as an alternate measure of central tendency.

A **weighted mean**, or weighted average, is a mean that uses "weighted" values. The formula is weighted mean $= \frac{w_1x_1+w_2x_2+w_3x_3...+w_nx_n}{w_1+w_2+w_3+\cdots+w_n}$. Weighted values, such as $w_1, w_2, w_3, ... w_n$ are assigned to each member of the set $x_1, x_2, x_3, ... x_n$. When calculating the weighted mean, make sure a weight value for each member of the set is used.

Review Video: All About Averages
Visit mometrix.com/academy and enter code: 176521

MEDIAN

The **statistical median** is the value in the middle of the set of data. To find the median, list all data values in order from smallest to largest or from largest to smallest. Any value that is repeated in the set must be listed the number of times it appears. If there are an odd number of data values, the median is the value in the middle of the list. If there is an even number of data values, the median is the arithmetic mean of the two middle values.

For example, the median of the data set {88, 72, 61, 90, 97, 68, 88, 79, 86, 93, 97, 71, 80, 84, 88} is 86 since the ordered set is {61, 68, 71, 72, 79, 80, 84, **86**, 88, 88, 88, 90, 93, 97, 97}.

The big disadvantage of using the median as a measure of central tendency is that is relies solely on a value's relative size as compared to the other values in the set. When the individual values in a set of data are evenly dispersed, the median can be an accurate tool. However, if there is a group of rather large values or a group of rather small values that are not offset by a different group of values, the information that can be inferred from the median may not be accurate because the distribution of values is skewed.

MODE

The **statistical mode** is the data value that occurs the greatest number of times in the data set. It is possible to have exactly one mode, more than one mode, or no mode. To find the mode of a set of data, arrange the data like you do to find the median (all values in order, listing all multiples of data values). Count the number of times each value appears in the data set. If all values appear an equal number of times, there is no mode. If one value appears more than any other value, that value is the mode. If two or more values appear the same number of times, but there are other values that appear fewer times and no values that appear more times, all of those values are the modes.

For example, the mode of the data set {**88**, 72, 61, 90, 97, 68, **88**, 79, 86, 93, 97, 71, 80, 84, **88**} is 88.

The main disadvantage of the mode is that the values of the other data in the set have no bearing on the mode. The mode may be the largest value, the smallest value, or a value anywhere in between in the set. The mode only tells which value or values, if any, occurred the greatest number of times. It does not give any suggestions about the remaining values in the set.

Review Video: Mean, Median, and Mode
Visit mometrix.com/academy and enter code: 286207

Vectors and Scalars in Force and Motion

VECTORS

Vectors are mathematical quantities with both **magnitude and direction**. A vector is most commonly described by the magnitude of its components in the relevant coordinate system. Vectors may exist in any number of dimensions, but for applications in mechanics they will most often be in either two or three. A vector is generally denoted by a letter either in boldface type or with an arrow above it.

Adding or subtracting vectors is as simple as adding or subtracting their components. For instance, given the two vectors $\mathbf{a} = \langle 1,5,7 \rangle$ and $\mathbf{b} = \langle 5,-3,3 \rangle$, $\mathbf{a} + \mathbf{b} = \langle (1+5), (5-3), (7+3) \rangle = \langle 6,2,10 \rangle$. If vectors are given as a length and an angle, it may be necessary to use trigonometry to convert these to orthogonal components.

Visually, adding a vector is accomplished by drawing the second vector starting from the endpoint of the first vector. To visually subtract a vector, draw both vectors starting from the origin. The difference will be the vector from the endpoint of the second to the endpoint of the first.

Vector addition has many of the same relevant properties as scalar addition. It is commutative, in that $\mathbf{a} + \mathbf{b} = \mathbf{b} + \mathbf{a}$, and associative, in that $(\mathbf{a} + \mathbf{b}) + \mathbf{c} = \mathbf{a} + (\mathbf{b} + \mathbf{c})$.

There are a few different ways to multiply vectors, though none of them is exactly the same as algebraic multiplication. For instance, one way to multiply vectors is to multiply a vector by a scalar. If we are to multiply vector **a** by scalar **s**, we can only multiply the magnitude of **a** by the absolute value of **s**. The direction of the product will be the same as **a** so long as **s** is positive; if **s** is negative, the resulting vector will be in the opposite direction. Remember that dividing **a** by **s**, is equivalent to multiplying **a** by $\frac{1}{\mathbf{s}}$. One common example of this kind of operation in physics is in the equation for force. To find force, we multiply mass (scalar) by acceleration (vector). Of course, since mass will always be positive, the direction of the resulting vector (force) will always be in the direction of the acceleration.

Resultant Force Vectors

Force has both magnitude and direction. Furthermore, multiple forces acting on one object combine in vector addition. This can be demonstrated by considering an object placed at the origin of the coordinate plane. If it is pushed along the positive direction of the *x*-axis, it will move in this direction. If the force acting on it is in the positive direction of the *y*-axis, it will move in that direction.

However, if both forces are applied at the same time, then the object will move at an angle to both the *x*- and *y*-axes, an angle determined by the relative amount of force exerted in each direction. In this way, we may see that the resulting force is a vector sum; a net force that has both magnitude and direction.

Resultant vectors from applied forces:

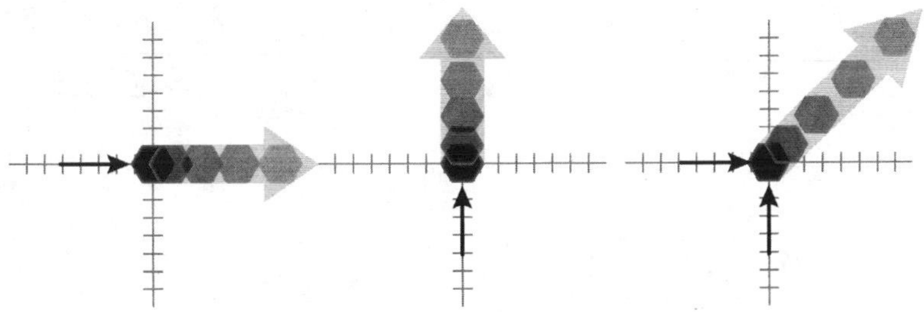

Review Video: Forces: Push-Pull
Visit mometrix.com/academy and enter code: 104731

Cross Products

When two vectors are being **multiplied for a vector product** ($\mathbf{a} \times \mathbf{b} = \mathbf{c}$), the equation will be written $\mathbf{c} = ab \sin \varphi$, where φ is the smaller of the two angles between **a** and **b**. Because in this form the multiplication of **a** and **b** is indicated with the $\times$, this resulting vector is often known as the cross product. Of course, if **a** and **b** are parallel, then $\mathbf{a} \times \mathbf{b} = 0$. The direction of **c** will be perpendicular to the plane that contains both **a** and **b** by the right-hand rule. It should be noted that the commutative law does not apply to this kind of multiplication. Instead, we may say that the cross product is an anticommutative function, meaning that $\mathbf{b} \times \mathbf{a} = -\mathbf{a} \times \mathbf{b}$. This kind of equation will be used in the formula for torque.

An alternative method for calculating the cross product is to take the determinant of a 3×3 matrix composed of the two vectors along with the unit vectors **i**, **j**, and **k**. So for vectors $\mathbf{a} = \langle 2,3,6 \rangle$ and $\mathbf{b} = \langle 1,1,4 \rangle$:

$$a \times b = \begin{vmatrix} \mathbf{i} & \mathbf{j} & \mathbf{k} \\ 2 & 3 & 6 \\ 1 & 1 & 4 \end{vmatrix} = \mathbf{i}(12-6) + \mathbf{j}(6-8) + \mathbf{k}(2-3)$$

So $\mathbf{a} \times \mathbf{b} = 6\mathbf{i} - 2\mathbf{j} - \mathbf{k}$. Conversely, $\mathbf{b} \times \mathbf{a} = -6\mathbf{i} + 2\mathbf{j} + \mathbf{k}$.

Dot Products

There are two different methods for multiplying two vectors: one way yields a **vector product**, and one way yields a **scalar product**. If we take the vectors **a** and **b** and decide to solve for a scalar product, we will set up this equation: $\mathbf{a} \cdot \mathbf{b} = ab \cos \varphi$. In this equation, a is the magnitude of the vector **a**, b is the magnitude of the vector **b**, and φ is the angle between **a** and **b**. Another way to arrive at the same scalar product is to multiply each component of one vector by the corresponding component in the other vector and sum the results: $\mathbf{a} \cdot \mathbf{b} = axbx + ayby + azbz$. Since there are only scalars on the right side of the equation, the resulting product will be a scalar. This product is often referred to as a dot product, since the left side of the equation is often written with the expression, "**a** · **b**" (a dot b). This kind of equation is exemplified by the formula for work, in which a scalar (work) is found by multiplying two vectors (force and displacement).

Chapter Quiz

Ready to see how well you retained what you just read? Scan the QR code to go directly to the chapter quiz interface for this study guide. If you're using a computer, simply visit the online resources page at **mometrix.com/resources719/ftcephysics** and click the Chapter Quizzes link.

Thermodynamics

Temperature, Scales, Heat, and Heat Capacity

Temperature Scales

Empirical or relative temperature scales, like Celsius (°C) and Fahrenheit (°F), can have a corresponding **absolute temperature scale**, which in this case would be Kelvin (K) and Rankine (R), respectively. A temperature of 0 K or 0 R is known as **absolute zero**, at which point atomic motion and thermal energy are, theoretically, at a minimum. Kelvins and degrees Celsius are related by the equation, $T_K = T_C + 273.15$. Similarly, Rankines and degrees Fahrenheit are related as $T_R = T_F + 459.67$. From these relations, we can see that within both individual pairs of temperature scales, the magnitude of the unit is the same; that is, an increase of 1 °C is the same an increase of 1 K, while an increase of 1 °F equals an increase of 1 R. Converting from Fahrenheit to Celsius is slightly more complicated: $T_C = \frac{5}{9}(T_F - 32)$, or in reverse, $T_F = \frac{9}{5}T_C + 32$. From these equations, we can see that a change of 1 °C is greater than a change of 1 °F .

Relationship between Heat and Temperature

It is often useful to know how much heat is required to cause a certain amount of material to reach a desired temperature. Each material has a property called specific heat, which allows this calculation. To bring about a temperature increase ΔT to a mass m made of a material with specific heat c, the required heat input is found by the equation $Q = mc\Delta T$. This equation can also be used to calculate the amount of heat absorbed during a given temperature increase. The amount of heat required to raise the temperature of 1 gram of water by 1 degree Celsius, or 1 Kelvin, is 1 calorie or 4.184 joules. Thus, the specific heat of water is 1 $\frac{\text{cal}}{\text{g K}}$ or 4.184 $\frac{\text{J}}{\text{g K}}$.

Note that since Kelvin and Celsius scales use the same unit size and the heat equation uses *change* in temperature, it is equally valid to use units of $\frac{\text{J}}{\text{g K}}$ or $\frac{\text{J}}{\text{g °C}}$.

Latent Heat and Specific Heat

Suppose we wish to convert ice initially at –5 °C to water at 5 °C. We must provide heat to accomplish this. The amount of heat energy required to raise the temperature of a given quantity of a material is a property known as **specific heat**. This is most often given on a mass basis, with units of $\frac{\text{J}}{\text{g K}}$, but may also be given as a molar property as $\frac{\text{J}}{\text{mol K}}$. If the given quantity of material and the given specific heat are not unit compatible, it will be necessary to multiply or divide by the molar weight of the material to achieve compatibility. Returning to the problem at hand, in order for ice initially at -5 °C to reach 5 °C, it must undergo a phase change from a solid to a liquid. When the ice is heated, it does not simply become water when it reaches 0 °C. In order for the ice to become water, additional heat must be added to break the bonds of the solid. This heat is called the **latent heat of fusion** and, like the specific heat, may be given on a mass or a molar basis, with common units of kJ/g or kJ/mol, respectively. This heat input for the phase change occurs while the material remains at a constant temperature. Once the phase change has been completed, the water temperature will begin to rise again with heat input, though the specific heat of liquid water will be different from that of ice. If the water need be heated above 100 °C, it will have to undergo a second phase change, overcoming the **latent heat of vaporization**, and its temperature will subsequently be governed by a third specific heat, that of the gas phase.

Thermal Expansion and Contraction

When the temperature of most materials changes, they will undergo some amount of size change called **thermal expansion**. Though generally quite small, it is important to know how much of an impact thermal expansion might have on the size of an object. Each material has a linear coefficient of thermal expansion α, generally having units of $°C^{-1}$ or $°F^{-1}$, that relates the change in length to the original length. The percentage change in length is found by the equation $\frac{\Delta L}{L_0} = \alpha\Delta T$, and the absolute change is found by a rearrangement of that equation, $\Delta L = L_0\alpha\Delta T$. Negative thermal expansion means that either ΔT is negative (i.e., getting colder) or the material has a negative α (some materials in specific conditions have this property).

Assuming that the material is able to expand in all directions, there will similarly be a change in **areas** and **volumes**. The change in an area A_0 will be $\Delta A = 2\alpha A_0\Delta T + \alpha^2\Delta T^2$. Because α is generally much less than 1, $\alpha^2\Delta T^2$ will most often be negligible. Thus, the change in area becomes $\Delta A = 2\alpha A_0\Delta T$. From this we can see that the area coefficient of thermal expansion is $\gamma = 2\alpha$, and $\Delta A = \gamma A_0\Delta T$. By making similar assumptions with the equation for change in volume, we find that the volume coefficient of thermal expansion is $\beta = 3\alpha$ and that $\Delta V = \beta V_0\Delta T$.

Various Sample Temperature Conversions

Convert 200.0 Degrees Fahrenheit to the Celsius Scale.

To convert from 200.0 °F to °C, use the equation $T_C = \frac{5}{9}(T_F - 32)$. Substituting 200.0 in for T_F yields $T_C = \frac{5}{9}(200.0 - 32) = \frac{5}{9}(168.0) = 93.33$ °C.

Convert 24.0 Degrees Celsius to the Fahrenheit Scale.

To convert from 24.0 °C to °F, use the equation $T_F = \frac{9}{5}T_C + 32$. Substituting 24.0 in for T_C yields $T_F = \frac{9}{5}(24.0) + 32 = 43.2 + 32 = 75.2$ °F

Convert 21.5 Degrees Celsius to the Kelvin Scale.

To convert from 21.5 °C to K, use the equation $T_K = T_C + 273.15$. Substituting 21.5 in for T_C yields $T_K = 21.5 + 273.15 = 294.65$ K.

Thermal Energy

Thermal energy is part of a system's **total internal energy**, which consists of potential and kinetic energy. Thermal energy is the total internal kinetic energy of a system due to the random motions of the particles. The thermal energy of a system is measured by its temperature, which is the average kinetic energy of the particles in that system. The flow of thermal energy is referred to as heat. Appropriate units for thermal energy include the joule (J), British thermal unit (Btu), calorie (cal), and kilocalorie (kcal).

$$1 \text{ Btu} = 1{,}055 \text{ J}$$
$$1 \text{ cal} = 4.184 \text{ J}$$
$$1{,}000 \text{ cal} = 1 \text{ kcal}$$

Heat Capacity and Specific Heat

Heat capacity is the amount of heat required to raise a sample of matter by 1 °C. Heat capacity is an extensive property and varies with the amount of matter in the sample. The greater the mass of the sample, the higher the heat capacity of the sample. This means that a specific type of matter will have different heat capacities depending on the size of the sample. Heat capacity may be represented by the formula $C = \frac{Q}{\Delta T}$, where Q is the heat in joules and ΔT is the change in temperature in degrees Celsius. Specific heat is the amount of heat required to raise the temperature of a unit mass by 1 °C. The formula for specific heat is $c = \frac{Q}{m\Delta T}$, where Q is the heat in joules, ΔT is the change in temperature in degrees Celsius, and m is the mass of the sample. Because the specific heat formula incorporates the mass of the sample, a specific type of substance will have a constant specific heat, making specific heat an intensive property.

Review Video: Specific Heat Capacity
Visit mometrix.com/academy and enter code: 736791

Explain How to Calculate the Amount of Heat Lost By a Piece of Copper with a Mass of 100.0 g When it Cools from 100.0°C to 20.0°C. The Specific Heat of Copper is 0.380 J/(g·°C).

To calculate the amount of heat lost by a piece of copper with a mass of 100.0 g when it cools from 100.0 °C to 20.0 °C, use the equation $Q = mc\Delta T$, where Q is the amount of heat lost in joules, m is the mass of the copper in grams, c is the specific heat of copper, and ΔT is the change in temperature $(T_2 - T_1)$ in degrees Celsius. Substituting these known values yields:

$$Q = (100.0\text{ g})\left(0.380\ \frac{\text{J}}{\text{g °C}}\right)\left((20.0\text{°C}) - (100.0\text{°C})\right) = -3{,}040\text{ J}$$

The negative value confirms that heat was lost as the copper cooled.

Finding the Specific Heat of a Substance with a Calorimeter

The specific heat of a substance can be determined using a calorimeter. A known amount of the substance is heated to a known temperature. In the classroom setting, this can be accomplished by placing the metal in a loosely stoppered test tube and then placing the test tube in boiling water. The calorimeter is prepared by placing water of a known amount and temperature in the calorimeter. The heated metal is carefully placed into the water in the calorimeter. The temperature of the water is carefully monitored until it stops rising. The final temperature of the metal will be equal to the final temperature of the water. The heat lost by the metal equals the heat gained by the water:

$$-Q_{\text{metal}} = Q_{\text{water}}$$

$$-m_{\text{metal}}c_{\text{metal}}\Delta T_{\text{metal}} = m_{\text{water}}c_{\text{water}}\Delta T_{\text{water}}$$

In these equations, Q is the amount of heat lost or gained in joules, m is the mass in grams, c is the specific heat, and ΔT is the change in temperature $T_2 - T_1$ in degrees Celsius.

Review Video: Using a Calorimeter
Visit mometrix.com/academy and enter code: 703935

Calculating the Specific Heat of an Unknown Metal:

- In a calorimetry experiment, the specific heat of an unknown metal dropped 20.0 °C.
- The mass of the unknown metal is 100.0 g.
- The temperature of the water with a mass of 100.0 g in the calorimeter increased 1.00 °C.
- The specific heat of water is 4.184 $\frac{\text{J}}{\text{g °C}}$.

The heat lost by the metal must equal the heat gained by the water, as shown in the equation $Q_{lost\ by\ metal} = Q_{gained\ by\ the\ water}$, where Q is the amount of heat lost or gained in joules. To calculate the specific heat of the metal, use $-m_{metal}c_{metal}\Delta T_{metal} = m_{water}c_{water}\Delta T_{water}$, where m is the mass of the metal or water in grams, c is the specific heat of the metal or water, and ΔT is the change in temperature $(T_2 - T_1)$ in degrees Celsius in the metal or water. Solving the equation for c_{metal} results in:

$$c_{metal} = -\frac{m_{water}c_{water}\Delta T_{water}}{m_{metal}\Delta T_{metal}}$$

Substituting in the given information yields:

$$c_{\text{metal}} = -\frac{(100.0\text{ g})\left(4.184\ \frac{\text{J}}{\text{g °C}}\right)(1.00\text{ °C})}{(100.0\text{ g})(-20.0\text{ °C})} = 0.209\ \frac{\text{J}}{\text{g °C}}$$

Heat Transfer

Heat transfer is the flow of thermal energy, which is measured by temperature. Heat will flow from warmer objects to cooler objects until an **equilibrium** is reached in which both objects are at the same temperature. Because the particles of warmer objects possess a higher kinetic energy than the particles of cooler objects, the particles of the warmer objects are vibrating more quickly and collide more often, transferring energy to the cooler objects in which the particles have less kinetic energy and are moving more slowly. Heat may be transferred by conduction, convection, or radiation. In **conduction**, heat is transferred by direct contact between two objects. In **convection**, heat is transferred by moving currents. In **radiation**, heat is transferred by electromagnetic waves.

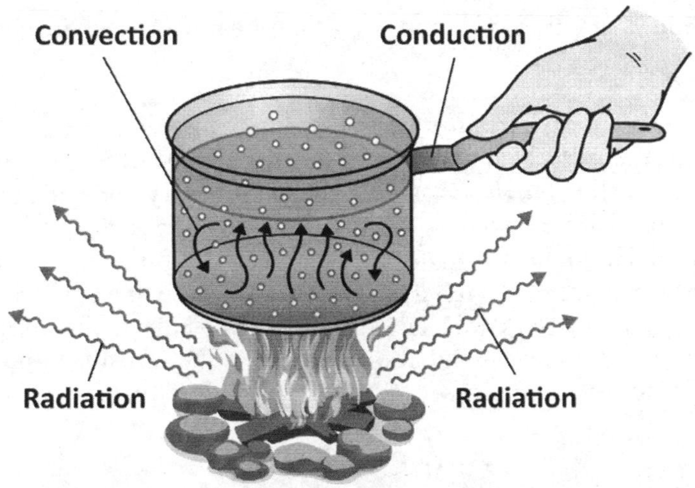

Review Video: Heat Transfer at the Molecular Level
Visit mometrix.com/academy and enter code: 451646

Convection

Heat always flows from a region of higher temperature to a region of lower temperature. If two regions are at the same temperature, there is a thermal equilibrium between them and there will be no net heat transfer between them. Convection is a mode of heat transfer in which a surface in contact with a fluid experiences a heat flow. The heat rate for convection is given as $q = hA\Delta T$, where h is the convection coefficient, and q is the heat transferred per unit of time. The convection coefficient is dependent on a number of factors, including the configuration of the surface and the nature and velocity of the fluid. For complicated configurations, it often has to be determined experimentally.

Convection may be classified as either free or forced. In free convection, when a surface transfers heat to the surrounding air, the heated air becomes less dense and rises, allowing cooler air to descend and come into contact with the surface. Free convection may also be called natural convection. Forced convection in this example would involve forcibly cycling the air: for instance, with a fan. While this does generally require an additional input of work, the convection coefficient is always greater for forced convection.

Conduction

Conduction is a form of heat transfer that requires contact. Since heat is a measure of kinetic energy, most commonly vibration, at the atomic level, it may be transferred from one location to another or one object to another by contact. The rate at which heat is transferred is proportional to the material's thermal conductivity k, cross-sectional area A, and temperature gradient $\frac{\Delta T}{\Delta x}$:

$$q = kA\left(\frac{\Delta T}{\Delta x}\right)$$

If two ends of a rod are each held at a constant temperature, the heat transfer through the rod will be given as $q = k\text{A}\left(\frac{T_H - T_L}{d}\right)$, where d is the length of the rod. The heat will flow from the hot end to the cold end. The thermal conductivity is generally given in units of $\frac{\text{W}}{\text{m K}}$. Metals are some of the best conductors, many having a thermal conductivity around 400 $\frac{\text{W}}{\text{m K}}$. The thermal conductivity of wood is very small, generally less than 0.5 $\frac{\text{W}}{\text{m K}}$. Diamond is extremely thermally conductive and may have a conductivity of over 2,000 $\frac{\text{W}}{\text{m K}}$. Although fluids also have thermal conductivity, they will tend to transfer heat primarily through convection.

Radiation

Radiation heat transfer occurs via electromagnetic radiation between two bodies. Unlike conduction and convection, radiation requires no medium in which to take place. Indeed, the heat we receive from the sun is entirely radiation since it must pass through a vacuum to reach us. Every body at a temperature above absolute zero emits heat radiation at a rate of $q = e\sigma AT^4$, where e is the surface emissivity and σ is the Stefan-Boltzmann constant. The net radiation heat-transfer rate for a body is given by $q = e\sigma A(T^4 - T_0^4)$, where T_0 is the temperature of the surroundings. Emissivity, which has a value between 0 and 1, is a measure of how well a surface absorbs and emits radiation. Dark-colored surfaces tend to have high emissivity, while shiny or reflective surfaces have low emissivity. In the radiation heat-rate equation, it is important to remember to use absolute temperature units, since the temperature value is being raised to a power.

Types of Energy

Chemical, Electrical, Electromagnetic, Nuclear, and Thermal Energy

Different types of energy may be associated with systems:

- **Chemical energy** is the energy that is stored in chemical bonds and intermolecular forces.
- **Electrical energy** is the energy associated with the movement of electrons or ions through a material.
- **Electromagnetic energy** is the energy of electromagnetic waves of several frequencies including radio waves, microwaves, infrared light, visible light, ultraviolet light, x-rays, and gamma rays.
- **Nuclear energy** is the binding energy that is stored within an atom's nucleus.
- **Thermal energy** is the total internal kinetic energy of a system due to the random motions of the particles.

Phase Transitions

States of Matter

The four states of matter are solid, liquid, gas, and plasma. **Solids** have a definite shape and a definite volume. Because solid particles are held in fairly rigid positions, solids are the least compressible of the four states of matter. **Liquids** have definite volumes but no definite shapes. Because their particles are free to slip and slide over each other, liquids take the shape of their containers, but they still remain fairly incompressible by natural means. **Gases** have no definite shape or volume. Because gas particles are free to move, they move away from each other to fill their containers. Gases are compressible. **Plasmas** are high-temperature, ionized gases that exist only under very high temperatures at which electrons are stripped away from their atoms.

Review Video: States of Matter
Visit mometrix.com/academy and enter code: 742449

Review Video: Properties of Liquids
Visit mometrix.com/academy and enter code: 802024

Review Video: States of Matter [Advanced]
Visit mometrix.com/academy and enter code: 298130

The following table shows similarities and differences between solids, liquids, and gases:

	Solid	Liquid	Gas
Shape	Fixed shape	No fixed shape (assumes shape of container)	No fixed shape (assumes shape of container)
Volume	Fixed	Fixed	Changes to assume volume of container
Fluidity	Does not flow easily	Flows easily	Flows easily
Compressibility	Hard to compress	Hard to compress	Compresses

Six Different Types of Phase Change

A substance that is undergoing a change from a solid to a liquid is said to be melting. If this change occurs in the opposite direction, from liquid to solid, this change is called freezing. A liquid which is being converted to a gas is undergoing vaporization. The reverse of this process is known as condensation. Direct transitions from gas to solid and solid to gas are much less common in everyday life, but they can occur given the proper conditions. Solid to gas conversion is known as sublimation, while the reverse is called deposition.

Review Video: Chemical and Physical Properties of Matter
Visit mometrix.com/academy and enter code: 717349

Phase Diagram and Critical Point

A **phase diagram** is a graph or chart of pressure versus temperature that represents the solid, liquid, and gaseous phases of a substance and the transitions between these phases. Typically, **pressure** is located on the vertical axis, and temperature is located along the horizontal axis. The curves drawn on the graph represent points at which different phases are in an equilibrium state. These curves indicate at which pressure and temperature the phase changes of sublimation, melting, and boiling occur. Specifically, the curve between the liquid and gas phases indicates the pressures and temperatures at which the liquid and gas phases are in equilibrium. The curve between the solid and liquid phases indicates the temperatures and pressures at which the solid and liquid phases are in equilibrium. The open spaces on the graph represent the distinct phases solid, liquid, and gas. The point at which the solid–liquid, solid–gas, and liquid–gas phase boundaries intersect is called the triple point. At the triple point, the solid, liquid, and gas phases all exist in equilibrium. The critical point, by contrast, is the endpoint of the liquid–gas coexistence curve, where the liquid and gas phases become indistinguishable and form a supercritical fluid.

LETTERED REGIONS OF A PHASE DIAGRAM

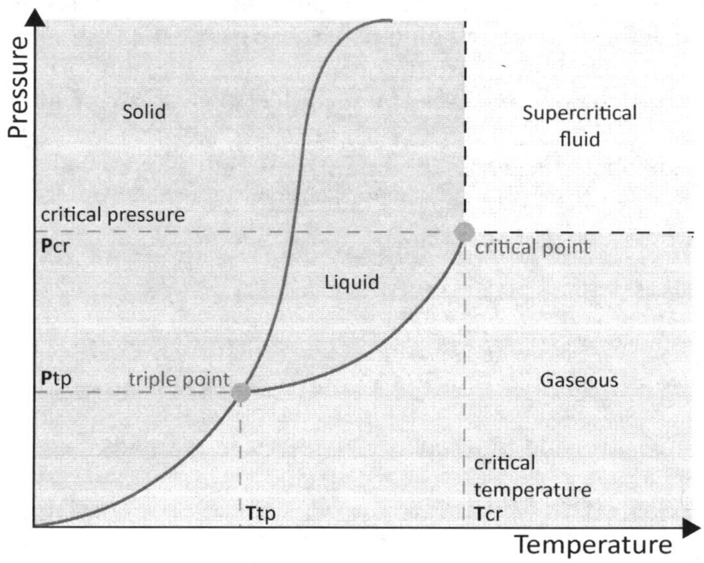

A—**Solid phase**: This is a region of high pressure and low temperature where the substance always exists as a solid.

B—**Liquid phase**: This is a region of pressure and temperature where the substance is in the liquid phase.

C—**Gas phase**: This is a region of pressure and temperature where the substance is in the gaseous phase.

D—**Sublimation point**: The portion of the curve that contains point D shows all the combinations of pressure and temperature at which the solid phase is in equilibrium with the gaseous phase.

E—**Triple point**: The point at which the solid, liquid, and gaseous phases are all in equilibrium.

F—**Boiling point**: The line that contains point F indicates all the combinations of pressure and temperature at which the liquid phase and gas phase are in equilibrium.

Calculating Phase Transitions

HEATING CURVE OF WATER FROM –40 °C TO 140 °C

In the first portion of the curve, the graph slants up and to the right as the ice is a solid that is increasing in temperature from –40 °C to 0 °C. In the second portion of the curve, the graph remains horizontal during the phase change from solid to liquid as the temperature remains constant at 0 °C. In the third portion of the curve, the graph slants up and to the right as the water now is in the liquid state and is increasing in temperature from 0 °C to 100 °C. In the fourth portion of the curve, the graph remains horizontal during the phase change from liquid to gas as the temperature remains at 100 °C. In the last portion of the curve, the graph slants up and to the right as water now is in the gaseous state and the steam is increasing in temperature from 100 °C to 140 °C

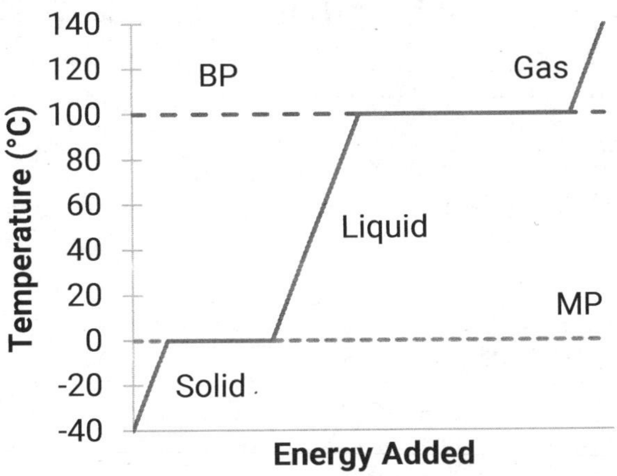

Calculating the Amount of Heat Corresponding to Each Portion of a Heating Curve

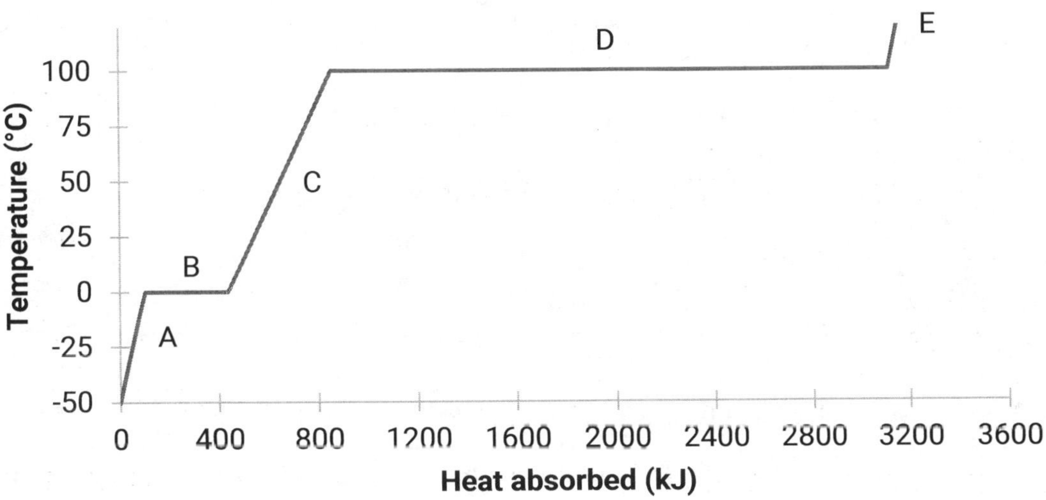

For portion A, $Q = mc_{ice}\Delta T$, where Q is the amount of heat gained in joules, m is the mass of the ice in grams, c_{ice} is the specific heat of ice, and ΔT is the temperature change in degrees Celsius.

For portion B, $Q = m\Delta H_{fus}$, where Q is the amount of heat gained in joules, m is the mass of the ice/water in grams, and ΔH_{fus} is the heat of fusion for water in joules per gram, $\frac{J}{g}$.

For portion C, $Q = mc_{water}\Delta T$, where Q is the amount of heat gained in joules, m is the mass of the water in grams, c_{water} is the specific heat of water, and ΔT is the temperature change in degrees Celsius.

For portion D, $Q = m\Delta H_{vap}$, where Q is the amount of heat gained in joules, m is the mass of the water/steam in grams, and ΔH_{vap} is the heat of vaporization for water in joules per gram, $\frac{J}{g}$.

For portion E, $Q = mc_{steam}\Delta T$, where Q is the amount of heat gained in joules, m is the mass of the steam in grams, c_{steam} is the specific heat of steam, and ΔT is the temperature change in degrees Celsius.

Heat of Vaporization, Heat of Fusion, and Heat of Sublimation

- The **heat of vaporization** (ΔH_{vap}) is the amount of heat that must be added to one mole of a substance to change the substance from the liquid phase to the gaseous phase.
- The **heat of fusion** (ΔH_{fus}) is the amount of heat that must be added to one mole of a substance to change the substance from the solid phase to the liquid phase.
- The **heat of sublimation** (ΔH_{sub}) is the amount of heat that must be added to one mole of a substance to change the substance directly from the solid phase to the gaseous phase without passing through the liquid phase.

Explain How to Calculate the Amount of Heat Required to Change 100.0 g of Ice at −10.0 °C to Water at 10.0 °C. $\left[\Delta H_{fus} = 334\ \frac{J}{g};\ c_{water} = 4.18\ \frac{J}{g\ °C},\ c_{ice} = 2.06\ \frac{J}{g\ °C}\right]$**.**

To calculate the amount of heat required to change 100.0 g of ice at −10.0 °C to water at 10.0 °C, it is necessary to calculate the heat required for each step along the way. Step 1 is to calculate the heat required to raise the temperature of the ice from −10.0 °C to 0.0 °C. Step 2 is to calculate the amount of heat required to melt the ice. Finally, step 3 is to calculate the amount of heat required to raise the temperature of the water from 0.0 °C to 10.0 °C.

For steps 1 and 3, the required equation is $Q = mc\Delta T$.

Because step 2 is a phase change, the required equation is $Q = m\Delta H_{fus}$.

For step 1: $Q_1 = (100.0\text{ g})\left(2.06\ \frac{J}{g\ °C}\right)(0.0°C - (-10.0°C)) = 2{,}060\text{ J}$.

For step 2: $Q_2 = m\Delta H_{fus} = (100.0\text{ g})\left(334\ \frac{J}{g}\right) = 33{,}400\text{ J}$.

For step 3: $Q_3 = (100.0\text{ g})\left(4.18\ \frac{J}{g\ °C}\right)(10.0\ °C - 0.0\ °C) = 4{,}180\text{ J}$.

Adding $Q_1 + Q_2 + Q_3 = 2{,}060\text{ J} + 33{,}400\text{ J} + 4{,}180\text{ J} = 39{,}640\text{ J}$.

Explain How to Calculate the Amount of Heat Required to Change 100.0 g of Water at 90.0 °C to Steam at 110.0 °C. $\left[\Delta H_{vap} = 2{,}260\ \frac{J}{g};\ c_{steam} = 1.86\ \frac{J}{g\ °C},\ c_{water} = 4.18\ \frac{J}{g\ °C}\right]$**.**

To calculate the amount of heat required to change 100.0 g of water at 90.0 °C to steam at 110.0 °C, it is necessary to calculate the heat required at each step along the way. Step 1 is to calculate the heat required to raise the temperature of the water from 90.0 °C to 100.0 °C. Step 2 is to calculate the amount of heat required to change the water to steam. Finally, step 3 is to calculate the amount of heat required to raise the temperature of the steam from 100.0 °C to 110.0 °C.

For steps 1 and 3, the required equation is $Q = mc\Delta T$.

Because Step 2 is a phase change, the required equation is $Q = m\Delta H_{vap}$.

For step 1: $Q_1 = (100.0\text{ g})\left(4.18\ \frac{J}{g\ °C}\right)(100.0\ °C - 90.0\ °C) = 4{,}180\text{ J}$.

For step 2: $Q_2 = m\Delta H_{vap} = (100.0\text{ g})\left(2{,}260\ \frac{J}{g}\right) = 226{,}000\text{ J}$.

For step 3: $Q_1 = (100.0\text{ g})\left(1.86\ \frac{J}{g\ °C}\right)(110.0°C - 100.0°C) = 1{,}860\text{ J}$.

Adding $Q_1 + Q_2 + Q_3 = 4{,}180\text{ J} + 226{,}000\text{ J} + 1{,}860\text{ J} = 232{,}040\text{ J}$.

Gas Laws

Kinetic Molecular Theory

The **kinetic molecular theory of gases** states that the pressure exerted by a gas is due to numerous collisions of molecules with one another and with container walls. This assertion led to the development of what is now known as the ideal gas law: $PV = nRT$, where P is **pressure,** V is **volume,** T is **temperature,** n is the number of moles of gas present, and R is the universal gas constant. Different aspects of this law have different names, but there are many simple relations that may be derived from it. For instance, if an ideal gas is contained such that no molecules can escape, then it may be said that $\frac{P_1V_1}{T_1} = \frac{P_2V_2}{T_2}$, where the subscripts indicate distinct sets of conditions. Generally, one of the three variables will be held constant while the other two change. If an ideal gas in a container with a constant volume is heated, the effect this has on the pressure can be determined both analytically and numerically. Additional energy imparted to the gas particles will cause them to move faster, and, according to the kinetic molecular theory, faster particles mean more collisions and a higher resulting pressure. This can be expressed numerically as $\frac{P_1}{T_1} = \frac{P_2}{T_2}$. This means that if T_2 is higher than T_1, then P_2 must be equivalently higher than P_1 to maintain the same ratio.

Other derivations from the ideal gas law include calculating molarity or moles per unit volume $\left(\frac{n}{V} = \frac{P}{RT}\right)$, gas density if the molecular weight (M) is known $\left(\rho = \frac{PM}{RT}\right)$, or molecular weight if the density is known $\left(M = \frac{\rho RT}{P}\right)$.

Ideal Gases

An **ideal gas** is a hypothetical or theoretical gas. Ideal gases are assumed to be a set of randomly moving point particles that do not interact with each other. The collisions of ideal gases are assumed to be completely elastic, and the intermolecular forces are assumed to be zero. Real gases show far more complex behaviors. The ideal gas laws tend to fail at low temperatures and high pressures when the effects of the particle size and intermolecular forces are more apparent. Also, the ideal gas assumptions do not account for phase transitions.

Avogadro's Law

Avogadro's law describes the relationship between the **volume** and **number of moles** of an ideal gas at a constant pressure and temperature. For an ideal gas, the volume and the number of moles are directly related. If the volume increases, the number of moles would have to increase in order to maintain the pressure and temperature. If the number of moles in the container increases, the volume will also need to increase to maintain the same pressure and temperature. The relationship between volume and the number of moles of a gas is represented by $V \propto n$, $V = kn$, or $\frac{V}{n} = k$. Because the quotient of the volume and the number of moles is a constant, Avogadro's law can be stated as:

$$\frac{V_i}{n_i} = \frac{V_f}{n_f}$$

Review Video: Avogadro's Hypothesis
Visit mometrix.com/academy and enter code: 968309

Boyle's Law

Boyle's law describes the relationship between the **volume** and **pressure** of an ideal gas at a constant temperature for a given amount of gas. For an ideal gas, volume and pressure are inversely related. Because gases are compressible, if the pressure of a gas sample is increased, the volume will decrease. If the pressure of a gas sample is decreased, the volume will increase. Conversely, if the volume of a gas sample is increased, the pressure will decrease. If the volume of a gas sample is decreased, the pressure will increase. For example, if the pressure of a gas sample is doubled, the volume decreases to one-half of the original volume. If the pressure of a gas sample is tripled, the volume decreases to one-third of the original volume. The relationship between volume and pressure is represented by $V \propto \frac{1}{P}$, $V = k\frac{1}{P}$, or $PV = k$. Because the product of the pressure and the volume is a constant, Boyle's law can be stated as $P_iV_i = P_fV_f$.

Review Video: Boyle's Law
Visit mometrix.com/academy and enter code: 115757

Charles's Law

Charles's law describes the relationship between the **volume** and **temperature** of an ideal gas at a constant pressure for a given amount of gas. For an ideal gas, volume and temperature are directly related. Because the kinetic energy of a gas is directly proportional to the absolute temperature, if the temperature increases, the average kinetic energy of the gas molecules increases. As the molecules move faster, they will spread farther apart as long as the pressure remains constant, which increases the volume. If the volume of the container were to increase, the temperature would also have to increase if it were to maintain a constant pressure, since the molecules must move faster to strike the container as often. The relationship between volume and temperature is represented by $V \propto T$, $V = kT$, or $\frac{V}{T} = k$. Because the quotient of the volume and the temperature is a constant, Charles's law can be stated as $\frac{V_i}{T_i} = \frac{V_f}{T_f}$, where the temperature is stated in Kelvin.

Combined Gas Law

The **combined gas law** combines Boyle's law and Charles's law. According to Boyle's law, **volume** and **pressure** are inversely related, or $V \propto \frac{1}{P}$. According to Charles's law, **volume** and **temperature** are directly related, or $V \propto T$. Combining these relationships into one yields $V \propto \frac{T}{P}$ or $V = k\frac{T}{P}$. Solving for k yields $\frac{PV}{T}$. Because $k = \frac{P_1V_1}{T_1}$ and $k = \frac{P_2V_2}{T_2}$, the combined gas law can be written as:

$$\frac{P_1V_1}{T_1} = \frac{P_2V_2}{T_2}$$

For situations in which $V_1 = V_2$, the combined gas law yields a relationship of $P \propto T$, indicating that for a constant volume, the pressure and temperature are directly related.

Ideal Gas Law

The **ideal gas law** combines Boyle's law, Charles's law, and Avogadro's law. According to Boyle's law, $V \propto \frac{1}{P}$. According to Charles's law, $V \propto T$. According to Avogadro's law, $V \propto n$. Combining these three relationships into one relationship yields $V \propto \frac{nT}{P}$. Multiplying through by P yields $PV \propto nT$, or $PV = nRT$, where R is the ideal gas constant of $0.0821\ \frac{\text{L atm}}{\text{K mol}}$, P is the pressure in atmospheres, V is the volume in liters, n is the number of moles, and T is the temperature in Kelvin.

Behavior of Real Gases

Although assuming that gases are ideal is appropriate for many situations, **real gases** behave differently than **ideal gases**. The collisions of real gases are not elastic. Real gases do have attractive and repulsive forces. Real gases have **mass**, whereas ideal gases do not. The atoms or molecules of real gases are not point particles, and they do interact with each other, especially under high pressures and low temperatures. Under the right conditions of pressure and temperature, real gases will undergo phase transitions and become liquids. The pressure of real gases is less than those of ideal gases due to the small attractive forces between the particles in the gases.

Review Video: Ideal Gas vs Real Gas
Visit mometrix.com/academy and enter code: 619477

A 5.0 L Gas Sample Has a Pressure of 1.0 Standard Atmosphere (atm). If the Pressure Is Increased to 2.0 atm, Find the New Volume. Assume That the Temperature Is Constant.

To find the new volume, use the equation associated with Boyle's law, $P_iV_i = P_fV_f$. Solving the equation for the unknown V_f yields $V_f = \frac{P_iV_i}{P_f}$. Substituting the given values, $P_i = 1.0$ atm, $V_i = 5.0$ L, and $P_f = 2.0$ atm, into the equation yields $V_f = \frac{(1.0 \text{ atm})(5.0 \text{ L})}{(2.0 \text{ atm})} = 2.5$ L. This checks out because the pressure increased and the volume decreased. More specifically, because the pressure was doubled, the volume was reduced to one-half of the original volume.

A Gas Sample Has a Volume of 10.0 L at 200.0 K. Find Its Volume If the Temperature Is Increased to 300.0 K.

To find the new volume, use the equation associated with Charles's law, $\frac{V_i}{T_i} = \frac{V_f}{T_f}$. Solving the equation for the unknown V_f yields $V_f = \frac{T_fV_i}{T_i}$. Substituting the given values, $V_i = 10.0$ L, $T_i = 200.0$ K, and $T_f = 300.0$ K, into the equation yields $V_f = \frac{(300.0 \text{ K})(10.0 \text{ L})}{(200.0 \text{ K})} = 15.0$ L. This checks out because the temperature increased and the volume increased. Also, note that if the temperature had not been stated in Kelvin, it would have to be converted to Kelvin before substituting the values into the equation.

Explain How to Find the Pressure That 0.500 mol of H_2 (g) Will Exert on a 500.0 mL Flask at 300.0 K.

To calculate the pressure that 0.500 mol of $H_2(g)$ will exert on a 500.0 mL flask at 300.0 K, use the ideal gas equation $PV = nRT$, where R is the ideal gas constant of 0.0821 $\frac{\text{L atm}}{\text{K mol}}$, P is the pressure in atmospheres, V is the volume in liters, n is the number of moles, and T is the temperature in Kelvin. Solving the ideal gas equation for P yields $P = \frac{nRT}{V}$. First, convert the 500.0 mL to 0.500 L. Substituting in $n = 0.500$ mol, $V = 0.500$ L, $T = 300.0$ K, and $R = 0.0821 \frac{\text{L atm}}{\text{K mol}}$ yields:

$$P = \frac{(0.500 \text{ mol})\left(0.0821 \frac{\text{L atm}}{\text{K mol}}\right)(300.0 \text{ K})}{(0.500 \text{ L})} = 24.6 \text{ atm}$$

Thermodynamic Processes of Gases

In discussing thermodynamic processes applied to gases, it is important to understand what is meant by some of the different types of processes that can take place. Most real processes do not strictly hold to one of these types, but most can be reasonably approximated by one of them. A process in which the pressure remains constant is known as an isobaric process. In this type of process, the volume-to-absolute-temperature ratio remains constant. In an isothermal process, the temperature remains constant, as does the product of the pressure and volume. For isothermal processes, the internal energy of the gas is constant, and, according to the first law of thermodynamics, the heat added is equal to the work done by the gas. An adiabatic process is one in which no heat is transferred between the gas or its surroundings. This does not mean that the temperature of the gas remains the same; rather, any temperature changes are due to changes in pressure or volume. According to the first law of thermodynamics, the change in internal energy of the gas is equal to the amount of work done on the gas by its surroundings.

Review Video: What is the Difference between Heat and Temperature?
Visit mometrix.com/academy and enter code: 879095

Heat Engines and the Carnot Cycle

A **heat engine** is a mechanical device that **takes in heat energy** (Q_H) from a high-temperature region and uses that energy to **produce work** (W). It then **expels heat** (Q_C) to a lower-temperature region. When the machine is operating at a steady state, such that it does not change temperature, the first law of thermodynamics tells us that the net heat input is equal to the work achieved:

$$Q_H - Q_C = W$$

We can define the efficiency of a heat engine as the work received divided by the work put in, or $\eta = \frac{W}{Q_H}$. The rejected heat Q_C is not considered work received because it is not usable for work. The efficiency may also be calculated as $\eta = 1 - \frac{Q_C}{Q_H}$. From this, we can see that 100% efficiency can only be achieved if $Q_C = 0$; however, constructing a heat engine that expels no heat is impossible.

A **Carnot engine** is a heat engine that operates on the Carnot cycle, an ideal reversible gas cycle that consists of the following processes: high-temperature isothermal expansion, adiabatic expansion, low-temperature isothermal compression, and adiabatic compression. The efficiency of this ideal engine is given as $\eta = 1 - \frac{T_C}{T_H}$, where T_C and T_H are the low and high temperatures of the gas during the cycle. Carnot's theorem states that no heat engine operating between T_C and T_H can have a higher efficiency than that of the Carnot engine.

Laws of Thermodynamics

First Law

The **first law of thermodynamics** states that energy cannot be **created** or **destroyed**, but only **converted** from one form to another. It is generally applied as $Q = \Delta U + W$, where Q is the net heat energy added to a system, ΔU is the change in internal energy of the system, and W is the work done by the system. For any input of heat energy to a system, that energy must be either converted to internal energy through a temperature increase or expended in doing work. For a system that gives off heat, either the temperature of the system must decrease or work must be done on the system by its surroundings. By convention, work done by the system is positive while work done on the system is negative.

For instance, suppose a gas is compressed by a piston while the gas temperature remains constant. If we consider the gas to be the system, the work is negative, since the work is being performed on the gas. Since the temperature remains constant, $\Delta U = 0$. Thus, Q must be a negative quantity, indicating that heat is lost by the gas. Conversely, if the gas does positive work on the piston while remaining at a constant temperature, the gas must be receiving heat input from the surroundings.

Second Law

The **second law of thermodynamics** is primarily a statement of the natural tendency of all things toward disorder rather than order. It deals with a quantity called **entropy**, which is an inverse measure of the remaining useful energy in a system. If we take a system of a pot of hot water and an ice cube, the system entropy initially has a value of s_1. After the ice cube melts in the water and the system reaches an equilibrium temperature, the system has larger entropy value s_2, which is the maximum entropy for the system. The system cannot return to its initial state without work put into the system to refreeze the ice cube and reheat the water. If this is done and the system returns to a state with entropy s_1, then the entropy of the surroundings must at the same time increase by more than $s_2 - s_1$, since the net entropy from any process is always greater than zero. Reversible processes are those that may be accomplished in reverse without requiring additional work input. These processes do not exist in the real world, but can be useful for approximating some situations. All real processes are irreversible, meaning they require additional work input to accomplish in reverse. Another important concept is that of spontaneity, the ability of a process to occur without instigation. An ice cube located in an environment at a temperature above the freezing point will spontaneously melt. Although some processes can decrease system entropy at a cost to the entropy of the surroundings, all spontaneous processes involve an increase in the total entropy of the universe.

Third and Zeroth Laws

The **third law of thermodynamics** regards the behavior of systems as they **approach absolute zero temperature**. Actually reaching a state of absolute zero is impossible. According to this law, all activity disappears as molecules slow to a standstill near absolute zero, and the system achieves a perfect crystal structure while the system entropy approaches its minimum value. For most systems, this would in fact be a value of zero entropy. Note that this does not violate the second law since causing a system to approach absolute zero would require an immense increase in the entropy of the surroundings, resulting in a positive net entropy. This law is used to determine the value of a material's standard entropy, which is its entropy at the standard temperature of 25 °C.

The **zeroth law of thermodynamics** deals with thermal equilibrium between two systems. It states that if two systems are both in thermal equilibrium with a third system, then they are in thermal equilibrium with each other. This may seem intuitive, but it is an important basis for the other thermodynamic laws.

> **Review Video: Laws of Thermodynamics**
> Visit mometrix.com/academy and enter code: 253607

Entropy

Entropy (S) is the amount of **disorder** or **randomness of a system**. According to the second law of thermodynamics, systems tend toward a state of greater entropy. The second law of thermodynamics can also be stated as $\Delta S > 0$. Processes with positive changes in entropy tend to be spontaneous. For example, melting is a process with a positive ΔS. When a solid changes into a liquid state, the substance becomes more disordered; therefore, entropy increases. Entropy also will increase in a reaction in which the number of moles of gases increases due to the amount of disorder increasing. Entropy increases when a solute dissolves into a solvent due to the increase in the number of particles. Entropy increases when a system is heated due to the particles moving faster and the amount of disorder increasing.

Spontaneous / Reversible Processes

Some chemical processes are **spontaneous**. According to the second law of thermodynamics, systems or processes always **tend to a state of greater entropy** or lower potential energy. Some exothermic chemical systems are spontaneous because they can increase their stability by reaching a lower potential energy. If processes or reactions have products at a lower potential energy, these processes tend to be spontaneous. Spontaneous reactions have only one direction as given by the second law of thermodynamics. Spontaneous processes go in the direction of greater entropy and lower potential energy. To be reversible, a reaction or process has to be able to go back and forth between two states. A spontaneous process is irreversible.

Concept of Change in Enthalpy

All chemical processes involve either the release or the absorption of heat. Enthalpy is this heat energy. **Enthalpy** is a state function that is equivalent to the amount of heat a system exchanges with its surroundings. For **exothermic processes**, which release heat, the change in enthalpy (ΔH) is negative because the final enthalpy is less than the initial enthalpy. For **endothermic processes**, which absorb heat, the change in enthalpy (ΔH) is positive because the final enthalpy is greater than the initial enthalpy.

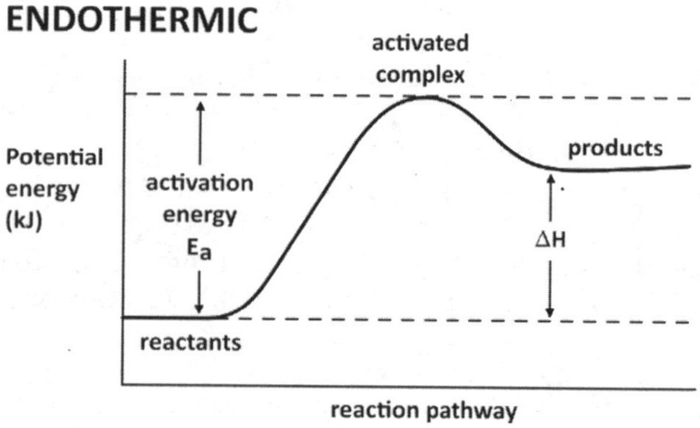

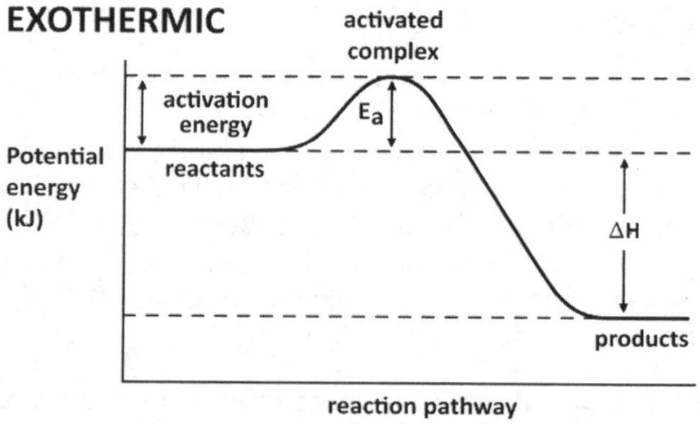

Review Video: Enthalpy
Visit mometrix.com/academy and enter code: 233315

Gibbs Energy

Gibbs energy (G), also known as Gibbs free energy, is the energy of the system that is available to do work. Gibbs energy determines the **spontaneity** of chemical and physical processes. Some processes are spontaneous because $\Delta H < 0$ or because $\Delta S > 0$. If one of the conditions is favorable but the other condition is not favorable, Gibbs energy can be used to determine if a process is spontaneous. Gibbs energy is given by $G = H - TS$. For processes that occur at constant temperature, $\Delta G = \Delta H - T\Delta S$. If ΔG is equal to zero, then the reaction is at equilibrium and neither the forward nor the reverse reaction is spontaneous. If ΔG is less than zero, then the forward reaction is spontaneous. If ΔG is greater than zero, then the reverse reaction is spontaneous.

Chapter Quiz

Ready to see how well you retained what you just read? Scan the QR code to go directly to the chapter quiz interface for this study guide. If you're using a computer, simply visit the online resources page at **mometrix.com/resources719/ftcephysics** and click the Chapter Quizzes link.

Mechanics

Work, Energy, and Power

Basic Equation for Work

The equation for **work** (W) is $W = \boldsymbol{Fd}$, where $\boldsymbol{F}$ is the force exerted and $\boldsymbol{d}$ is the displacement of the object on which the force is exerted. For the simplest case, when the vectors of force and displacement have the same direction, the work done is equal to the product of the magnitudes of the force and displacement. If this is not the case, then the work may be calculated as $W = \boldsymbol{Fd}\cos\theta$, where θ is the angle between the force and displacement vectors. If force and displacement have the same direction, then work is positive; if they are in opposite directions, however, work is negative; and if they are perpendicular, the work done by the force is zero.

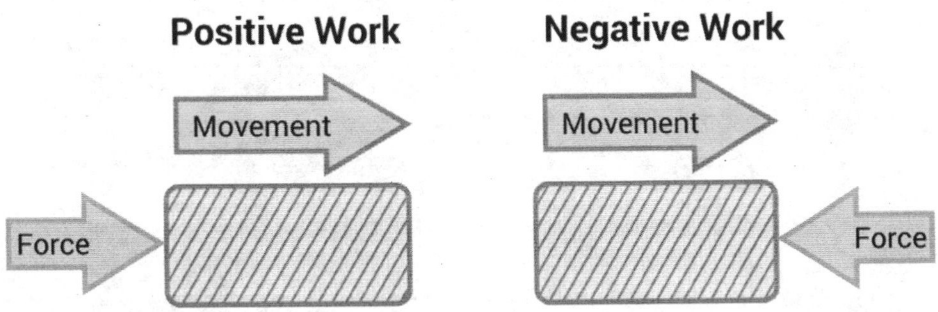

Review Video: Work
Visit mometrix.com/academy and enter code: 681834

For example, if a man pushes a block horizontally across a surface with a constant force of 10 N for a distance of 20 m, the work done by the man is 200 N-m or 200 J. If instead the block is sliding and the man tries to **slow its progress** by pushing against it, his work done is –200 J, since he is pushing in the direction opposite the motion. Also, if the man pushes vertically downward on the block while it slides, his work done is zero, since his force vector is perpendicular to the displacement vector of the block. It is important to note in each of these cases that neither the mass of the block nor the elapsed time is considered when calculating the amount of work done by the man.

Review Video: Push and Pull Forces
Visit mometrix.com/academy and enter code: 104731

Power

Put simply, **power** is the **rate at which work is done**. Power, like work, is a scalar quantity. If we know the amount of work, W, that has been performed in a given amount of time, Δt, then we may find average power, $P_{avg} = \frac{W}{\Delta t}$. If we are instead looking for the instantaneous power, there are two possibilities. If the force on an object is constant, and the object is moving at a constant velocity, then the instantaneous power is the same as the average power. If either the force or the velocity is varying, the instantaneous power should be computed by the equation $P = \boldsymbol{Fv}$, where $\boldsymbol{F}$ and $\boldsymbol{v}$ are the instantaneous force and velocity, respectively. This equation may also be used to compute average power if the force and velocity are constant. Power is typically expressed in joules per second, or watts.

Simple Machines

Simple machines include the pulley, lever, wheel and axle, wedge, inclined plane, and screw. These simple machines have no internal source of energy. More complex or compound machines can be formed from them. Simple machines provide a mechanical advantage and make it easier to accomplish a task. Single or double pulleys allow for easier direction of force. A lever enables a multiplication of force. The wheel and axle allows for movement with less resistance. The inclined plane enables a force less than an object's weight to be used to push it to a greater height. The wedge and screw are forms of the inclined plane. A wedge turns a smaller force working over a greater distance into a larger force. The screw is similar to an incline that is wrapped around a shaft.

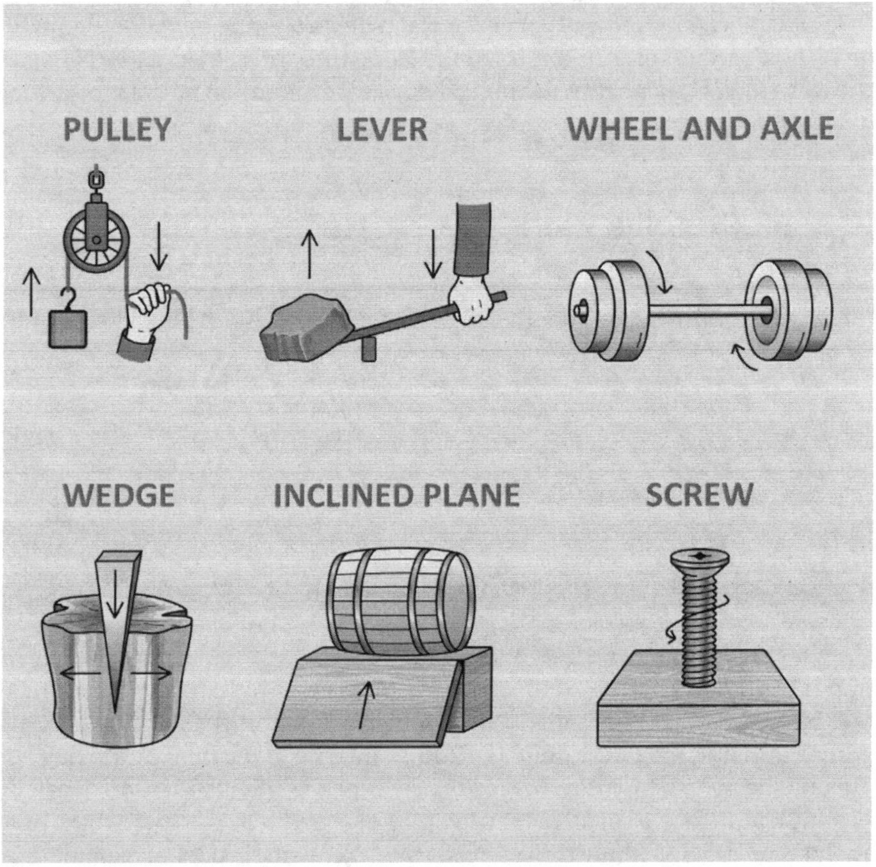

Review Video: Simple Machines
Visit mometrix.com/academy and enter code: 950789

Mechanical Advantage

There is a certain amount of **work** required to move an object that cannot be reduced. However, using one or more simple machines can increase either the distance or force needed. Since work is defined as a force multiplied by a distance, force and distance are inversely proportional.

$$\mathbf{Work_{input} = Work_{output}}$$

$$\mathbf{force_{input} \times distance_{input} = force_{output} \times distance_{output}}$$

Simple machines can either reduce the amount of input force needed by increasing the input distance or they can reduce the input distance needed by increasing the required input force. The ratio of the output force over the input force is a measure of the **mechanical advantage** of a machine. Due to the inverse relationship between force and distance for these machines, mechanical advantage can also be expressed as the ratio of input distance over the output distance.

$$\textbf{Mechanical Advantage} = \frac{\textbf{force}_{\textbf{output}}}{\textbf{force}_{\textbf{input}}} = \frac{\textbf{distance}_{\textbf{input}}}{\textbf{distance}_{\textbf{output}}}$$

LEVERS

The **lever** is the most common kind of simple machine. See-saws, shovels, and baseball bats are all examples of levers. There are three classes of levers which are differentiated by the relative orientations of the fulcrum, resistance, and effort. The **fulcrum** is the point at which the lever rotates, the **effort** is the point on the lever where force is applied, and the **resistance** is the part of the lever that acts in response to the effort.

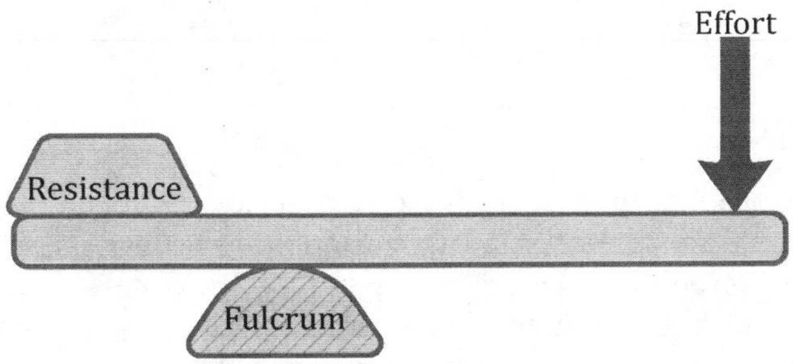

The mechanical advantage of a lever depends on the distances of the effort and resistance from the fulcrum.

$$\textbf{Mechanical Advantage} = \frac{\textbf{effort distance}}{\textbf{resistance distance}}$$

In a **first-class lever**, the fulcrum is between the effort and the resistance. A seesaw is a good example of a first-class lever when effort is applied to force one end up, the other end goes down, and vice versa. The shorter the distance between the fulcrum and the resistance, the easier it will be to move the resistance. As an example, consider whether it is easier to lift another person on a see saw when they are sitting close to the middle or all the way at the end. A little practice will show you that it is much more difficult to lift a person the farther away he or she is on the see-saw.

First-Class Lever

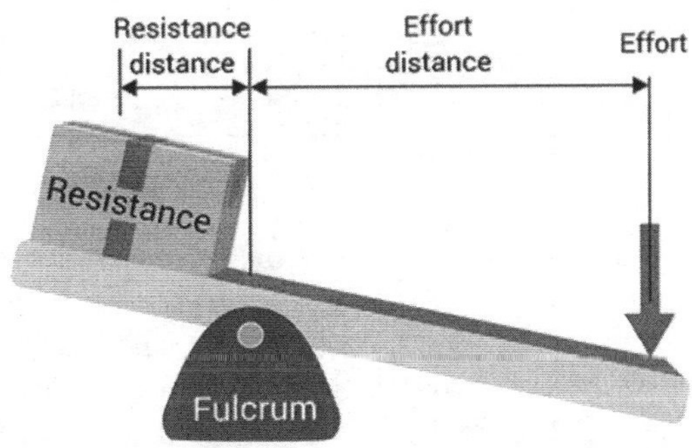

In a **second-class lever**, the resistance is in between the fulcrum and the effort. While a first-class lever is able to increase force and distance through mechanical advantage, a second-class lever is only able to increase force. A common example of a second-class lever is the wheelbarrow; the force exerted by your hand at one end of the wheelbarrow is magnified at the load. Basically, with a second-class lever, you are trading distance for force; by moving your end of the wheelbarrow a bit farther, you produce greater force at the load.

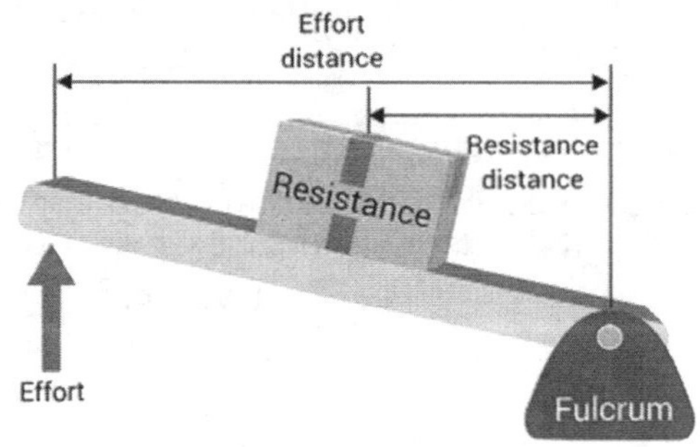

Third-class levers are used to produce greater distance. In a third-class lever, the force is applied in between the fulcrum and the resistance. A baseball bat is a classic example of a third-class lever; the bottom of the bat, below where you grip it, is considered the fulcrum. The end of the bat, where the ball is struck, is the resistance. By exerting effort at the base of the bat, close to the fulcrum, you are able to make the end of the bat fly quickly through the air. The closer your hands are to the base of the bat, the faster you will be able to make the other end of the bat travel.

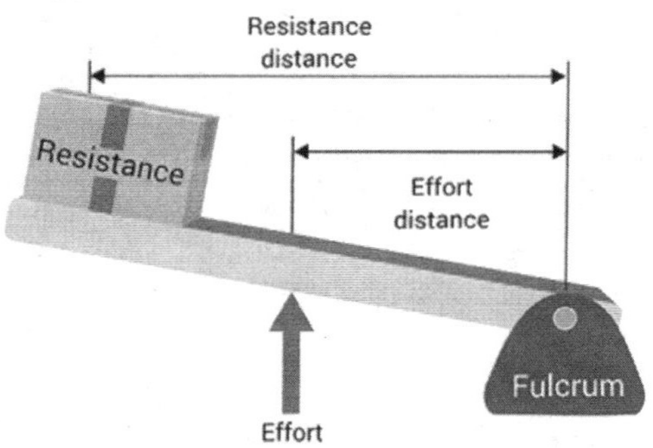

Review Video: Levers
Visit mometrix.com/academy and enter code: 103910

Wheel and Axle

Another basic arrangement that makes use of simple machines is called the wheel and axle. When most people think of a wheel and axle, they immediately envision an automobile tire. The steering wheel of the car, however, operates on the same mechanical principle, namely that the force required to move the center of a circle is much greater than the force required to move the outer rim of a circle. When you turn the steering wheel, you are essentially using a second-class lever by increasing the output force by increasing the input distance. The force required to turn the wheel from the outer rim is much less than would be required to turn the wheel from its center.

The equation for the mechanical advantage of a wheel and axle is:

$$\textbf{Mechanical Advantage} = \frac{\textbf{radius}_{\textbf{wheel}}}{\textbf{radius}_{\textbf{axle}}}$$

For instance, a steering wheel with a radius of 12 inches has a greater mechanical advantage than a steering wheel with a radius of 10 inches; the same amount of force exerted on the rim of each wheel will produce greater force on the axle of the larger wheel.

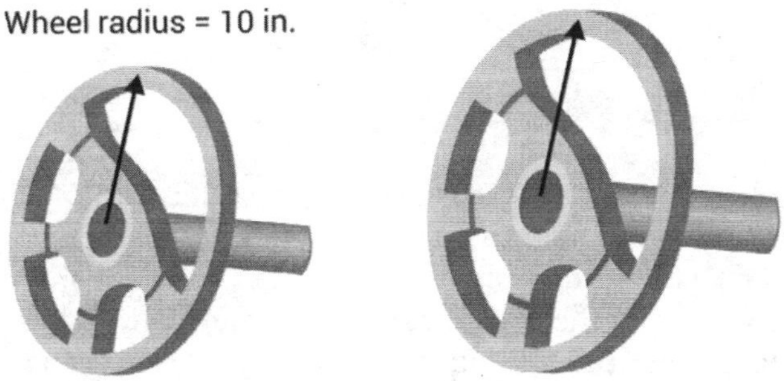

Thus, the mechanical advantage for each is:

$$\frac{10 \text{ inches}}{2 \text{ inches}} = 5 \qquad \frac{12 \text{ inches}}{2 \text{ inches}} = 6$$

Review Video: Wheel and Axle
Visit mometrix.com/academy and enter code: 574045

PULLEYS

The pulley is a simple machine in which a rope is carried by the rotation of a wheel. Another name for a pulley is a block. Pulleys are typically used to allow the force to be directed from a convenient location. For instance, imagine you are given the task of lifting a heavy and tall bookcase. Rather than tying a rope to the bookcase and trying to lift it, it would make sense to tie a pulley system to a rafter above the bookcase and run the rope through it, so that you could pull down on the rope and lift the bookcase. Pulling down allows you to incorporate your weight (normal force) into the act of lifting, thereby making it easier.

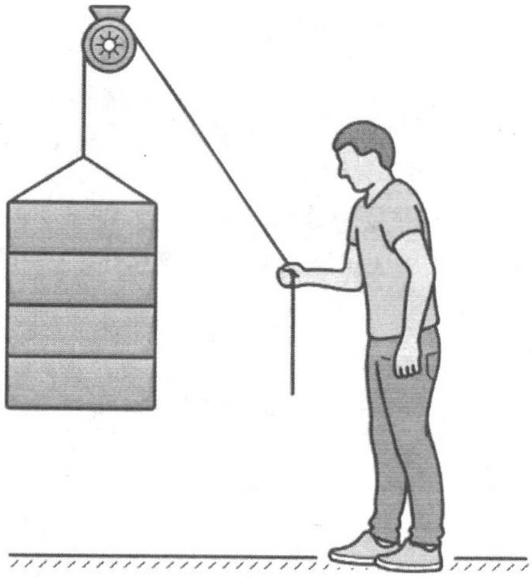

If there is just one pulley above the bookcase, you have created a first-class lever that will not diminish the amount of force that needs to be applied to lift the bookcase. There is another way to use a pulley, however, that can make the job of lifting a heavy object considerably easier. First, tie the rope directly to the rafter. Then, attach a pulley to the top of the bookcase and run the rope through it. If you can then stand so that you are above the bookcase, you will have a much easier time lifting this heavy object. This is because the weight of the bookcase is now being distributed: half of it is acting on the rafter, and half of it is acting on you. In other words, this arrangement allows you to lift an object with half the force. This simple pulley system, therefore, has a mechanical advantage of 2. Note that in this arrangement, the unfixed pulley is acting like a second-class lever. The price you pay for your mechanical advantage is that whatever distance you raise your end of the rope, the bookcase will only be lifted half as much.

Of course, it might be difficult for you to find a place high enough to enact this system. If this is the case, you can always tie another pulley to the rafter and run the rope through it and back down to the floor. Since this second pulley is fixed, the mechanical advantage will remain the same.

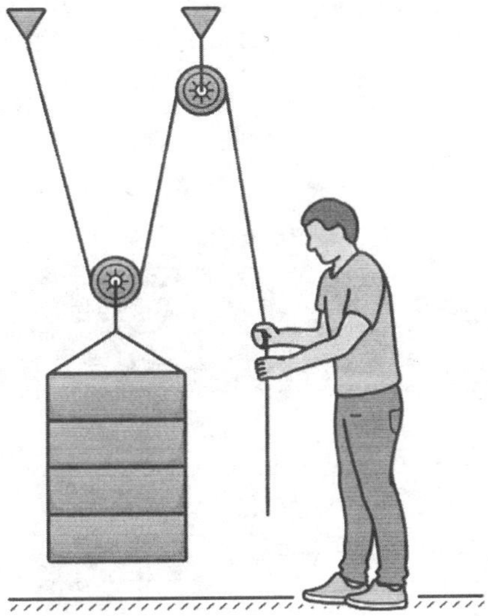

Inclined Plane

The inclined plane is perhaps the most common of the simple machines. It is simply a flat surface that elevates as you move from one end to the other. Consider how much easier it is for a person to walk up a long ramp than to climb a shorter but steeper flight of stairs; this is because the force required is diminished as the distance increases. Indeed, the longer the ramp, the easier it is to ascend.

Inclined planes often used to move heavy objects. For instance, moving a heavy box onto the back of a truck requires less force when pushing it up a ramp than when lifting it directly onto the truck bed. The longer the ramp, the greater the mechanical advantage, and the easier it will be to move the box. The mechanical advantage of an inclined plane is equal to the slant length divided by the rise of the plane.

$$\textbf{Mechanical Advantage} = \frac{\textbf{slant length}}{\textbf{rise}}$$

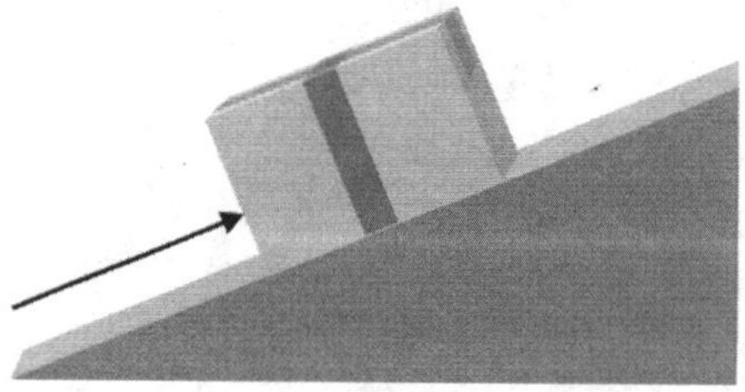

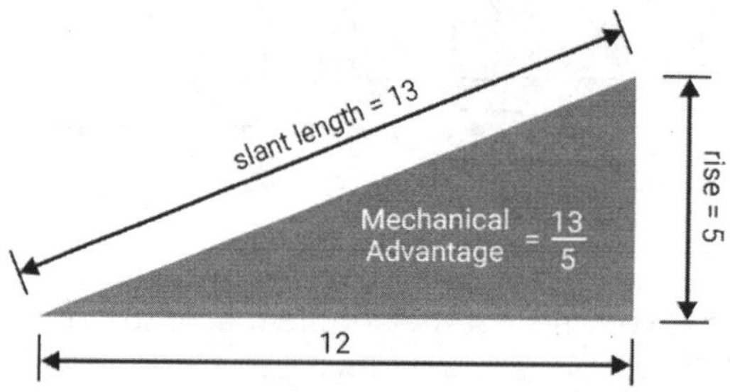

Screw

A screw is simply an inclined plane that has been wound around a cylinder so that it forms a sort of spiral.

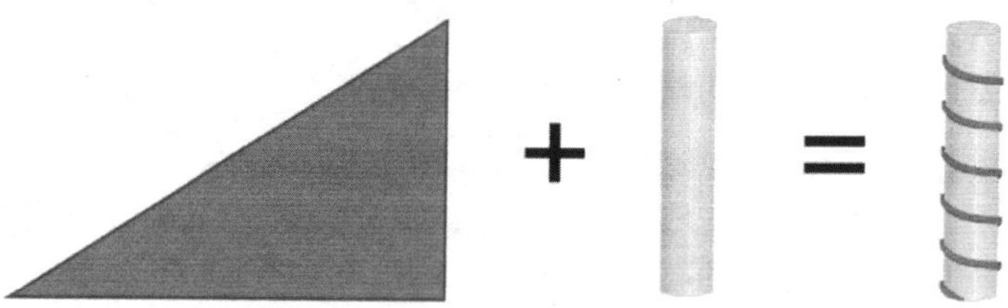

When it is placed into some medium, as for instance wood, the screw will move either forward or backward when it is rotated. The principle of the screw is used in a number of different objects, from jar lids to flashlights. The equation for the mechanical advantage is a modification of the inclined plane's equation.

Because the rise of the inclined plane is the length along a screw, length between rotations is the rise. The slant length is equal the circumference of one rotation ($2\pi r$).

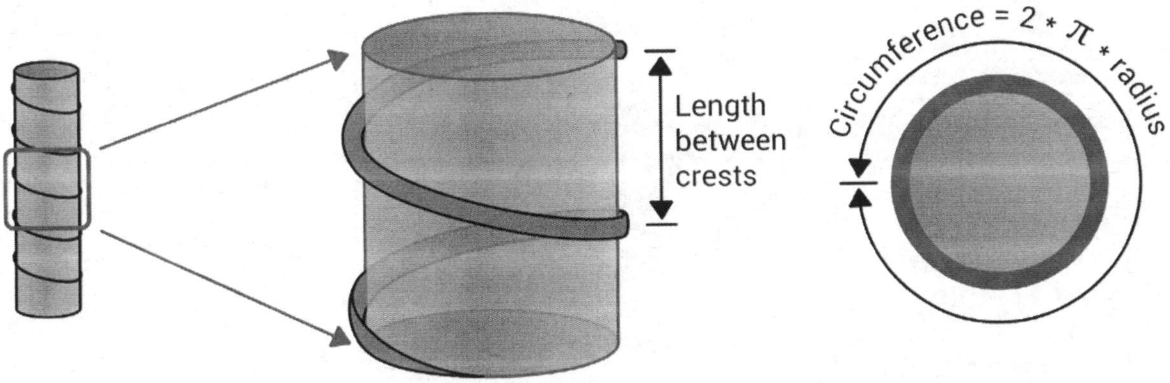

$$\text{Mechanical Advantage} = \frac{2 \times \pi \times \text{radius}}{\text{length between crests}}$$

Wedge

A wedge is a variation on the inclined plane, in which the wedge moves between objects or parts and forces them apart. The unique characteristic of a wedge is that, unlike an inclined plane, it is designed to move. Perhaps the most familiar use of the wedge is in splitting wood. A wedge is driven into the wood by hitting the flat back end. The thin end of a wedge is easier to drive into the wood since it has less surface area and, therefore, transmits more force per area. As the wedge is driven in, the increased width helps to split the wood.

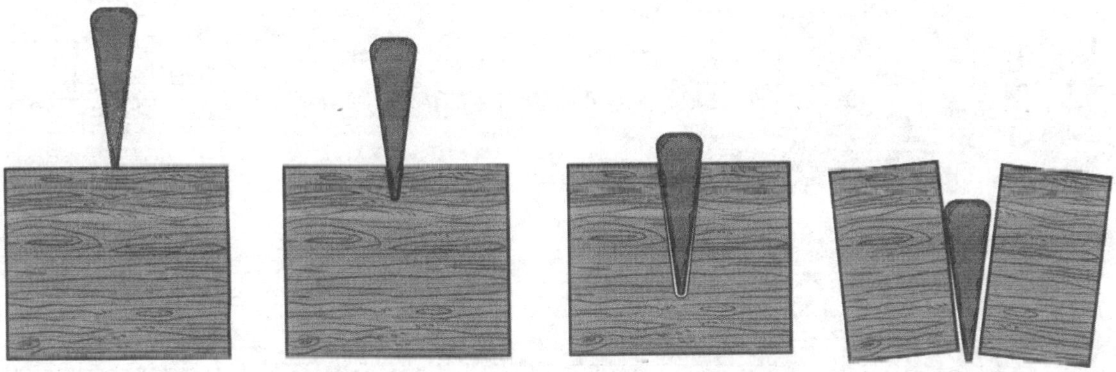

The longer and thinner the wedge, the greater the mechanical advantage. The equation for mechanical advantage of a wedge is:

$$\text{Mechanical Advantage} = \frac{\text{length}}{\text{width}}$$

Gears

Gears are a system of interlocking wheels that can create immense mechanical advantages. The amount of mechanical advantage, however, will depend on the gear ratio; that is, on the relation in size between the gears.

When a small gear is driving a big gear, the speed of the big gear is relatively slow; when a big gear is driving a small gear, the speed of the small gear is relatively fast.

The equation for the mechanical advantage is:

$$\textbf{Mechanical Advantage} = \frac{\text{torque}_{output}}{\text{torque}_{input}} = \frac{r_{output}}{r_{input}} = \frac{\#\text{ of teeth}_{output}}{\#\text{ of teeth}_{input}}$$

Note that mechanical advantage is greater than 1 when the output gear is larger. In these cases, the output velocity (ω) will be lower. The equation for the relative speed of a gear system is:

$$\frac{\omega_{input}}{\omega_{output}} = \frac{r_{output}}{r_{input}}$$

$$\text{Mechanical Advantage} = \frac{\text{teeth}_{output}}{\text{teeth}_{input}} = \frac{20}{10} = 2$$

$$\text{Mechanical Advantage} = \frac{\text{teeth}_{output}}{\text{teeth}_{input}} = \frac{16}{8} = 2$$

Gear Ratios

A gear ratio is a measure of how much the speed and torque are changing in a gear system. It is the ratio of output speed to input speed. Because the number of teeth is directly proportional to the speed in meshing gears, a gear ratio can also be calculated using the number of teeth on the gears. When the driving gear has 30 teeth and the driven gear has 10 teeth, the gear ratio is 3:1.

$$\text{Gear Ratio} = \frac{\#\text{ of teeth}_{driving}}{\#\text{ of teeth}_{driven}} = \frac{30}{10} = \frac{3}{1} = 3:1$$

This means that the smaller, driven gear rotates 3 times for every 1 rotation of the driving gear.

Uses of Gears

Gears are used to change the direction, location, and amount of output torque, as well as change the angular velocity of output.

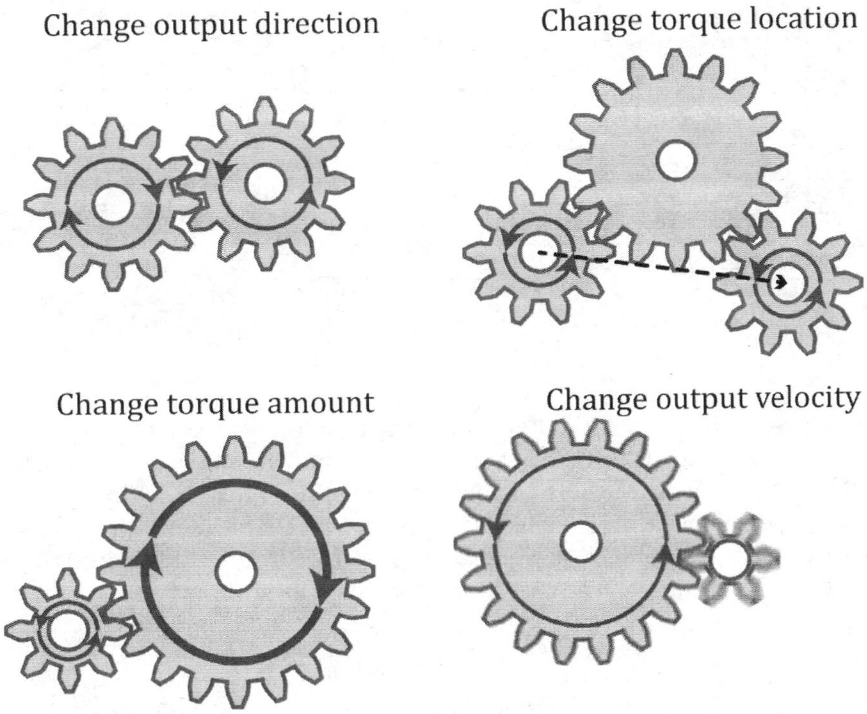

Cams

In the study of motion, a final application often tested is the cam. A cam and follower system allows mechanical systems to have timed, specified, and repeating motion. Although cams come in varied forms, tests focus on rotary cams. In engines, a cam shaft coordinates the valves for intake and exhaust. Cams are often used to convert rotational motion into repeating linear motion.

Cams rotate around one point. The follower sits on the edge of the cam and moves along with the edge. To understand simple cams, count the number of bumps on the cam. Each bump will cause the follower to move outwards.

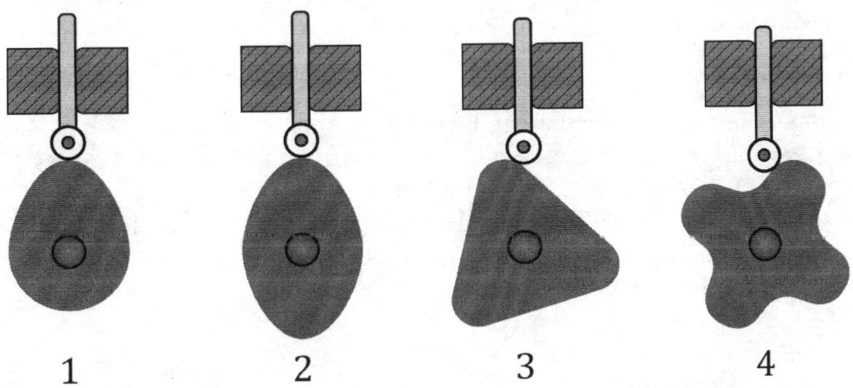

Another way to consider cams is to unravel the cam profile into a straight object. The follower will then follow the top of the profile.

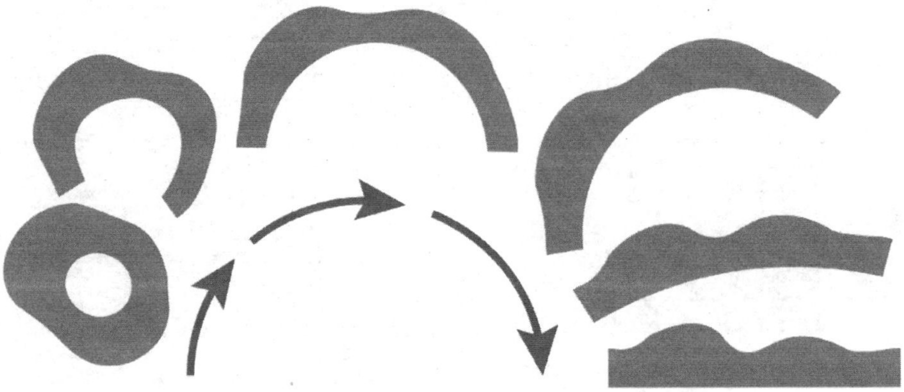

ENERGY

Energy is a word that has developed several different meanings in the English language, but in physics, it refers to the measure of a body's ability to do work. In physics, energy may not have a million meanings, but it does have many forms. Each of these forms, such as chemical, electric, and nuclear, is the capability of an object to perform work. However, the most commonly used concepts are mechanical energy and mechanical work. **Mechanical energy** is the sum of an object's kinetic and potential energies. While kinetic energy is linked to an object's motion, potential energy can be in a few different forms. The common forms of potential energy are gravitational and elastic.

KINETIC ENERGY

The **kinetic energy of an object** is that quality of its motion that can be related in a qualitative way to the amount of work performed on the object. Kinetic energy can be defined as $KE = \frac{mv^2}{2}$, in which m is the mass of an object and v is the magnitude of its velocity. Kinetic energy cannot be negative, since it depends on the square of velocity. Units for kinetic energy are the same as those for work: joules. Kinetic energy is a scalar quantity.

Changes in kinetic energy occur when a force does work on an object, such that the speed of the object is altered. This change in kinetic energy is equal to the amount of work that is done, and can be expressed as $W = KE_f - KE_i = \Delta KE$. This equation is commonly referred to as the work-kinetic energy theorem. If there are several different forces acting on the object, then W in this equation is the total work done by all the forces, or by the net force. This equation can be very helpful in solving some problems that would otherwise rely solely on Newton's laws of motion.

POTENTIAL ENERGY

Potential energy is the amount of energy that can be ascribed to a body or bodies based on configuration. There are a couple of different kinds of potential energy. **Gravitational potential energy** is the energy associated with the separation of bodies that are attracted to one another gravitationally. Any time you lift an object, you are increasing its gravitational potential energy. Gravitational potential energy can be found by the equation $PE = mgh$, where m is the mass of an object, $\boldsymbol{g}$ is the gravitational acceleration, and h is its height above a reference point, most often the ground.

Another kind of potential energy is **elastic potential energy**; elastic potential energy is associated with the compression or expansion of an elastic, or spring-like, object. Physicists will often refer to potential energy as being stored within a body, the implication being that it could emerge in the future.

Review Video: Potential and Kinetic Energy
Visit mometrix.com/academy and enter code: 491502

Elastic Potential Energy

Elastic potential energy is the potential for a certain amount of work to be done by one object on another using elastic compression or tension. The most common example is the spring. A spring will resist any compression or tension away from its equilibrium position (natural position). A small buggy is pressed into a large spring. The spring contains a large amount of elastic potential energy. If the buggy and spring are released, the spring will exert a force on the buggy, pushing it for a distance. This work will put kinetic energy into the buggy. The energy can be imagined as a liquid poured from one container into another. The spring pours its elastic energy into the buggy, which receives the energy as kinetic energy.

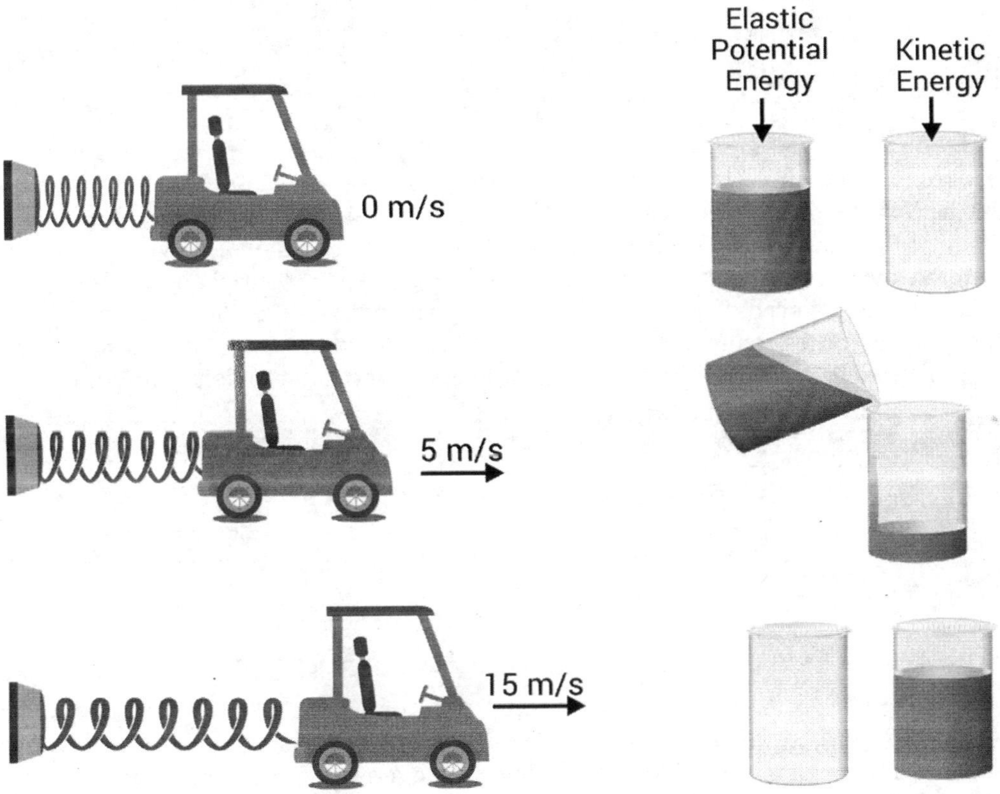

Conservative and Non-Conservative Forces

Forces that change the state of a system by changing kinetic energy into potential energy, or vice versa, are called **conservative forces**. This name arises because these forces conserve the total amount of kinetic and potential energy. Every other kind of force is considered non-conservative. One example of a conservative force is gravity. Consider the path of a ball thrown straight up into the air. Since the ball has the same amount of kinetic energy when it is thrown as it does when it returns to its original location (known as completing a closed path), gravity can be said to be a conservative force. More generally, a force can be said to be conservative if the work it does on an object through a closed path is zero. Frictional force would not meet this standard, of course, because it is only capable of performing negative work.

For example, imagine a ball moving perpendicular to the surface of the Earth, in other words straight up and down, with its weight being the only force acting on it. As the ball rises, the weight will be doing work on the ball, decreasing its speed and its kinetic energy and slowing it down until it momentarily stops. During this ascent, the potential energy of the ball will be rising. Once the ball begins to fall back down, it will lose potential energy as it gains kinetic energy. Mechanical energy is conserved throughout; the potential energy of the ball at its highest point is equal to the kinetic energy of the ball at its lowest point, just before to impact.

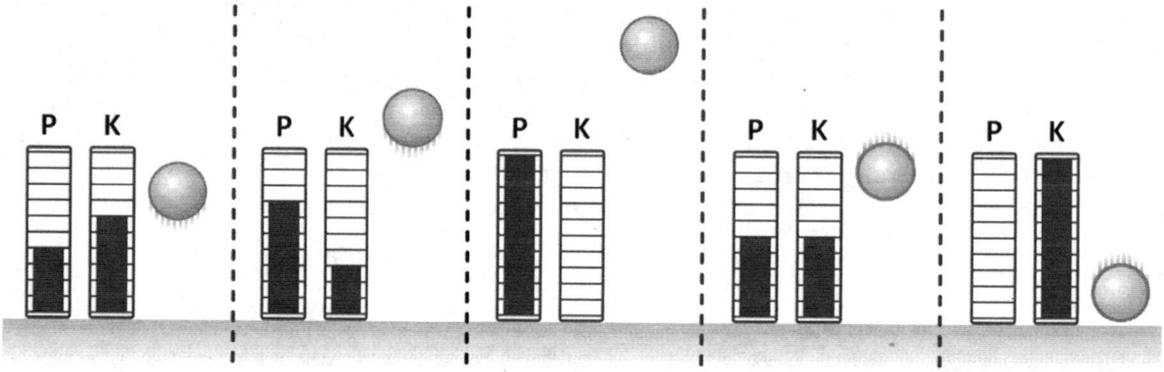

In systems where friction and air resistance are not negligible, we observe a different sort of result. For example, imagine a block sliding across the floor until it comes to a stop due to friction. Unlike a compressed spring or a ball flung into the air, there is no way for this block to regain its energy with a return trip. Therefore, we cannot say that the lost kinetic energy is being stored as potential energy. Instead, it has been dissipated and cannot be recovered. The total mechanical energy of the block-floor system has been not conserved in this case but rather reduced. The total energy of the system has not decreased, since the kinetic energy has been converted into thermal energy, but that energy is no longer useful for work.

One-Dimensional Analysis of Work Done By a Variable Force

If the force on an object varies across the distance the object is moved, then a simple product will not yield the work. If we consider the work performed by a variable force in one dimension, then we are assuming that the directions of the force and the displacement are the same. The magnitude of the force will depend on the position of the particle. In order to calculate the amount of work performed by a variable force over a given distance, we should first divide the total displacement into a number of intervals, each with a width of Δx. We may then say that the amount of work performed during any one interval is $\Delta W = \boldsymbol{F}_{avg}\Delta x$, where $\boldsymbol{F}_{avg}$ is the average force over the interval Δx. We can then say that the total amount of work performed is the sum of all work performed during the various intervals. By reducing the interval to an infinitesimal length, we obtain the integral:

$$W = \int_{x_1}^{x_2} \boldsymbol{F}_x dx$$

This integral requires that the force be a known function of x.

Work Performed by a Spring

If we move a block attached to a spring from point x_i to point x_f, we are doing work on the block, and the spring is also doing work on the block. To determine the work done by the spring on the block, we can substitute ***F*** from Hooke's law into our equation for work performed by a variable force, and arrive at this measure: $W = \frac{k(x_i{}^2 - x_f{}^2)}{2}$. This work will be positive if $x_i{}^2 > x_f{}^2$, and negative if the opposite is true. If $x_i = 0$ and we decide to call the final position x, then we may change our equation: $W = \frac{-kx^2}{2}$. It is important to keep in mind that this is the work done by the spring. The work done by the force that moves the block to its final position will be a positive quantity.

Like all simple harmonic oscillators, springs operate by **storing and releasing potential energy**. The amount of energy being stored or released by a spring is equal to the magnitude of the work done by the spring during that same operation. The total potential energy stored in a spring can be calculated as $PE = \frac{kx^2}{2}$. Neglecting the effects of friction and drag, an object oscillating on a spring will continue to do so indefinitely, since total mechanical energy (kinetic and potential) is conserved. In such a situation, the period of oscillation can be calculated as $T = 2\pi \times \sqrt{\frac{m}{k}}$.

Displacement, Velocity, and Acceleration

Displacement

When something changes its location from one place to another, it is said to have undergone **displacement**. If we can determine the original and final position of the object, then we can determine the total displacement with the equation $\Delta \boldsymbol{x} = x_f - x_i$, where x_f is the final position and x_i is the initial position.

If the object has moved in the positive direction, then the final position will be greater than the original position, so we can say that the change was positive. If the final position is less than the original, however, displacement will be negative. Displacement along a straight line is an example of a vector quantity; it has both a magnitude and a direction. If an object travels from position $x = -5$ cm to $x = 5$ cm, it has undergone a displacement of 10 cm. If it traverses the same path in the opposite direction, its displacement is -10 cm. A vector that spans the object's displacement in the direction of travel is known as a displacement vector, with units of length.

Review Video: Displacement in Physics
Visit mometrix.com/academy and enter code: 236197

Determining Position

In order to determine anything about the motion of an object, we must first locate it. In other words, we must be able to describe its position relative to some reference point, often called an **origin**. If we consider the origin as the zero point of an axis, then positive values correspond to the location of an object one direction, and negative values are locations in the exact opposite direction. If a particle is located 5 cm from the origin in the positive direction of the x-axis, its location is said to be $x = 5$ cm. If another particle is 5 cm from the origin in the negative direction of the x-axis, its position is $x = -5$ cm. These two particles are 10 cm apart. A vector whose starting point is the origin and whose endpoint is the location of an object is that object's position vector, with units of length.

Velocity

Difference between Speed and Velocity

Often, people confuse the words *speed* and *velocity*. There is a significant difference. The average velocity is based on the amount of displacement, a vector. Alternately, the average speed is based on the distance covered or the path length. The equation for speed is:

$$\textbf{average speed} = \frac{\textbf{total distance traveled}}{\textbf{change in time}}$$

Notice that we used total distance and *not* change in position, because speed is path-dependent.

If the plane traveling between cities had needed to fly around a storm on its way, making the distance traveled 50 miles greater than the distance the car traveled, the plane would still have the same total displacement as the car.

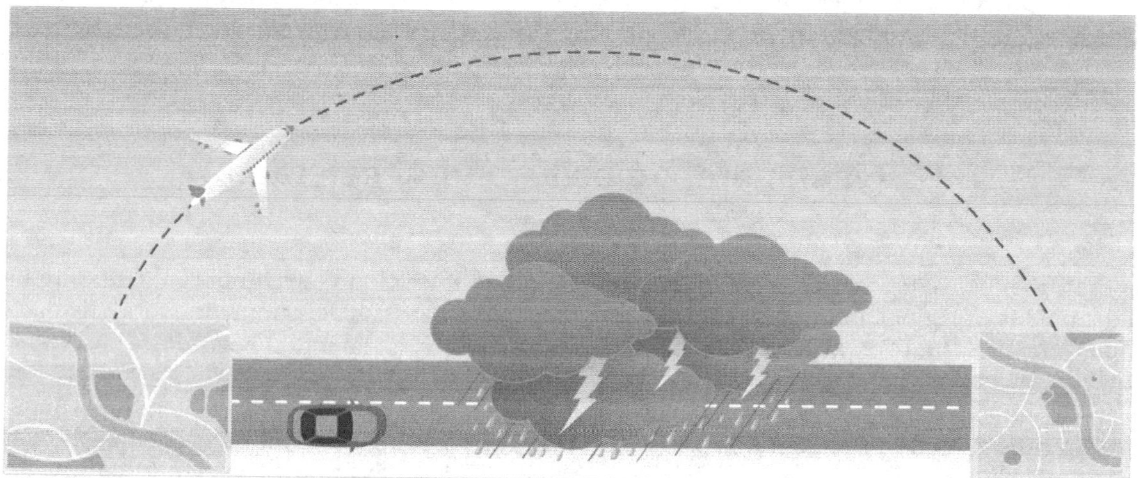

For this reason, the average speed can be calculated:

$$\text{plane average speed} = \frac{150 \text{ miles}}{1 \text{ hour}} = 150 \text{ miles per hour}$$

$$\text{car average speed} = \frac{100 \text{ miles}}{2 \text{ hours}} = 50 \text{ miles per hour}$$

Instantaneous Velocity

There are two types of velocity that are commonly considered in physics: average velocity and instantaneous velocity. In order to obtain the **instantaneous velocity** of an object, we must find its average velocity and then try to decrease Δt as close as possible to zero. As Δt decreases, it approaches what is known as a limiting value, bringing the average velocity very close to the instantaneous velocity. Instantaneous velocity is most easily discussed in the context of calculus-based physics.

Average Velocity

If we want to calculate the **average velocity** of an object, we must know two things. First, we must know its **displacement**, or the distance it has covered relative to a starting point. Second, we must know the **time it took to cover this distance**. Once we have this information, the formula for average velocity is: $\boldsymbol{v}_{avg} = \frac{(x_f - x_i)}{(t_f - t_i)}$, where the subscripts i and f denote the initial and final values of the position and time. In other words, the average velocity is equal to the change in position divided by the change in time. This calculation will indicate the average distance that was covered per unit of time. Average velocity is a vector and will always point in the same direction as the displacement vector (since time is a scalar and always positive).

Acceleration

Acceleration is the **change in the velocity** of an object. Like velocity, acceleration may be computed as an average or an instantaneous quantity. To calculate average acceleration, we may use the equation $\boldsymbol{a}_{avg} = \frac{\boldsymbol{v}_f - \boldsymbol{v}_i}{t_f - t_i}$, where the subscripts i and f denote the initial and final values of the velocity and time. The so-called instantaneous acceleration of an object can be found by reducing the time component to the limiting value until instantaneous velocity is approached. Acceleration will be expressed in units of distance divided by time squared; for instance, meters per second squared. Like position and velocity, acceleration is a vector quantity and will therefore have both magnitude and direction.

Review Video: Velocity and Acceleration
Visit mometrix.com/academy and enter code: 671849

Kinematics

Kinematic Equations

The phenomenon of constant acceleration allows physicists to construct a number of helpful equations. Perhaps the most fundamental equation of an object's motion is the **position equation**:

$$x_f = x_i + \boldsymbol{v}_i t + \frac{1}{2}\boldsymbol{a}t^2$$

If the object is starting from rest at the origin, this equation reduces to $x_f = \frac{at^2}{2}$. The position equation can be rearranged to give the **displacement equation**:

$$\Delta \boldsymbol{x} = \boldsymbol{v}_i t + \frac{1}{2}\boldsymbol{a}t^2$$

If the object's acceleration is unknown, the position or displacement may be found by the equation:

$$\Delta \boldsymbol{x} = \frac{(\boldsymbol{v}_f + \boldsymbol{v}_i)t}{2}$$

If the position of an object is unknown, the velocity may be found by the equation:

$$\boldsymbol{v}_f = \boldsymbol{v}_i + \boldsymbol{a}t$$

Similarly, if the time is unknown, the velocity after a given displacement may be found by the equation:

$$\boldsymbol{v}_f = \sqrt{(\boldsymbol{v}_i{}^2 + 2\boldsymbol{a}\Delta \boldsymbol{x})}$$

Concept of Projectile Motion

When we discuss **projectile motion**, we are referring to the movement of an object through two dimensions during a free fall. Two-dimensional motion may be described using the same equations as one-dimensional motion, but two equations must be considered simultaneously. For basic equations for projectile motion, it is often assumed that the rate of gravitational acceleration on the Earth is $\boldsymbol{g} = 9.8 \text{ m/s}^2$, and that the effect of air resistance can be ignored (Note: take care with the sign on gravitational acceleration make sure that it always points toward the Earth). If a projectile is launched under such ideal conditions, we may say that its initial velocity is $\boldsymbol{v}_0 = v_0 \cos\theta\, \mathbf{i} + v_0 \sin\theta\, \mathbf{j}$. These two velocity components are sometimes written as $\boldsymbol{v}_{0x}$ and $\boldsymbol{v}_{0y}$, respectively.

PROJECTILE MOTION EXAMPLE

Simple projectile motion occurs when an object is in the air and experiencing only the force of gravity. We will disregard drag for this topic. Some common examples of projectile motion are thrown balls, flying bullets, and falling rocks. The characteristics of projectile motion are:

1. The horizontal component of velocity doesn't change
2. The vertical acceleration due to gravity affects the vertical component of velocity

Because gravity only acts downwards, objects in projectile motion only experience acceleration in the y-direction (vertical). The horizontal component of the object's velocity does not change in flight. This means that if a rock is thrown out off a cliff, the horizontal velocity (think of the shadow if the sun is directly overhead) will not change until the ball hits the ground.

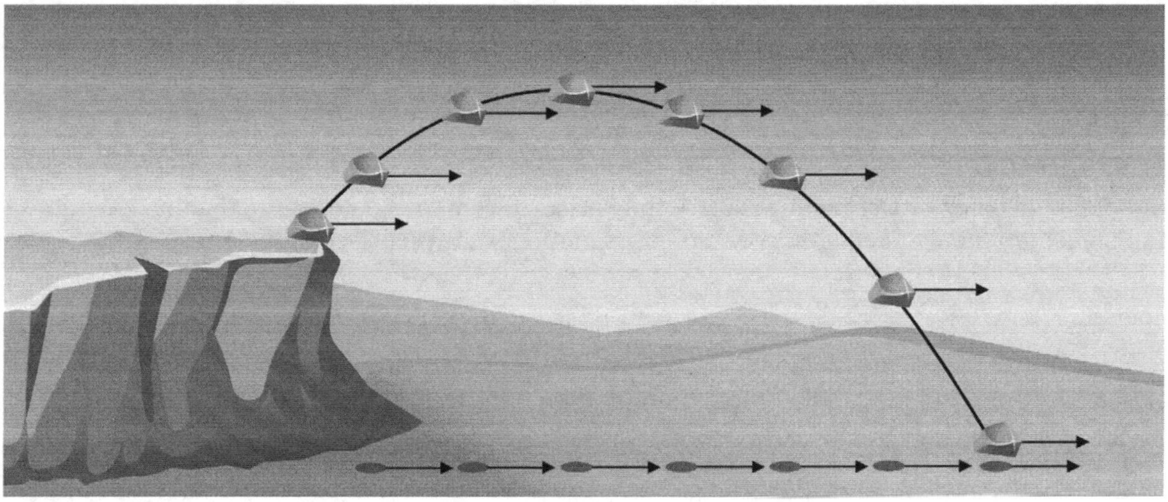

The velocity in the vertical direction is affected by gravity. Gravity imposes an acceleration of $g = 9.8\frac{\text{m}}{\text{s}^2}$ or $32\frac{\text{ft}}{\text{s}^2}$ downward on projectiles. The vertical component of velocity at any point is equal to:

$$\textbf{vertical velocity} = \textbf{original vertical velocity} - \textbf{g} \times \textbf{time}$$

When these characteristics are combined, there are three points of particular interest in a projectile's flight. At the beginning of a flight, the object has a horizontal component and a vertical component giving it a large speed. At the top of a projectile's flight, the vertical velocity equals zero, making the top the slowest part of travel. When the object passes the same height as the launch, the vertical velocity is opposite of the initial vertical velocity, making the speed equal to the initial speed.

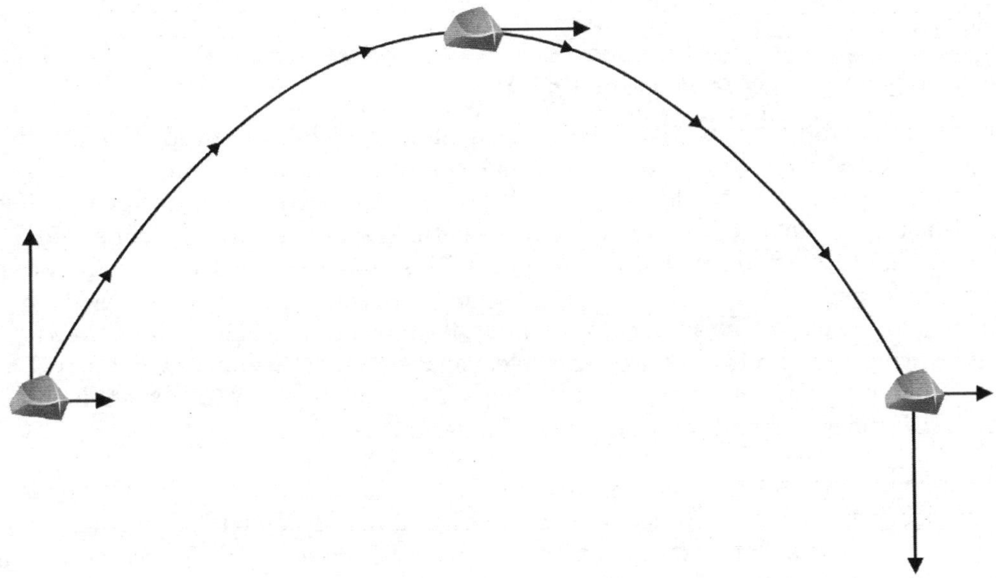

If the object continues falling below the initial height from which it was launched (e.g., it was launched from the edge of a cliff), it will have an even greater velocity than it did initially from that point until it hits the ground.

Review Video: Projectile Motion
Visit mometrix.com/academy and enter code: 719700

Example: If a cannon located at a height of 5 m above ground level fires a cannonball 250 m/s at an angle of $\frac{\pi}{6}$ from the horizontal, how far will the cannonball travel before hitting the ground?

When the cannonball hits the ground, it has been displaced by –5 m in the y-direction. Solving for the components of initial velocity yields $\boldsymbol{v}_{0x} = 216.5$ m/s and $\boldsymbol{v}_{0y} = 125$ m/s. Setting up the y-direction displacement equation results in the following: $-5 = 125t_f - 4.9t_f^{\,2}$. Solving for t_f yields an impact time of around 25.5 seconds. To find the horizontal distance covered, set up the displacement equation for the x-direction: $\Delta\boldsymbol{x} = \boldsymbol{v}_{0x}t_f + \frac{1}{2}\boldsymbol{a}_x(t_f)^2$. Since we ignore the effects of air resistance, acceleration in the x-direction is zero, yielding a flight distance of 5,530 m.

Uniform Circular Motion

We may say that a particle is in **uniform circular motion** when it is traveling in a circle, or circular arc, and at a constant speed. Crucially, we must note that such a particle is accelerating, even though the magnitude of its velocity does not change. This is because velocity is a vector, and consequently, any change in its direction is an acceleration. So, if we take two points on an arc of radius, r, separated by an angle, θ, and want to determine the time it will take a particle to move between these two points at a constant speed, $|\boldsymbol{v}|$, we can use the equation: $\Delta t = \frac{r\theta}{|\boldsymbol{v}|}$. The quantity $\frac{|\boldsymbol{v}|}{r}$ is often written as $\boldsymbol{\omega}$, or angular velocity, having units of radians per second, so the time may also be computed as $\Delta t = \frac{\theta}{\boldsymbol{\omega}}$. The speed, or absolute value of the velocity, of an object in uniform circular motion is also called the tangential speed, because the object is always moving in a direction tangent to the circle. Similarly, an increase in the magnitude of this velocity is called **tangential acceleration**.

A very important component of uniform motion is the centripetal acceleration. This is the acceleration that changes the direction of the velocity vector to follow the circular arc. It is directed toward the center of the circle or arc and is described by $\boldsymbol{a}_c = \frac{|v|^2}{r} = r\boldsymbol{\omega}^2$.

Relative Motion and Inertial Reference Frames

When we describe motion as being **relative**, we mean that it can only be measured in relation to something else. If a moving object is considered as it relates to some stationary object or arbitrary location, it will have a different measured velocity than it would if it were compared to some other object that is itself in motion. In other words, the measure of an object's velocity depends entirely on the reference frame from which the measurement is taken. When performing measurements of this kind, we may use any reference point we like. However, once we have decided on a reference point, we must be consistent in using it as the basis for all of our measurements, or else we will go astray. Additionally, if we want to be able to apply Newton's laws of motion or Galilean principles of relativity, we must select an **inertial reference frame**: that is, a reference frame that is not accelerating or rotating. A car traveling at a constant speed in a straight line is an inertial reference frame. A car moving in uniform circular motion is not.

An object's velocity with respect to a frame fixed to the Earth can be computed by measuring its velocity from any inertial reference frame and combining that velocity by vector addition with the velocity of the inertial frame with respect to the Earth. For instance, if a man is traveling in the x-direction at 20 m/s, and he throws a rock out the window at a relative velocity of 15 m/s in the y-direction, the rock's velocity with respect to the Earth is found by adding the two vectors:

$$\boldsymbol{v}_r = 20\mathbf{i} + 15\mathbf{j} \text{ m/s}$$

Laws of Motion

Newton's Laws

Newton's First Law

Before Newton formulated his laws of mechanics, it was generally assumed that some force had to act on an object continuously in order to make the object move at a **constant velocity**. Newton, however, determined that unless some other force acted on the object (most notably friction or air resistance), it would continue in the direction it was pushed at the same velocity forever.

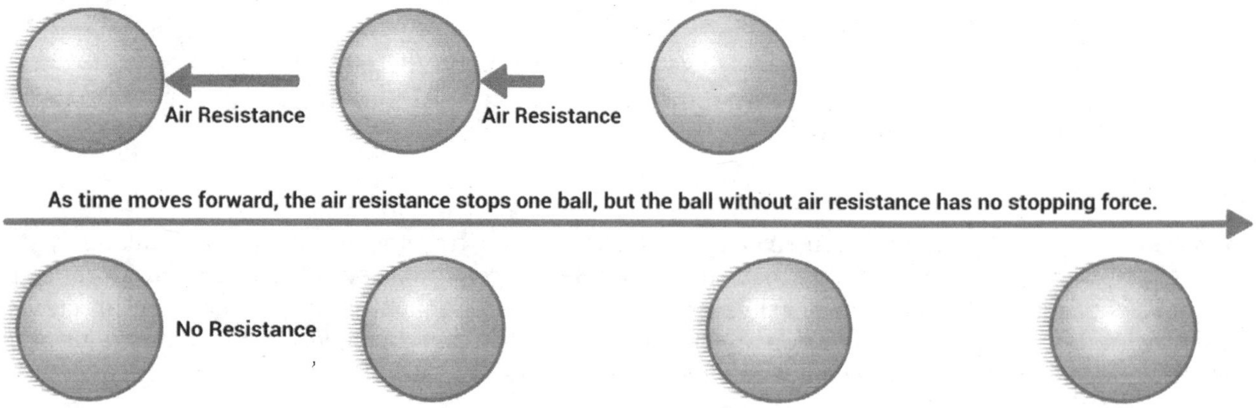

In this light, a body at rest and a body in motion are not all that different, and Newton's first law makes little distinction. It states that a body at rest will tend to remain at rest, while a body in motion will tend to remain in motion. This tendency of a body to remain in its present state of motion is referred to as **inertia**. In order for the body's state of motion to change, it must be acted on by a non-zero net force. **Net force** is the vector sum of all forces acting on a body. If this vector sum is zero, then there is no unbalanced force, and the body will remain in its present state of motion. It is important to remember that this law only holds in inertial reference frames.

> **Review Video: Newton's First Law of Motion**
> Visit mometrix.com/academy and enter code: 590367

NEWTON'S SECOND LAW

Newton's second law states that an **object's acceleration** is directly proportional to the net force acting on the object, and inversely proportional to the object's mass. It is generally written in equation form $\boldsymbol{F} = m\boldsymbol{a}$, where $\boldsymbol{F}$ is the net force acting on a body, m is the mass of the body, and $\boldsymbol{a}$ is its acceleration. It is important to note from this equation that since the mass is always a positive quantity, the acceleration vector is always pointed in the same direction as the net force vector. Of course, in order to apply this equation correctly, one must clearly identify the body to which it is being applied. Once this is done, we may say that $\boldsymbol{F}$ is the vector sum of all forces acting on that body, or the net force. This measure includes only those forces that are external to the body; any internal forces, in which one part of the body exerts force on another, are discounted.

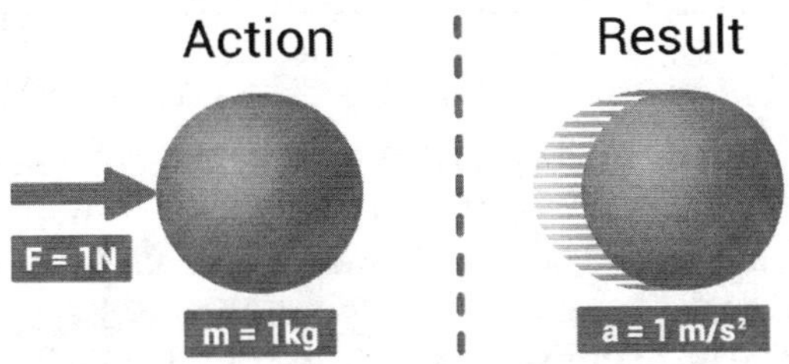

Newton's second law somewhat encapsulates his first, because it includes the principle that if no net force is acting on a body, the body will not accelerate. As was the case with his first law, Newton's second law may only be applied in inertial reference frames.

> **Review Video: Newton's Second Law of Motion**
> Visit mometrix.com/academy and enter code: 737975

NEWTON'S THIRD LAW

Newton's third law of motion can be stated as: **for every force, there is an equal and opposite force**. When a hammer strikes a nail, the nail hits the hammer just as hard. If we consider two objects, A and B, then we may express any contact between these two bodies with the equation $\boldsymbol{F}_{AB} = -\boldsymbol{F}_{BA}$. It is important to note in this kind of equation that the order of the subscripts denotes which body is exerting the force. Although the two forces are often referred to as the **action** and **reaction** forces, in physics there is really no such thing. There is no implication of cause and effect in the equation for Newton's third law. At first glance, this law might seem to forbid any movement at all. We must remember, however, that these equal, opposite forces are exerted on different bodies with different masses, so they will not cancel each other out.

As an example, consider two spring-based scales, both tipped on their sides, with the weighing surfaces facing each other. If scale #1 is pressing scale #2 into the wall, it exerts a force on scale #2, measurable by the reading on scale #2. However, because scale #1 is exerting a force on scale #2, scale #2 is exerting a force on scale #1 with an opposite direction, but the same magnitude.

Review Video: Newton's Third Law of Motion
Visit mometrix.com/academy and enter code: 838401

Equilibrium and Friction

Normal Force

The word *normal* is used in mathematics to mean perpendicular, and so the force known as normal force should be remembered as the perpendicular force exerted on an object that is resting on some other surface. For instance, if a box is resting on a horizontal surface, we may say that the normal force is directed upwards through the box (the opposite, downward force is the weight of the box). If the box is resting on a wedge, the normal force from the wedge is not vertical but is perpendicular to the surface.

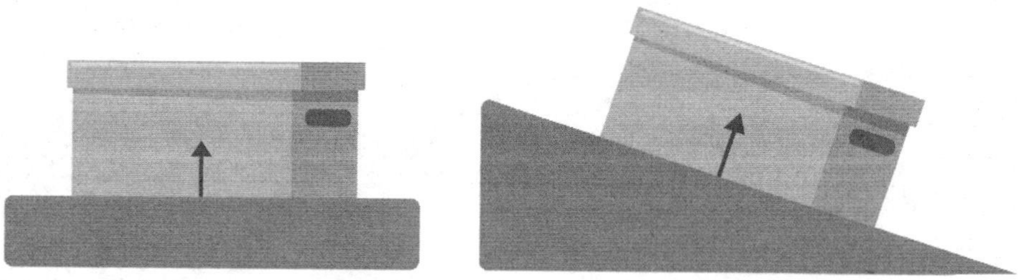

Static and Kinetic Frictional Forces

In order to illustrate the concept of friction, let us imagine a book resting on a table. As it sits there, the force of its weight ($\boldsymbol{W}$) is equal and opposite to the normal force ($\boldsymbol{N}$). If, however, we were to exert a force ($\boldsymbol{F}$) on the book, attempting to push it to one side, a frictional force ($\boldsymbol{f}$) would arise, equal and opposite to our force. This kind of frictional force is known as **static frictional force**.

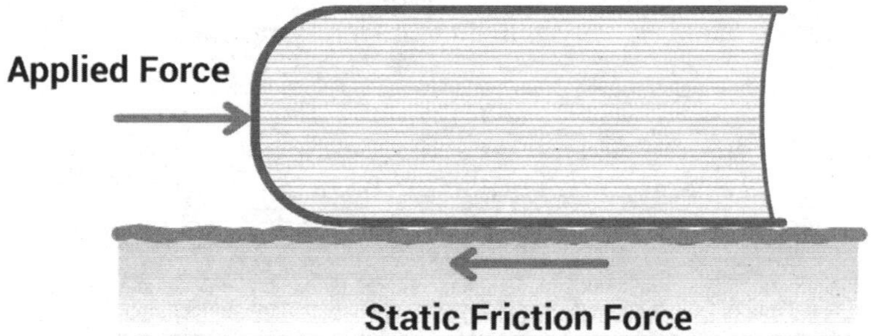

As we increase our force on the book, however, we will eventually cause it to accelerate in the direction of our force. At this point, the frictional force opposing us will be known as **kinetic frictional force**.

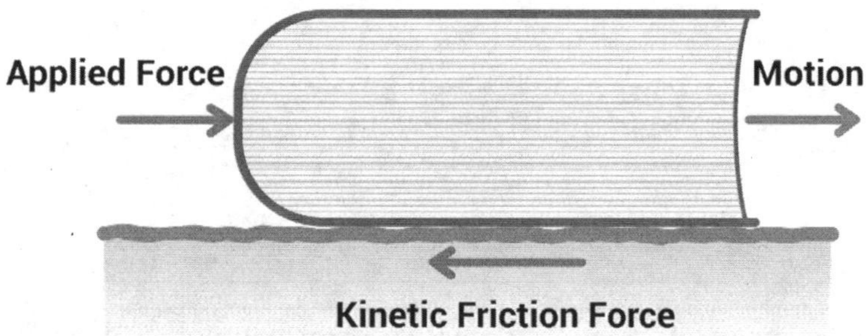

For the most part, kinetic frictional force is lower than static frictional force, and so the amount of force needed to maintain the movement of the book will be less than that needed to initiate movement. For wheels and spherical objects on a surface, static friction at the point of contact allows them to roll, but there is a frictional force that resists the rolling motion as well, due primarily to deformation effects in the rolling material. This is known as rolling friction, and tends to be much smaller than either static or kinetic friction.

Coefficient of Friction

If an object does not move when a horizontal force $\boldsymbol{F}$ is applied, then the **static frictional force** ($\boldsymbol{f}_s$) is exactly equal and opposite to $\boldsymbol{F}$, i.e., $\boldsymbol{f}_s = -\boldsymbol{F}$. Static frictional force has a maximum value, however, which is expressed as $\boldsymbol{f}_{s,max} = \mu_s N$, in which μ_s is the coefficient of static friction, and N is the magnitude of the normal force. If the magnitude of horizontal force applied to an object exceeds the maximum value of static friction, the object will begin to move. Once the object has begun to slide, the frictional force will generally decrease. The value to which the frictional force will diminish is expressed as $\boldsymbol{f}_k = \mu_k N$, in which μ_k is the coefficient of kinetic friction. For objects inclined to roll, such as balls or wheels, there is a rolling frictional force that resists the continued rolling of such an object. This force is expressed by $\boldsymbol{f}_r = \mu_r N$, in which μ_r is the coefficient of rolling friction. All of these frictional coefficients are dimensionless. Since the value of the frictional force depends on the interaction of the body and the surface, it is usually described as friction between the two.

Review Video: Friction
Visit mometrix.com/academy and enter code: 716782

Equilibrium

We may say that an object is in a **state of equilibrium** when it has a **constant linear momentum** ($\boldsymbol{p}$) at its center of mass, or when **angular momentum** ($\boldsymbol{L}$) **is also constant about the center of mass**. In other words, a wheel may be in equilibrium when it is spinning at a constant speed, and a hockey puck may be in equilibrium as it slides across ice. These are both examples of **dynamic equilibrium**. The phrase **static equilibrium**, however, is reserved for objects in which both linear and angular momentum are at zero. An object sitting on a table could be considered as being in static equilibrium.

BALANCED FORCES

An object is in equilibrium when the sum of all forces acting on the object is zero. When the forces on an object sum to zero, the object does not accelerate. Equilibrium can be obtained when forces in the y-direction sum to zero, forces in the x-direction sum to zero, or forces in both directions sum to zero.

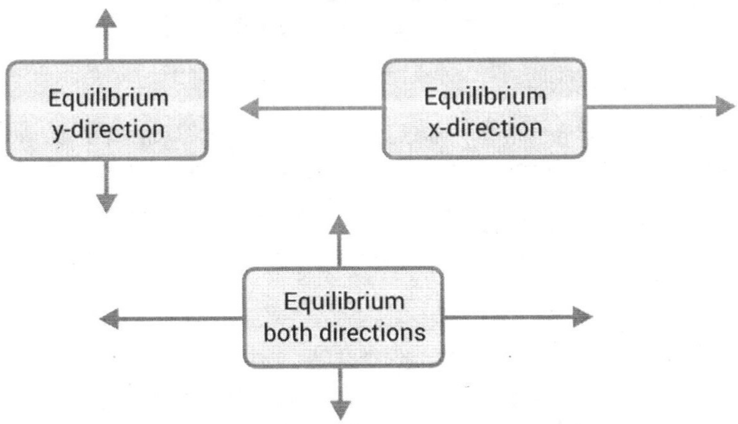

In most cases, a problem will provide one or more forces acting on an object and ask for a force to balance the system. The force will be the opposite of the current force or sum of current forces.

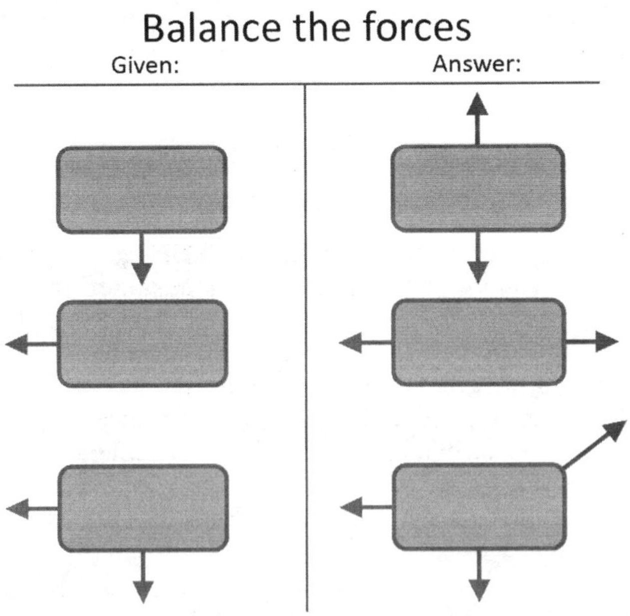

USING EQUILIBRIUM CONDITIONS

For a **body in equilibrium**, the net force vector and the net torque vector will both be equal to zero. For the most common cases, two-dimensional systems, these conditions can be fully expressed by one or two force summation equations and one torque summation equation. Torque summations may be taken about any point on the body, though strategic placement can make calculations simpler. To determine the **torque exerted by a**

force, multiply the magnitude of the force by the perpendicular distance to the point of interest. It will be necessary to decide in advance which direction of torque (clockwise or counterclockwise) will be considered positive.

For example, if we have a bar of known mass, m, that is suspended by cables at each end and whose center of mass is two thirds of the way along its length, L, we can use the equilibrium conditions to determine the tension in each cable. Gravity exerts a force of $-m\boldsymbol{g}$ on the bar's center of mass. Translational equilibrium conditions tell us that $\boldsymbol{T}_1 + \boldsymbol{T}_2 - m\boldsymbol{g} = 0$. Setting the total torque about the center of mass equal to zero, considering counterclockwise torque to be positive, yields the equation $\boldsymbol{T}_2\left(\frac{L}{3}\right) - \boldsymbol{T}_1\left(\frac{2L}{3}\right) = 0$. Solving these equations results in $\boldsymbol{T}_1 = \frac{mg}{3}$ and $\boldsymbol{T}_2 = \frac{2mg}{3}$. This result makes sense since the center of mass is closer to the second cable.

Translational and Rotational Equilibrium

If a body is in **translational equilibrium**, then its linear momentum will be constant, and there will be a net force of zero. Likewise, a body in rotational equilibrium will have a constant angular momentum, and again there will be a net torque of zero. Both of these equations are vector equations, and as such are both equivalent to three scalar equations for the three dimensions of motion, though in most instances, only one or two dimensions will be considered at a time. We may say that the two requirements for a body to be in equilibrium are that the vector sum of all the external forces acting on the body must be zero, and the vector sum of all the external torques acting on the body must also be zero. Conversely, if we are told that a body is in equilibrium, we may assume that both of these conditions will hold, and that we can use them to find unknown forces or torques.

Harmonic and Circular Motion

Polar Coordinate System

Polar coordinates were designed to be useful in situations in which circular arcs are more common than straight lines and right angles. Instead of having x- and y-coordinates, an object's location is described by its **distance from the origin**, r, and the angle between its position vector and the positive x-axis, commonly denoted as θ.

The two coordinate systems are related by the following equations:

$$x = r\cos\theta, y = r\sin\theta$$

$$r = \sqrt{(x^2 + y^2)}, \theta = \tan^{-1}\left(\frac{y}{x}\right)$$

The direction and nature of the conversion will dictate which set of equations to use.

The polar coordinate system simplifies many calculations of **circular motion**. Instead of a velocity in the x- or y-direction, velocity may be described by motion toward or away from the origin and an increase or decrease in the angle θ. For **uniform circular motion**, the change in r is zero, and the rate of change of angle θ is constant. The only acceleration on the body is the centripetal acceleration, given by $\boldsymbol{a}_c = \frac{|\boldsymbol{v}|^2}{r} = r\boldsymbol{\omega}^2$, where $\boldsymbol{\omega}$ is the rate of change in angle θ, known as the rotational velocity, keeping the body in its circular arc. This acceleration is caused by a centripetal force that pulls the object toward the center of the circle. By Newton's second law, this force has a magnitude given by $\boldsymbol{F} = m\boldsymbol{a}_c = \frac{m|\boldsymbol{v}|^2}{r} = mr\boldsymbol{\omega}^2$.

Simple Harmonic Motion

Simple harmonic motion in a single dimension, x, is described by the equation $x = A\cos(\omega t + \varphi)$, where A is the amplitude of oscillation, ω is the angular frequency of oscillation, and φ is the phase. The particular trigonometric operator used in the equation is not of great importance as sine may be substituted for cosine given a proper modification of the phase. Graphically, the motion of a harmonic oscillator starting from rest at maximum displacement is shown by the graph below. This graph assumes no energy lost to friction or drag.

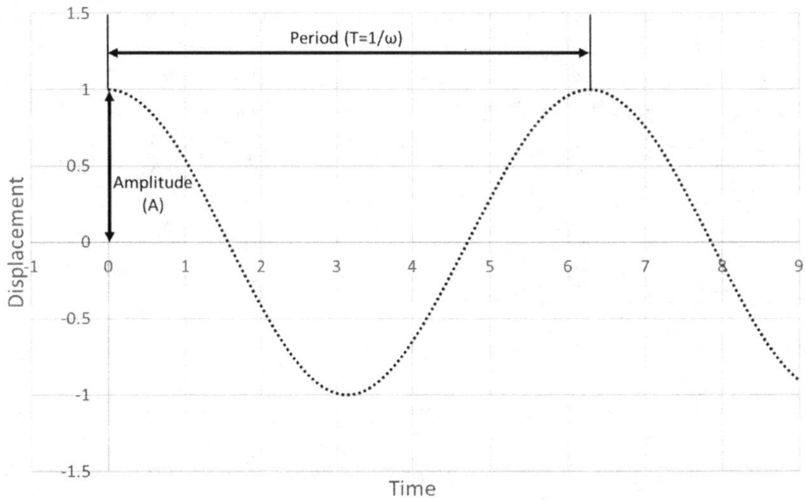

Hooke's Law

The work performed by a spring is one of the classic examples of **work performed by variable force**. When a spring is neither compressed nor extended, we may say that it is in a relaxed state. Any time the spring is taken out of this state, whether by being stretched or compressed, it will exert what is called a restoring force, as it attempts to return to its relaxed state. In most cases, we can say that the force, $\boldsymbol{F}$, exerted by the spring is proportional to the displacement of the free end from its position during the relaxed state. This is known as Hooke's law, and is expressed $\boldsymbol{F} = -k\boldsymbol{x}$, where k is the spring constant or stiffness. The x-coordinate in this equation corresponds to an axis where $\boldsymbol{x} = 0$ is the coordinate of the relaxed position. The negative sign in this equation indicates that the force is always opposite to the displacement.

Simple Pendulum

A **pendulum** is a **harmonic oscillator** that depends on the force of gravity for its motion. If we consider a simple pendulum composed of a mass hanging from an inelastic, massless string, then we may describe its restoring force as $\boldsymbol{F} = -m\boldsymbol{g} \sin\theta$, in which θ is the angle by which the mass is removed from its resting position. If the angle is very small, less than 15° or $\frac{\pi}{12}$, then $\theta \approx \sin\theta$, and the motion of the pendulum is like that of a simple harmonic oscillator. If this is the case, then the period of our simple pendulum can be found as $T = 2\pi\sqrt{\left(\frac{L}{g}\right)}$, where L is the length of the string. Again, this only holds if the angular amplitude θ_{max} is very small.

Like springs, pendulums operate by **converting energy** between kinetic and potential. Unlike springs, the potential energy stored in pendulums is gravitational potential energy. As the mass is displaced from its resting state, its height above ground increases. The potential energy stored in a simple pendulum can be calculated as $PE = mgL(1 - \cos\theta)$.

Linear Momentum and Impulse

In physics, **linear momentum** can be found by **multiplying the mass and velocity** of a particle ($\boldsymbol{p} = m\boldsymbol{v}$). Momentum is measured in kg·m/s. Like velocity, momentum is a vector quantity and will always have the same direction as the velocity. Newton's second law describes **momentum**, stating that the rate of change of momentum is proportional to the force exerted and is in the direction of the force. Impulse is the application of force over a period of time, Δt. If a constant net force of 10 N is exerted on an object for 5 seconds, it gives the object an impulse of 50 N-s. An impulse of 50 N-s corresponds to a change in momentum of 50 kg·m/s in the direction of the force. In equation form, $\boldsymbol{F}\Delta t = m\Delta \boldsymbol{v}$, where $\boldsymbol{F}$ is a constant net force. If the force is varying, it will be necessary to integrate the force over time.

For example, suppose a 2-kg block is initially at rest on a frictionless surface and a constant net force of 8 N is exerted on the block for 5 seconds. In order to determine how fast the block is moving, we need to calculate the impulse that was given to it ($\boldsymbol{F}\Delta t = 40$ N-s). This means that the change in momentum of the block was 40 kg·m/s. Since the block has a mass of 2 kg, this translates to an increase in velocity of 20 m/s. Thus, the block will be traveling at 20 m/s after 5 seconds.

Linear Momentum and Collisions

In a closed and isolated system (i.e., one in which no particles leave or enter and on which the sum of external forces is zero), we can assume that the momentum of the system will neither increase nor decrease. If we write the equation for the linear momentum of the system such that the net external force is equal to zero, we will find that linear momentum, $\boldsymbol{p}$, is a constant. The equation for linear momentum is a vector equation, and, as such, it can be divided into component equations for each dimension.

Some of the most popular examples used to demonstrate conservation of linear momentum involve two objects colliding on a frictionless surface. These collisions are generally categorized as either elastic or inelastic. In a perfectly **elastic** collision, both total momentum and total kinetic energy of the system are conserved. In a perfectly **inelastic** collision, only the total momentum of the system is conserved, as the two bodies combine to form a single body; however, in reality, most actual collisions fall somewhere between these two extremes. Unless a collision is specified as being perfectly elastic, it should be assumed that only momentum is conserved.

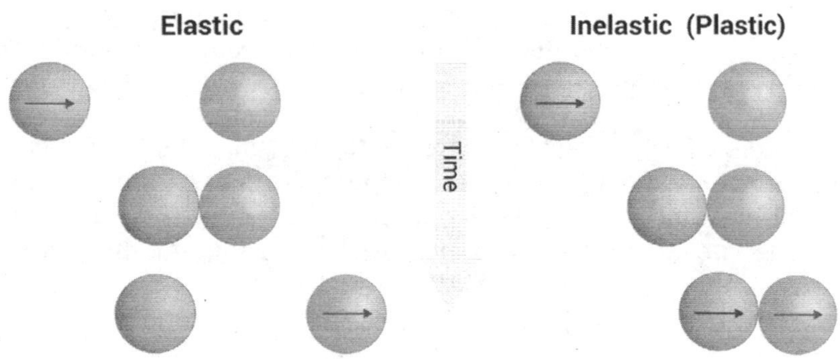

Examples of One-Dimensional Collisions

All examples assume a frictionless surface.

A 0.01-kg bullet traveling at 400 m/s strikes a stationary block of wood that weighs 10 kg and buries itself in the wood. What is the final velocity of the block and the bullet?

The bullet initially has 4 kg·m/s of momentum. The block of wood, beginning at rest, has no momentum. Thus, the final momentum is 4 kg·m/s. Given the new combined mass of 10.01 kg, the final velocity is approximately 0.4 m/s.

Two blocks, with masses of 10 kg and 40 kg, are traveling toward one another at -20 m/s and 10 m/s, respectively. Assuming the collision was perfectly elastic, find the final velocities of each body. Assuming it was perfectly inelastic, find the final velocity of the resulting single body.

For elastic collisions, two conditions hold: $KE_i = KE_f$ and $\boldsymbol{p}_i = \boldsymbol{p}_f$. Calculating initial conditions yields $KE_i = 4{,}000$ J and $\boldsymbol{p}_i = 200 \text{ kg} \cdot \text{m/s}$ for both blocks. Equating these to the final values of each yields $5\boldsymbol{v}_{1f}{}^2 + 20\boldsymbol{v}_{2f}{}^2 = 4{,}000$ and $10\boldsymbol{v}_{1f} + 40\boldsymbol{v}_{2f} = 200$. Solving both equations simultaneously gives $\boldsymbol{v}_{1f} = 28$ m/s and $\boldsymbol{v}_{2f} = -2$ m/s.

The inelastic case is much simpler. Since the two blocks merge to form one, the final momentum, 200 kg · m/s, is divided by the combined mass to give the final velocity of 4 m/s.

Conservation of Energy and Momentum

Applying Conservation of Rotational Energy and Angular Momentum

A metal hoop of mass m and radius r is released from rest at the top of a hill of height h. Assuming that it rolls without sliding and does not lose energy to friction or drag, what will be the hoop's angular and linear velocities upon reaching the bottom of the hill?

The hoop's initial energy is all potential energy, $PE = mgh$. As the hoop rolls down, all of its energy is converted to **translational** and **rotational kinetic energy**. Thus, $mgh = \frac{1}{2}m\boldsymbol{v}^2 + \frac{1}{2}I\boldsymbol{\omega}^2$. Since the moment for a hoop is $I = mr^2$, and $\boldsymbol{\omega} = \frac{v}{r}$, the equation becomes $mgh = \frac{1}{2}m\boldsymbol{v}^2 + \frac{1}{2}mr^2\left(\frac{v^2}{r^2}\right)$, which further simplifies to $gh = \boldsymbol{v}^2$. Thus, the resulting velocity of the hoop is $\boldsymbol{v}_f = \sqrt{gh}$, with an angular velocity of $\boldsymbol{\omega}_f = \frac{v_f}{r}$. Note that if you were to forget about the energy converted to rotational motion, you would calculate a final velocity of $\boldsymbol{v}_f = \sqrt{2gh}$, which is the **impact velocity** of an object dropped from height h.

Angular momentum, $\boldsymbol{L}$, of an object is defined as its moment of inertia multiplied by its angular velocity, or $\boldsymbol{L} = I\boldsymbol{\omega}$. Consider a planet orbiting the sun with an elliptical orbit where the small radius is r_S and large radius is r_L. Find the angular velocity of the planet when it is at distance r_S from the sun if its velocity at r_L is $\boldsymbol{\omega}_L$.

Since the size of a planet is almost insignificant compared to the interplanetary distances, the planet may be treated as a single particle of mass m, giving it a moment about the sun of $I = mr^2$. Since the gravitational force is incapable of exerting a net torque on an object, we can assume that the planet's angular momentum about the sun is a constant, $\boldsymbol{L}_L = \boldsymbol{L}_S$. Thus, $mr_L{}^2\boldsymbol{\omega}_L = mr_S{}^2\boldsymbol{\omega}_S$. Solving this equation for $\boldsymbol{\omega}_S$ yields $\boldsymbol{\omega}_S = \boldsymbol{\omega}_L\left(\frac{r_L}{r_S}\right)^2$.

Mass-Energy Relationship

Because mass consists of atoms, which are themselves formed of subatomic particles, there is an energy inherent in the composition of all mass. In other words, it would require a significant input of energy to form all the atoms in a given mass from their most basic particles. This rest energy is the energy that Einstein refers to in his famous mass-energy relation $E = mc^2$, where c is the speed of light in a vacuum. In theory, if all the particles in a given mass were converted directly to energy (e.g., by matter-antimatter annihilation), it would give off energy $E = mc^2$. For example, if this were to happen to a single gram of mass, the resulting outburst of energy would be $E = 9 \times 10^{13}$ J, enough energy to provide power for over 2,000 average households for a whole year.

In some nuclear reactions, small amounts of mass are converted to energy. The amount of energy released can be calculated through the same relation, $E = mc^2$. Most such reactions involve mass losses on the order of 10^{-30} kg.

Fluid Mechanics

Basics of Fluids

While it may sound obvious, fluids can best be defined as **substances that flow**. A fluid will conform, slowly or quickly, to any container in which it is placed. This is because a fluid is unable to maintain a force tangential to its surface. In other words, **fluids cannot withstand shearing stress**. They can, on the other hand, exert a force perpendicular to their surface. Both liquids and gases are considered to be fluids. Fluids, essentially, are those substances in which the atoms are not arranged in any permanent, rigid way. In ice, for instance, molecules are all lined up in a crystalline lattice, while in water and steam, the only intermolecular arrangements are haphazard connections between neighboring molecules.

Fluid Density and Pressure

The **density of a fluid** is generally expressed with the symbol ρ. The density may be found with the simple equation $\rho = \frac{m}{V}$, mass per unit volume. Density is a scalar property, meaning that it has no direction component. It is typically measured in SI units of kilograms per cubic meter. While the density of a gas will tend to fluctuate considerably depending on the level of pressure, the density of a liquid is comparatively stable. The density of water is most often taken to be 1,000 kg/m^3.

The **pressure of a fluid** is calculated as $P = \frac{F}{A}$, force per unit area. To find the pressure at a given depth in a fluid, or the hydrostatic pressure, the pressure can be calculated as $P = \rho g h$, where h is the fluid depth. For instance, the pressure of water is greater the deeper you are below the surface.

Pressure, like fluid density, is a scalar, and does not have a direction. The equation for pressure is concerned only with the magnitude of the force, not with the direction in which it is pointing. The SI unit of pressure is the Newton per square meter, or pascal.

Archimedes' Principle

If an object is submerged in water, it will have a **buoyant force** exerted on it in the upward direction. This force is caused by the water pressure acting on the bottom surface of the object. The deeper the object is submerged, the greater the pressure at the bottom surface. Often, of course, this buoyant force is much too small to keep an object from sinking to the bottom. This idea of buoyancy is summarized in **Archimedes'**

principle: a body wholly or partially submerged in a fluid will be buoyed up by a force equal to the weight of the fluid displaced by the body.

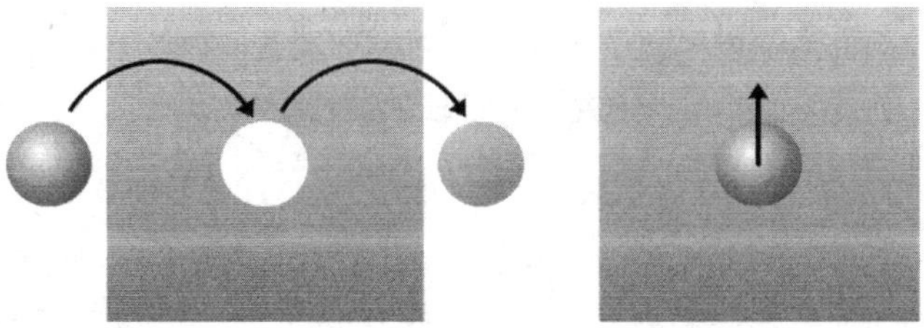

Thus, an object's ability to remain afloat in a fluid depends on its density relative to that of the fluid. If the fluid has a higher density than the object then the object will float. Otherwise, the object will sink. This principle can also be used to find the weight of a floating object by calculating the volume of fluid that it has displaced. For instance if a cube with a volume of 1 m^3 is floating in water to a depth of 0.25 m, the cube is displacing 0.25 m^3 of water. This is the equivalent of 250 kg of water, creating a buoyancy force of 2,450 N. Thus, the block weighs 2,450 N, has a mass of 250 kg, and has a density of 250 kg/m^3.

Pascal's Principle

Pascal's principle states that a change in the pressure applied to an enclosed fluid is **transmitted** undiminished to **every portion** of the fluid, as well as to the walls of the containing vessel. Imagine, for instance, a container filled with liquid, on top of which rests a piston loaded down with a lead weight. The atmosphere, lead weight, and piston will combine to exert pressure P_{ext} on the liquid, so the total pressure will be $P = P_{ext} + \rho g h$, for every point at height h within the fluid. Imagine again, an enclosed fluid in a container with two pistons on top, one with area $A_1 = 2 \text{ m}^2$ and the other with area $A_2 = 4 \text{ m}^2$. Since the pressure will be the same at both pistons, the upward force on the larger piston will be twice that of the smaller, since it has a larger area and the force is equal to the pressure times the area over which it is applied.

Drag Force

Friction can also be generated when an object is moving through air or liquid. A drag force occurs when a body moves through some fluid (either liquid or gas) and experiences a force that opposes the motion of the body. The drag force is greater if the air or fluid is thicker or is moving in the direction opposite to the object. Obviously, the higher the drag force, the greater amount of positive force required to keep the object moving forward. This is one reason ideal fluid questions assume that the fluids are non-viscous.

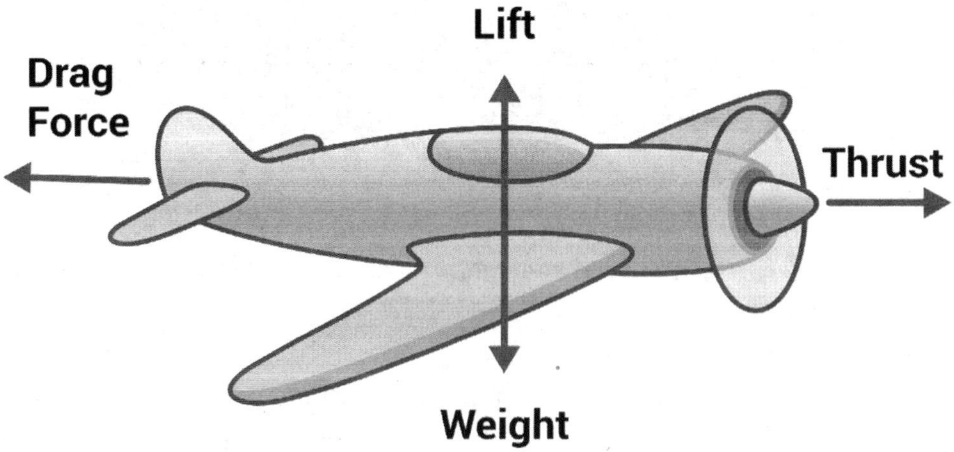

Ideal Fluids in Motion

Since the motion of actual fluids is extremely complex, physicists usually refer to **ideal fluids** when they make their calculations. Using ideal fluids in equations is a bit like discounting friction in other calculations; it tends to make the process more mathematically manageable. So, when we deal with ideal fluids, we are making four assumptions. First, we are assuming that the **flow is steady**; in other words, the velocity of every part of the fluid is the same. Second, we assume that fluids are **incompressible**, and therefore have a consistent density. Third, we assume that fluids are **non-viscous**, meaning that they flow easily and without resistance. Finally, we assume that the flow of ideal fluids is **irrotational**: that is, particles in the fluid will not rotate around a center of mass.

Flow Rates

When liquids flow in and out of containers at certain rates, the change in volume is the volumetric flow in minus the volumetric flow out. Volumetric flow is essentially the amount of volume moved past some point divided by the time it took for the volume to pass.

$$\textbf{Volumetric flow rate} = \frac{\textbf{volume moved}}{\textbf{time for the movement}}$$

If the flow into a container is greater than the flow out, the container will fill with the fluid. However, if the flow out of a container is greater than the flow into a container, the container will drain of the fluid.

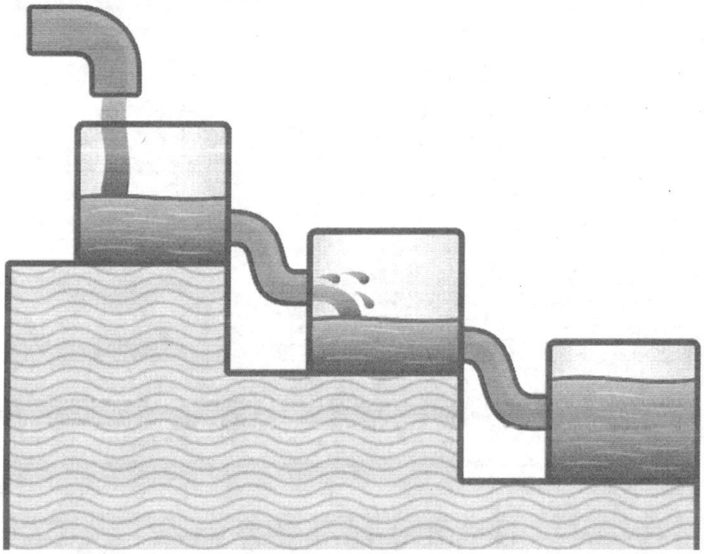

Streamlines, Tube of Flow, Volume Flow Rate, and the Equation of Continuity

A **streamline** is the path traced out by a very small unit of fluid, which we will refer to as a particle. Although the velocity of a particle may change in both magnitude and direction, streamlines will never cross one another. In many instances of flow, several streamlines will group together to form what is called a tube of flow. If we were to make two cross-sections of a tube of flow, with areas A_1 and A_2, we would find that since fluid is incompressible, the same amount of fluid passes through the two cross-sections over the same interval of time. This is expressed by the equation $Q = Av$, in which Q is known as the volumetric flow rate and is constant for a given tube of flow. This equation is known as the **equation of continuity**; it suggests that flow will be faster in areas of the tube that are narrower. One very important equation derived from this principle is $A_1v_1 = A_2v_2$. Given that a pipe narrows its cross-section from A_1 to A_2, and the fluid velocity in A_1 is v_1, the velocity in A_2 must be $v_2 = \frac{A_1v_1}{A_2}$. Also important to note is that the mass flow rate is directly related to the volumetric flow rate by the equation $m_{flow} = \rho vA = \rho Q$.

Bernoulli's Equation

Let us imagine an ideal fluid in a tube of flow. By applying the **law of conservation of energy** with ideal fluid assumptions, we can arrive at **Bernoulli's equation**: $P + \rho gh + \frac{\rho v^2}{2} = C$, where C is a constant for a given tube of flow. Basically, this equation states that in the absence of an external input of energy or a significant elevation change, any increase in velocity will require a decrease in fluid pressure. And under similar circumstances, an increase in pressure will necessarily cause a decrease in velocity. It is essentially just a reformulation of the law of conservation of mechanical energy for fluid mechanics. Bernoulli's principle is used to explain a number of physical phenomena, including the lift force on the wings of an aircraft.

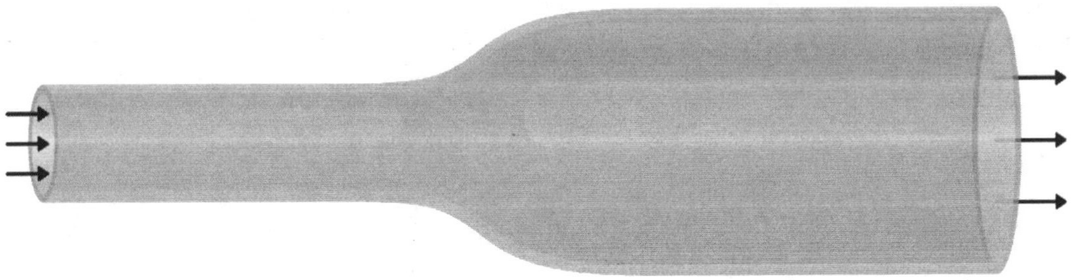

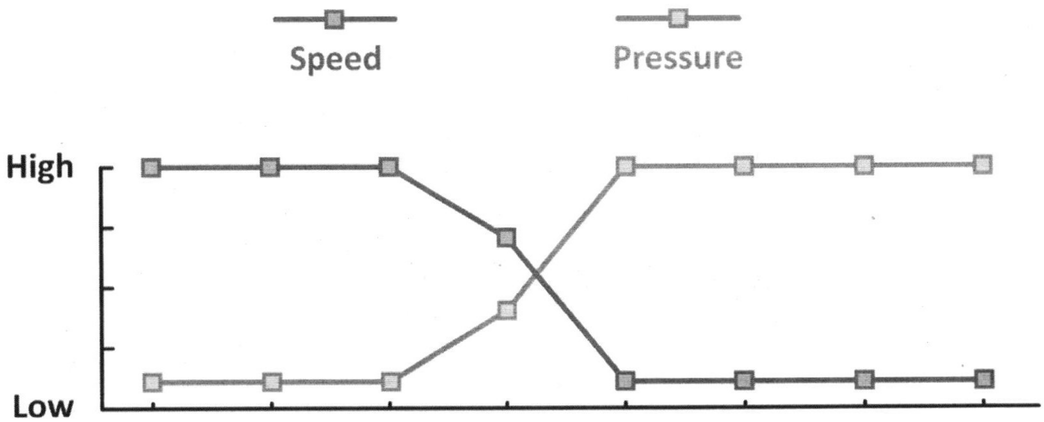

Rotational Motion

Angular Motion and the Axis of Rotation

When a body is moving in a straight line, it is said to be moving in **translation**. When, on the other hand, it is moving around some fixed axis, it is said to be in **rotation**. For a rotating object, the fixed axis is called the axis of rotation. Every point on the body will move in a circle that has this axis as its center, and every point will move through the same angle over the same interval of time. Angles may be measured in one of three units: degrees, radians, or revolutions. A full rotation is equal to 360 degrees, 2π radians, or 1 revolution. On a circle, one radian is the angle that measures an arc length equal to the radius of the circle. Since a circle's circumference is 2π times the radius, one full rotation is equal to 2π radians.

Angular motion has many correlations to linear motion. For an angle of rotation, θ, the linear distance traveled is $\boldsymbol{x} = r\theta$. For angular velocity, $\boldsymbol{\omega}$, the linear velocity is $\boldsymbol{v} = r\boldsymbol{\omega}$. For angular acceleration, $\boldsymbol{\alpha}$, the linear acceleration is $\boldsymbol{a} = r\boldsymbol{\alpha}$. When discussing angular motion in this way, the angular unit is always radians.

Rotational Kinematics

Concept: Increasing the radius increases the linear speed

Calculation: Linear speed = radius × rotational speed

In practice, simple rotation is when an object rotates around a point at a constant speed. Most questions covering rotational kinematics will provide the distance from a rotating object to the center of rotation (radius) and ask about the linear speed of the object. A point will have a greater linear speed when it is farther from the center of rotation.

If a potter is spinning his wheel at a constant speed of one revolution per second, the clay six inches away from the center will be going faster than the clay three inches from the center. The clay directly in the center of the wheel will not have any linear velocity.

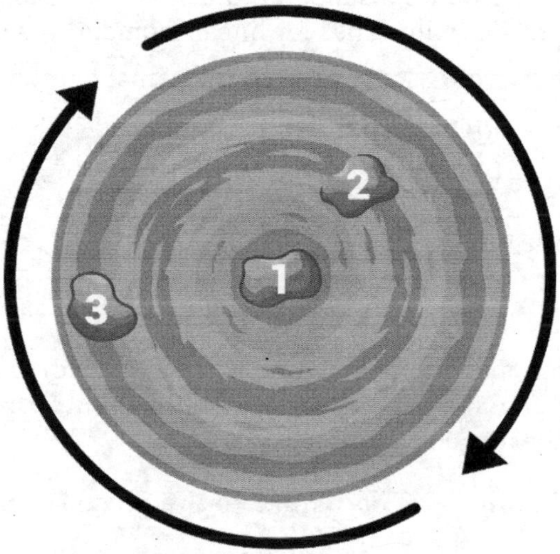

To find the linear speed of rotating objects using radians, we use the equation:

$$\textbf{linear speed} = (\textbf{rotational speed [in radians]}) \times (\textbf{radius})$$

Using degrees, the equation is:

$$\textbf{linear speed} = (\textbf{rotational speed [in degrees]}) \times \frac{\boldsymbol{\pi}\ \textbf{radians}}{\textbf{180 degrees}} \times (\textbf{radius})$$

To find the speed of the pieces of clay, we use the known values (rotational speed of 1 revolution per second, radii of 0 inches, 3 inches, and 6 inches) and the knowledge that one revolution = 2π.

$$\text{clay \#1 speed} = \left(2\pi\frac{\text{rad}}{\text{s}}\right) \times (0 \text{ inches}) = 0\frac{\text{inches}}{\text{second}}$$

$$\text{clay \#2 speed} = \left(2\pi\frac{\text{rad}}{\text{s}}\right) \times (3 \text{ inches}) = 18.8\frac{\text{inches}}{\text{second}}$$

$$\text{clay \#3 speed} = \left(2\pi\frac{\text{rad}}{\text{s}}\right) \times (6 \text{ inches}) = 37.7\frac{\text{inches}}{\text{second}}$$

Review Video: Linear Speed
Visit mometrix.com/academy and enter code: 327101

ROTATIONAL MOTION

Newton's second law, commonly stated as $\boldsymbol{F} = m\boldsymbol{a}$, is applied to rotational motion by the equation $\boldsymbol{\tau} = I\boldsymbol{\alpha}$. That is, the torque is equal to the moment of inertia times the angular acceleration. **Torque** is calculated as the magnitude of an applied force times its perpendicular distance from the body's center of mass. A body's moment of inertia depends on both its mass and its configuration. Each particle in a body contributes a moment of $I = mr^2$, where m is the particle's mass and r is its distance from the center of mass. Thus, for a thin ring or a thin, hollow sphere, the moment for the body is $I = mr^2$. Some other commonly encountered shapes are spheres $\left(I = \left(\frac{2}{5}\right) mr^2\right)$ and disks $\left(I = \left(\frac{1}{2}\right) mr^2\right)$. A closely related property of these shapes is the radius of gyration, k. This quantity is the average distance of mass from the center. It can be found by the equation $k = \sqrt{\left(\frac{I}{M}\right)}$. Similarly, the moment of inertia may be found as $I = mk^2$.

Another important corollary with linear motion is momentum. An object's angular momentum may be calculated as $\boldsymbol{L} = I\boldsymbol{\omega}$. All the same conservation rules for linear momentum apply to angular momentum as well. Additionally, there is a kinetic energy associated with rotational motion. It is calculated as $KE_r = \frac{I\omega^2}{2}$. When calculating kinetic energy for an object that is in both linear and angular motion, the total kinetic energy is the sum of the translational and rotational kinetic energy, $KE = \frac{mv^2}{2} + \frac{I\omega^2}{2}$.

Concept: Torque is a twisting force on an object

Calculation: Torque = radius × force

Torque, like force, is a vector and has magnitude and direction. As with force, the sum of torques on an object will affect the angular acceleration of that object. The key to solving problems with torque is understanding the lever arm. A better description of the torque equation is:

Torque = force × the distance perpedicular to the force from the center of rotation

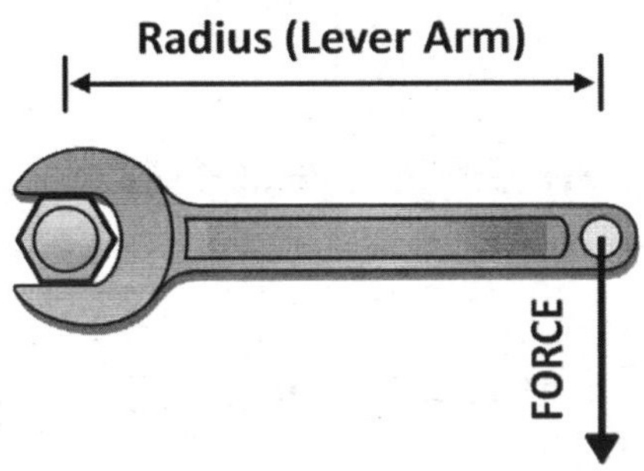

Because torque is directly proportional to the radius, or lever arm, a greater lever arm will result in a greater torque with the same amount of force. The wrench on the right has twice the radius and, as a result, twice the torque.

Alternatively, a greater force also increases torque. The wrench on the right has twice the force and twice the torque.

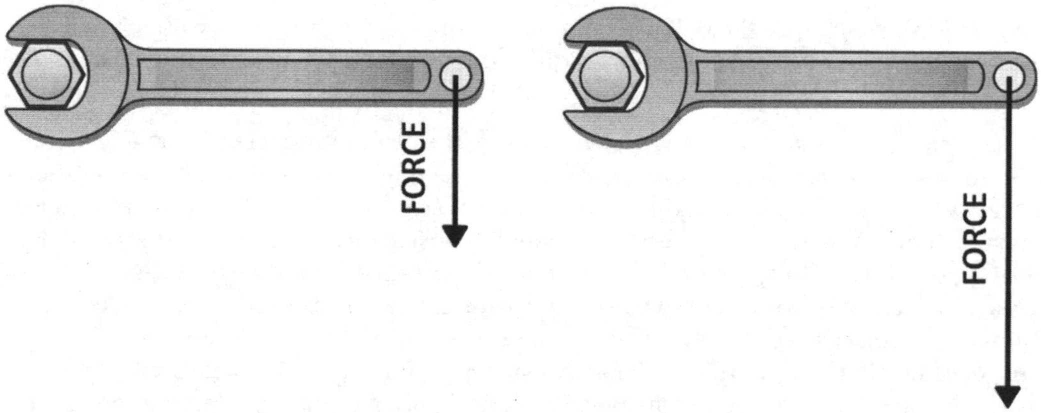

Two-Dimensional Collisions

All examples assume a frictionless surface.

Two blocks weighing 5 kg and 10 kg with velocities of $v_1 = 9\mathbf{i}$ m/s and $v_2 = 3\mathbf{j}$ m/s, respectively, are on a collision course. Assuming the collision is perfectly inelastic, find the velocity of the combined block after collision.

Since each block initially has velocity in only one dimension, it is a simple calculation to find the initial momentum values: $\boldsymbol{p}_x = 45\ \text{kg}\cdot\text{m/s}$ and $\boldsymbol{p}_y = 30\ \text{kg}\cdot\text{m/s}$. With the new combined mass of 15 kg, the final velocity vector will be $\boldsymbol{v}_f = 3\mathbf{i} + 2\mathbf{j}$ m/s.

Two hockey pucks both weighing 0.15 kg with velocity vectors $v_1 = 20\mathbf{i} + 30\mathbf{j}$ m/s and $v_2 = -50\mathbf{i} - 10\mathbf{j}$ m/s are headed toward a collision. Suppose that the final velocity of one puck is $v_{2f} = -10\mathbf{i} + 15\mathbf{j}$ m/s. Find the final velocity vector of the other puck.

We must ensure that momentum is conserved in both dimensions. The initial momentum in the x- and y-directions is calculated to be $\boldsymbol{p}_{xi} = -4.5\ \text{kg}\cdot\text{m/s}$ and $\boldsymbol{p}_{yi} = 3\ \text{kg}\cdot\text{m/s}$. Since we know the final velocity of one of the pucks, we can find the other's final velocity to be $\boldsymbol{v}_{1f} = -20\mathbf{i} + 5\mathbf{j}$ m/s.

Universal Gravitation and Orbital Motion

Newton's Law of Gravitation

One of Newton's major insights into the behavior of physical objects was that every object in the universe exerts an **attractive force on every other body**. In quantitative terms, we may say that the gravitational force with which particles attract one another is given by $\boldsymbol{F} = \frac{Gm_1m_2}{r^2}$, in which r is the distance between the particles, m_1 and m_2 are the masses of the particles, and G is the gravitational constant, $G = 6.674 \times 10^{-11}$ N-m^2/kg^2. Newton expressed this relation by saying that a uniform spherical shell of matter attracts a particle outside the shell as if all the shell's matter were concentrated at its center. In the case of gravitation on Earth, objects behave as if there was a single particle located at the center of the Earth with the mass of the entire Earth (M_E). Thus, regardless of an object's distance from the surface of the Earth, it can be approximated as a particle due to the effective distance from the Earth's center of mass. The difference in the gravitational pull on an object at sea level and at the highest point on the Earth's surface is about 0.25%. Thus, the gravitational acceleration anywhere on the Earth's surface is considered to be a constant 9.81 m/s^2. For an object orbiting the Earth, such as a satellite, its period of orbit can be found by equating the gravitational force to the centripetal force, giving the equation $\frac{GM_Em}{r^2} = mr\omega^2 = mr\left(\frac{2\pi}{T}\right)^2$. Solving for the period yields $T = \sqrt{\frac{4\pi^2r^3}{GM_E}}$.

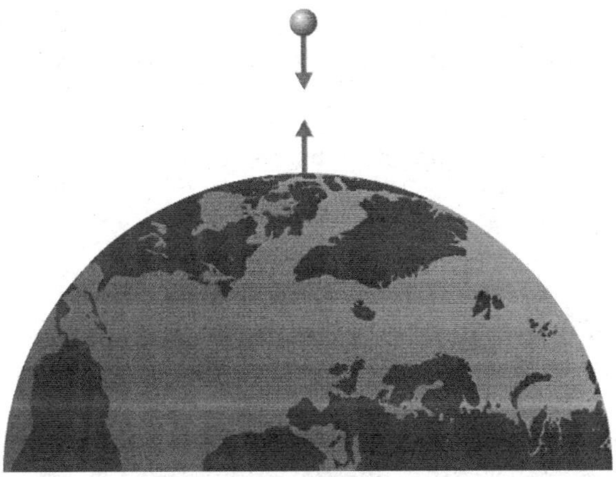

Review Video: Newton's Law of Gravitation
Visit mometrix.com/academy and enter code: 709086

Kepler's Laws

Kepler's First Law

Kepler's first law describing the movement of planets states that **all planets move in elliptical orbits**, with the sun at one focus. If we are to consider the motion of one planet around the sun, we will assume that its mass is much smaller than that of the sun, such that the center of mass of the system is almost in the middle of the sun. The orbit of the planet will then be defined by the semimajor axis, a (that is, half the length of the ellipse), the semiminor axis, b (half the width of the ellipse), and the eccentricity, e (the degree to which the orbit is not circular, $e = \sqrt{1 - \frac{b^2}{a^2}}$). The orbits of the planets are only slightly elliptical, though they are often exaggerated on diagrams. In a planetary orbit, the distance from the center of the ellipse to either focus is $d = ae$. The maximum and minimum distances of a planet from the sun are given by $r_{max} = \frac{b^2}{(a-d)}$ and $r_{min} = \frac{b^2}{(a+d)}$.

Kepler's Second Law

Kepler's second law for planets and satellites states that any line connecting a planet to the sun will sweep out **equal areas in equal times**, regardless of where the planet is in its orbit. In other words, the planet will move most slowly when it is far away from the sun, and fastest when it is closest. This law is directly connected to the law of conservation of angular momentum.

Kepler's Third Law

Kepler's third law for planets states that the square of the period of any planet is proportional to the cube of the semimajor axis of its orbit. This relation can be expressed $T^2 = \left(\frac{4\pi^2}{Gm}\right) r^3$. The quantity in parentheses in this equation is a constant, its only variable being the mass of the central body. This equation holds up for elliptical orbits as well.

Weight and Mass

Weight

Not to be confused with mass (quantity of matter), weight the term for the force due to the gravitational attraction between the masses of the two bodies. This force is described by the expression $\frac{Gm_1m_2}{r^2}$, where G is the gravitational constant, m_1 and m_2 are the masses of the two objects, and r is the distance between the centers of mass. Since the majority of humans are concerned with events close to the surface of the Earth, one of the masses (M_E) and the distance (R_E) are essentially constant and are combined into $\boldsymbol{g}$, which is the acceleration due to gravity near the surface of the Earth $\left(\boldsymbol{g} = \frac{GM_E}{(R_E)^2}\right)$. Thus, we can express weight as $\boldsymbol{W} = m\boldsymbol{g}$. Since it is a force, the SI unit for weight is the Newton. As a vector, $\boldsymbol{W}$ can be expressed as either $-mg\mathbf{j}$ or $-W\mathbf{j}$, in which $\mathbf{j}$ is the direction on the axis pointing away from the Earth.

Review Video: Mass, Weight, Volume, Density, and Specific Gravity
Visit mometrix.com/academy and enter code: 920570

Chapter Quiz

Ready to see how well you retained what you just read? Scan the QR code to go directly to the chapter quiz interface for this study guide. If you're using a computer, simply visit the online resources page at **mometrix.com/resources719/ftcephysics** and click the Chapter Quizzes link.

Waves and Optics

Types of Waves and their Characteristics

Transverse and Longitudinal Waves

Transverse waves have oscillations that are **perpendicular** to the direction of motion. A light wave is an example of a transverse wave. A group of light waves traveling in the same direction will be oscillating in several different planes. Light waves are said to be polarized when they are filtered such that only waves oscillating in a particular plane are allowed to pass, with the remainder being absorbed by the filter. If two such polarizing filters are employed successively and aligned to allow different planes of oscillation, they will block all light waves.

Longitudinal waves are waves that oscillate in the **same direction** as their primary motion. Their motion is restricted to a single axis, so they may not be polarized. A sound wave is an example of a longitudinal wave.

Velocity, Amplitude, Wavelength, and Frequency

- The **velocity of a wave**, v, is the rate at which it travels in a given medium. It is defined in the same way that velocity of physical objects is defined, a change in position divided by a change in time. A single wave may have a different velocity for every medium in which it travels. Some types of waves, such as light waves, do not require a medium.
- **Amplitude**, A, is one measure of a wave's strength. It is half the verticle distance between the highest and lowest points on the wave, the crest and trough, respectively. The vertical midpoint, halfway between the crest and trough, is sometimes called an equilibrium point, or a node.
- The **wavelength**, λ, is the horizontal distance between successive crests or troughs, or the distance between the first and third of three successive nodes.
- **Frequency**, f, is the number of crests or troughs that pass a particular point in a given period of time. It is the inverse of the period, the time required for the wave to cycle from one crest or trough to the next. Frequency is generally measured in hertz, or cycles per second.

Velocity, wavelength, and frequency are not independent quantities. They are related by the expression $v = \lambda f$. Note that amplitude, however, is independent from these quantities.

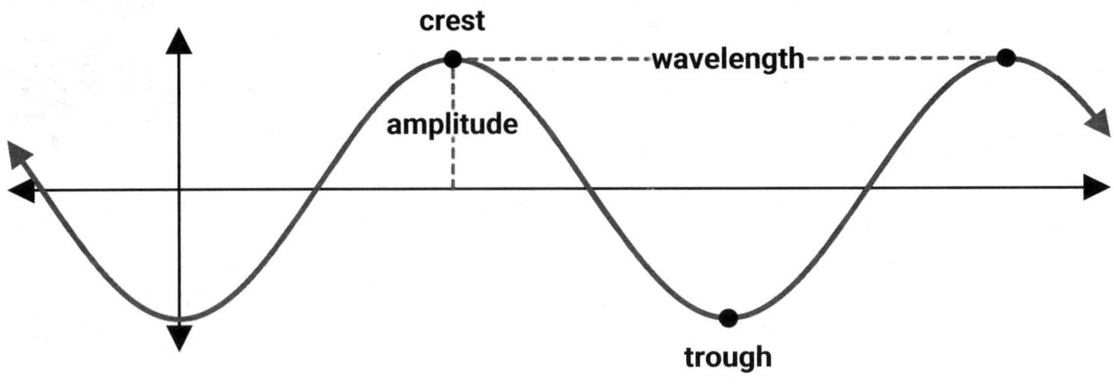

Intensity

The **intensity** I of a wave is equivalent to the flux through a given area over a period of time. It may also be defined as the energy density of a wave times its velocity. Intensity has units of watts per square meter. This can be seen in light waves as well. The intensity of light decreases as the distance from the light source increases. The inverse square law states that the intensity is inversely proportional to the square of the distance from the source. It is also directly proportional to the power P of the light source. This is shown mathematically by the expression $I = \frac{CP}{r^2}$, where C is the proportionality constant. This may be better understood by imagining the light waves emanating from a source as an expanding sphere. As their distance r from the source increases, the area over which they must divide themselves increases at a rate of $4\pi r^2$.

Standing Waves

A **standing wave** is the result of **interference** between two waves of the same frequency moving in opposite directions. These waves, although in constant motion, have certain points on the path where the amplitude is zero referred to as **nodes**. One example of a standing wave is a plucked guitar string. Since the string is attached at both ends, the fixed ends will be nodes. The primary tone will be that of the fundamental, or first harmonic, shown in the first figure below. It has a wavelength of twice the length of the string, L. The other three pictures below are those of the second through fourth harmonics. The nth harmonic has wavelength and frequency of $\lambda_n = \frac{2L}{n}$ and $f_n = \frac{nv}{2L}$, where v is wave velocity.

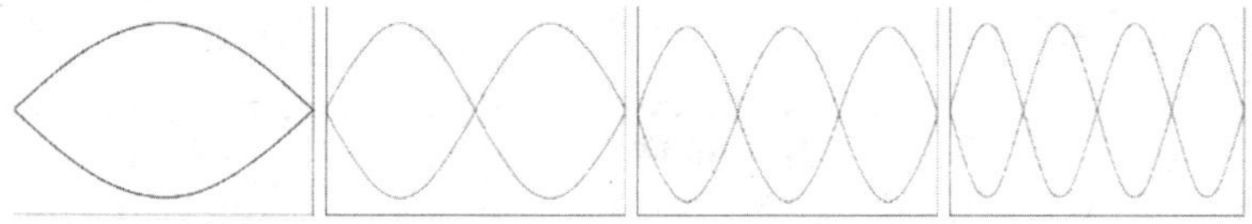

This same phenomenon occurs inside the tubes of wind instruments, though it is much more difficult to visualize. With a tube, however, there will be one or two open ends. Rather than a node, each open end will coincide with an **antinode**: that is, a crest or trough. For waves in a tube with two open ends, the wavelength and frequency calculations are the same as those for the plucked string. For the case with one open end, only the odd harmonics will be seen. The frequency of the nth harmonic becomes $f_n = \frac{nv}{4L}$, where n is odd.

Reflection, Refraction, Interference, and Diffraction of Waves

Reflection, Transmission, and Absorption

When light waves make contact with matter, they are either reflected, transmitted, or absorbed. If the light is **reflected** from the surface of the matter, the **angle** at which it hits the surface will be the same as the angle at which it leaves. If the ray of light is perpendicular to the surface, it will be reflected back in the direction from which it came.

When light is **transmitted** from one medium to another, its direction may be **altered** upon entering the new medium. This is known as **refraction**. The degree to which the light is refracted depends on the index of refraction, n, for each medium.

Light that is neither reflected nor transmitted will be **absorbed** by the surface and **stored as heat** energy. Because there are no ideal surfaces, most light and matter interaction will be a combination of two or even all three of these. Another result of imperfect surfaces is **scattering**, which occurs when waves are reflected in multiple directions. Rayleigh scattering is the specific case of a light wave being scattered by tiny particles that single out particular wavelengths. Dust particles in the atmosphere scatter primarily the blue wavelength of sunlight to give our sky a predominantly blue hue.

Review Video: Reflection, Transmission, and Absorption of Light
Visit mometrix.com/academy and enter code: 109410

Snell's Law

When light is transmitted from one medium to another, its direction may be altered upon entering the new medium. This is known as **refraction**. The degree to which the light is refracted depends on the index of refraction, n, for each medium. The **index of refraction** is a ratio of the speed of light in a vacuum to the speed of light in the medium in question, $n = \frac{c}{v_m}$. Since light can never travel faster than it does in a vacuum, the index of refraction is always greater than one. Snell's law gives the equation for determining the angle of refraction: $n_1 \sin(\theta_1) = n_2 \sin(\theta_2)$, where n is the index of refraction for each medium, and θ is the angle the light makes with the normal vector on each side of the interface between the two media.

We will examine a special case by trying to determine the angle of refraction for light traveling from a medium with $n_1 = 3$ to another medium with $n_2 = 1.5$. The light makes an angle $\theta_1 = 35°$ with the normal. Using Snell's law, we find that $\sin(\theta_2) = 1.15$. Since this is not mathematically possible, we conclude that the light cannot be refracted. This case is known as total internal reflection. When light travels from a more dense medium to a less dense medium, there is a minimum angle of incidence, beyond which all light will be reflected. This critical angle is $\theta_1 = \sin^{-1}\left(\frac{n_2}{n_1}\right)$. Fiber-optic cables make use of this phenomenon to ensure that the signal is fully reflected internally when it veers into the outer walls of the fiber.

Resonance and Natural Frequency

Every physical object has one or more **natural frequencies**, or frequencies at which it will naturally vibrate. The natural frequency is based on the object's dimensions, density, orientation, and other factors. If the object is acted on by a periodic force, it will vibrate at its natural frequency, regardless of the forcing frequency. If the excitation force is operating at the object's natural frequency, the object will experience **resonance**, in which the object receives all of the energy exerted by the excitation force. The amplitude of the vibration will increase rapidly and without bound until either the excitation force changes frequency or the natural frequency of the object is altered.

Diffraction and Dispersion

Diffraction occurs when a wave encounters a physical object. It includes phenomena such as bending, diverging, and other aperture effects. When light emerges from a single small slit, a rippling effect may be observed. The results of Young's double-slit experiment are due to diffraction as the light waves from these slits diverge. Similarly, light emerging from a circular aperture will project concentric light and dark rings due to diffraction. Diffraction grating is an arrangement of material whose reflective properties are intentionally varied at equally spaced intervals. Due to the arrangement, incident light is reflected in specific directions, known as diffraction orders, based on its wavelength.

Dispersion occurs when light consisting of multiple wavelengths enters a medium whose propagation behavior depends on the wavelength of transmitted light. This is what is observed when light passes through a prism, splitting it into its component colors.

Review Video: Diffraction of Light Waves
Visit mometrix.com/academy and enter code: 785494

Young's Double-Slit Experiment

Thomas Young's **double-slit experiment** visually demonstrated the interference between two sets of light waves. It consisted of shining light through two thin, closely spaced parallel slits and onto a screen. The interference between light waves from the two slits caused a pattern of alternately light and dark bands to appear on the screen, due to constructive and destructive interference, respectively. The dimensions of the experimental setup can be used to determine the wavelength of the light being projected onto the screen. This is given by the equation $\lambda = y\frac{d}{x}$, where y is the distance between the centers of two light bands, d is the distance between the slits, and x is the distance from the slits to the screen. Thin-film interference is caused when incident light is reflected both by a partially reflective thin layer on a surface and by the surface itself. This interference may be constructive or destructive.

WAVE SUPERPOSITION AND INTERFERENCE

The principle of **linear superposition** states that two or more waves occupying the same space create an effect equal to the sum of their individual amplitudes at that location. This is known as interference. If the resultant amplitude is larger than either individual amplitude, it is constructive interference. Similarly, if the interference reduces the effect, it is considered destructive.

Some special cases of interference are standing waves and beats, in which two waves having the same and nearly the same frequency, respectively, interfere with one another. Another concept related to interference is phase. If two waves with the same frequency are in phase, then they have perfectly constructive interference. The nodes in each wave will line up, as will the respective crests and troughs. If those same two waves are 180 degrees out of phase, they will experience perfectly destructive interference. The nodes will still line up, but each crest will be aligned with a trough, and vice versa. From this it can be seen that constructive interference results in a larger wave amplitude than destructive interference. If two identical waves are 180 degrees out of phase, the resultant wave will have zero amplitude. This effect is the design impetus for some noise-cancellation technology.

Doppler Effect

One common phenomenon of wave motion is the **Doppler effect**. It occurs when there is a **disparity** between the emitted frequency and the observed frequency of a wave. It is the caused by **relative motion** between the **wave source** and the **observer**. If the source and observer are both moving toward one another, the observed frequency is determined by the following equation: $f_o = f_e \frac{(v_w + v_o)}{(v_w - v_s)}$, where v_w is the speed of the wave. If the source or the observer is moving in the opposite direction, its sign must be reversed. The Doppler effect can occur with any wave (light, water, pressure, etc.), but it is most commonly observed when sound waves change pitch due to an observer's change in position relative to a loud train horn or emergency vehicle siren. The effect is also employed in the operation of speed-detecting radar guns. Microwaves are emitted at a known frequency and, after being reflected by the target, return at a different frequency, giving the object's speed.

Sound Waves

The **pitch of a sound** as it reaches one's ear is based on the frequency of the sound waves. A high-pitched sound has a higher frequency than a low-pitched sound. Like all waves, sound waves transmit energy. The rate at which this energy is transmitted is the sonic power. Loudness, or intensity of sound, is the sonic power received per unit area.

When a pair of sound waves with slightly different frequencies interfere with one another causing a periodic variation in sound intensity or a **beat**. The frequency of the variation, called the **beat frequency**, is equal to the difference between frequencies of the two sound waves. The phenomenon is used when tuning two instruments to one another. As the two pitches get closer, the beat frequency will become smaller and smaller until it disappears entirely, indicating that the instruments are in tune.

Review Video: Sound
Visit mometrix.com/academy and enter code: 562378

Electromagnetic Waves and Electromagnetic Spectrum

Electromagnetic Spectrum

The **electromagnetic spectrum** is the range of all wavelengths and frequencies of known electromagnetic waves. Visible light occupies only a small portion of the electromagnetic spectrum. Some of the common classifications of electromagnetic waves are listed in the table below with their approximate frequency ranges.

Classification	Freq. (Hz)
Gamma Rays	$\sim 10^{19}$
X-Rays	$\sim 10^{17} - 10^{18}$
Ultraviolet	$\sim 10^{15} - 10^{16}$
Visible Light	$\sim 10^{14}$
Infra-red	$\sim 10^{11} - 10^{14}$
Microwaves	$\sim 10^{10} - 10^{11}$
Radio/TV	$\sim 10^{6} - 10^{9}$

Electromagnetic waves travel at the speed of light, $c = 3 \times 10^8$ m/s. To find the wavelength of any electromagnetic wave, simply divide c by the frequency. Visible light occupies a range of wavelengths from approximately 380 nm (violet) to 740 nm (red). The full spectrum of color can be found between these two wavelengths.

Review Video: Electromagnetic Spectrum
Visit mometrix.com/academy and enter code: 771761

Review Video: Light
Visit mometrix.com/academy and enter code: 900556

Geometric Optics

Thin Lenses

A **lens** is an optical device that **redirects light** to either converge or diverge in specific geometric patterns. Whether the lens converges or diverges is dependent on the lens being **convex** or **concave**, respectively. The particular angle of redirection is dictated by the lens's focal length. For a **converging lens**, this is the distance from the lens that parallel rays entering from the opposite side would intersect. For a **diverging lens**, it is the distance from the lens that parallel rays entering the lens would intersect if they were reverse extrapolated. However, the focal length of a diverging lens is always considered to be negative. A thin lens is a lens whose focal length is much greater than its thickness. By making this assumption, we can derive many helpful relations.

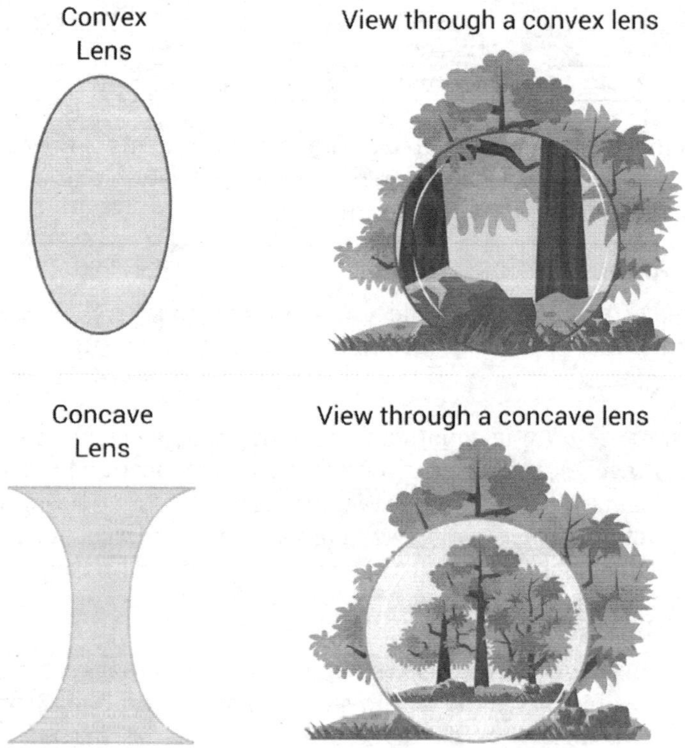

Real and Virtual Images

In optics, an **object's image** is what is seen when the object is viewed through a lens. The location of an object's image is related to the lens's **focal length** by the equation $\frac{1}{d_o} + \frac{1}{d_i} = \frac{1}{f}$, where f is the focal length, and d_o and d_i are the distance of the object and its image from the lens, respectively. A positive d_i indicates that the image is on the opposite side of the lens from the object. If the lens is a magnifying lens, the height of the object may be different from that of its image, and may even be inverted. The object's magnification, m, can be found as $m = \frac{-d_i}{d_o}$. The value for the magnification can then be used to relate the object's height to that of its image: $m = \frac{y_i}{y_o}$. Note that if the magnification is negative, then the image has been inverted.

Images may be either **real** or **virtual**. Real images are formed by light rays passing through the image location, while virtual images are only perceived by reverse extrapolating refracted light rays. Diverging lenses cannot create real images, only virtual ones. Real images are always on the opposite side of a converging lens from the object and are always inverted.

Concave Mirrors

Concave mirrors will create an image of an object in varying ways depending on the location of the object. The table below details the location, orientation, magnification, and nature of the image. The five object locations to be examined are between the mirror and the focal point (1), at the focal point (2), between the focal point and the center of curvature, or twice the focal point (3), at the center of curvature (4), and beyond the center of curvature (5).

Object	Image Location	Orientation	Magnification	Type
1	$d_i < 0$	upright	$m > 1$	virtual
2	none	none	none	none
3	$d_i > 2f$	inverted	$m < -1$	real
4	$d_i = 2f$	inverted	$m = -1$	real
5	$f < d_i < 2f$	inverted	$0 > m > -1$	real

Note in case 5 that the image may effectively be located at the focal point. This is the case for objects at extremely great, or near infinite, distances from the mirror. The magnification at these distances will be very small and a true infinite distance would result in a magnification of zero.

Plane Mirrors and Spherical Mirrors

Plane mirrors have very simple properties. They reflect only **virtual images**, they have no magnification, and the object's distance from the mirror is always equal to that of its image. Plane mirrors will also appear to reverse the directions left and right.

Spherical mirrors follow the same governing equations for finding image height, location, orientation, and magnification as do thin lenses; however, the sign convention for image location is reversed. A positive image location denotes that it is on the same side as the object. Spherical mirrors may be either **concave** or **convex**. Convex mirrors are by far the simpler of the two. They will always reflect virtual, upright images with magnification between zero and one. Concave mirrors have varying behavior based on the object location.

Simple Magnifier, the Microscope, and the Telescope

A simple magnifier, or commonly a **magnifying glass**, is a converging lens that creates an enlarged virtual image near the observer's eye. The object must be within a certain distance, about 25 cm or 10 inches, from the magnifier for it to operate properly. Otherwise, the image will be blurry.

A **microscope** is a magnifying device that is used to examine very small objects. It uses a series of lenses to capture light coming from the far side of the sample under examination. Often microscopes will have interchangeable magnification lenses mounted on a wheel, allowing the user to adjust the level of magnification by rotating in a different lens. Optical microscopes will generally be limited to a magnification of 1,500.

Telescopes are used to view very distant objects, most often celestial bodies. Telescopes use both lenses and mirrors to capture light from a distant source, focus it, and then magnify it. This creates a virtual image that is very much smaller than the object itself, and yet much larger than the object appears to the naked eye.

Prisms

Prisms are optical devices that alter the path or nature of light waves. Glass and plastic are the two most prevalent materials used to make prisms. There are three different types of prisms in common use. The most familiar of these is the dispersive prism, which splits a beam of light into its constituent wavelengths. For sunlight, this results in the full spectrum of color being displayed. These prisms are generally in the familiar triangular prism shape.

Polarizing prisms, as their name suggests, polarize light, but without significantly reducing the intensity, as a simple filter would. Waves that are oscillating in planes other than the desired plane are caused to rotate, so that they are oscillating in the desired plane. This type of prism is commonly used in cameras.

Reflective prisms are much less common than either of the others. They reflect light, often through the use of the total internal reflection phenomenon. Their primary use is in binoculars.

Chapter Quiz

Ready to see how well you retained what you just read? Scan the QR code to go directly to the chapter quiz interface for this study guide. If you're using a computer, simply visit the online resources page at **mometrix.com/resources719/ftcephysics** and click the Chapter Quizzes link.

Electricity and Magnetism

Electrostatics

Electric Field Equation

In order to define a particular **electric field**, we may place an object with positive charge, q_0, called a test charge, somewhere near the charged particle, and then measure the **force exerted** on the object. We may then say that electric field $\boldsymbol{E}$ at that point is $\boldsymbol{E} = \frac{\boldsymbol{F}}{q_0}$. Electric field is a vector, and the direction of $\boldsymbol{E}$ will be the direction of the force acting on the test charge. If we want to fully define some region of an electric field, we must find measures for the field at every point within that region. The SI units for electric field are Newtons per coulomb (N/C). When performing this operation, we will assume that the presence of the test charge does not affect in any way the charge distribution of the electric field.

Coulomb's Law

If two particles have charge magnitudes q_1 and q_2, and are separated by distance r, then the electrostatic force of attraction or repulsion between them can be calculated as $\boldsymbol{F} = \frac{kq_1q_2}{r^2}$, in which the constant k is approximately $9 \times 10^9\ \frac{\text{N}\cdot\text{m}^2}{\text{C}^2}$. This is known as **Coulomb's law**. We should note the similarity to Newton's equation for the gravitational force between two particles, $\boldsymbol{F} = \frac{Gm_1m_2}{r^2}$. The main difference between these two equations is that while electrical force may be attractive or repulsive, **gravitational force is always attractive**. No experiment has ever contradicted Coulomb's law, even those conducted at the subatomic level. The constant k in the equation is called Coulomb's constant or the electrostatic constant. An important principle when calculating electrostatic force, if more than two particles are involved, is the law of superposition. If we are looking for the force exerted on a particle by two or more other particles, we must determine the individual force from each of the other particles, and take the vector sum of those forces to determine the total effect.

Review Video: Static Electricity
Visit mometrix.com/academy and enter code: 113722

Gauss's Law for Electric Flux

Flux is a concept that is applicable in many areas of science. It is a measure of flow through a given area. Electric flux, Φ, is a measure of the electric field flowing perpendicularly through a particular area. It can be calculated by the equation $\Phi = \boldsymbol{E} \cdot \boldsymbol{A} = \boldsymbol{EA} \cos\theta$, where θ is the angle between the direction of $\boldsymbol{E}$ and $\boldsymbol{A}$ (the normal vector of the area).

Gauss's law states that the electric flux through an enclosing surface is directly related to charge enclosed by the surface. This relation is given by the equation $\Phi = \frac{Q}{\varepsilon_0}$, where Q is the total enclosed carge and ε_0 is a constant known as the permittivity of free space. The shape of the enclosing surface should be chosen to accommodate the finding of $\boldsymbol{E} \cdot \boldsymbol{A}$. Most often, this will be a sphere or cylinder, since these surfaces are perpendicular to field lines emanating from a point or line charge, respectively. Combining the the flux equation with Gauss's law yields the relation, $\frac{Q}{\varepsilon_0} = \boldsymbol{E} \cdot \boldsymbol{A}$. Units for electric flux are $\frac{\text{N}\cdot\text{m}^2}{\text{C}}$.

Electrical Properties of Materials

Common Means of Transferring Electrical Charge

Charge is transferred in three common ways: conduction, induction, and friction. **Conduction**, as the name implies, takes place between conductive materials. There must be a point of contact between the two materials and a potential difference, such as when a battery is connected to a circuit. **Induction also requires conductive materials. It occurs when a conductive material encounters a changing magnetic field**. The change can be the result of a changing magnetic field or the material moving within a constant magnetic field. Charge transfer due to **friction** does not require conductive materials. When two materials are rubbed together, electrons may be transferred from one to the other, leaving the two materials with equal and opposite charges. This is observed when shoes are dragged across a carpeted floor.

Review Video: Charging by Conduction
Visit mometrix.com/academy and enter code: 502661

Conductors, Insulators, and Semiconductors

In many materials, electrons are able to move freely; these are known as **conductors**. Due to their atomic structure and delocalized electrons, **metals** tend to be the best conductors, particularly copper and silver. Highly conductive wires are instrumental in creating low-resistance pathways for electrons to travel along within a circuit.

Other materials naturally inhibit the movement of charge and are known as **insulators**. Their electrons are tightly held by the individual constituent atoms. Glass, pure water, wood, and plastic are all insulators. Insulators are necessary in circuits to prevent charge from escaping to undesirable places, such as an operator's hand. For this reason, most highly conductive materials are covered by insulators.

Semiconductors, as the name suggests, are materials that only partially conduct electrical charge. The elements silicon and germanium are both common semiconductors, and are frequently used in microelectronic devices because they allow for tight control of the rate of conduction. In many cases, the conduction ability of semiconductors can be controlled by adjusting the temperature of the material.

Doping Semiconductors

Resistivity is the physical property of resistance of different materials: metals, which easily conduct electricity, have low resistivity; insulators have high resistivity; and the resistivity of **semiconductors** falls in between (example: silicon). **Doping** is the process of mixing different semiconductor atoms in order to control conductivity of the material. **N-type semiconductors** have an excess of electrons as a result of the doping process; when an electric field is applied, a negative pole forms due to the buildup of negatively charged electrons (example: silicon doped with antimony). **P-type semiconductors** have a shortage of electrons; when an electric field is applied, a positive pole forms (example: silicon doped with boron).

Introduction to Circuits and Current

Electric Current

Charge is a physical property of particles. For the particles of an atom, protons have a positive charge of +1, neutrons have no charge, and **electrons** have a negative charge of −1. Like charges repel each other (positive and positive or negative and negative), and opposite charges attract (negative and positive). The **net charge** of an atom or molecule can be found by adding up all the protons and electrons that it contains. When dealing with charge on the macro level, it is helpful to aggregate the charges in a material with different units. The coulomb is the SI unit for charge and is equivalent to about 6.24×10^{18} charged particles.

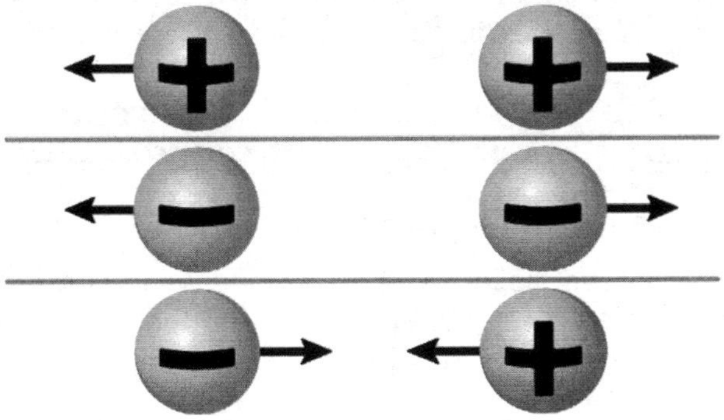

Electric current is the net rate of flow of charge (electrons) past a specific point, as in a wire or circuit. Current (represented by I in equations) is measured in amperes or amps (A). An ampere is equal to one coulomb per second $\left(A = \frac{C}{s}\right)$. Ammeters are tools that can be used to measure current.

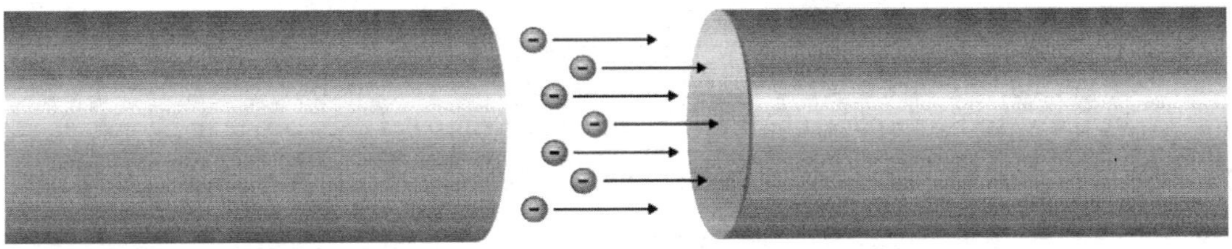

Electric current carries energy much like moving balls carry energy.

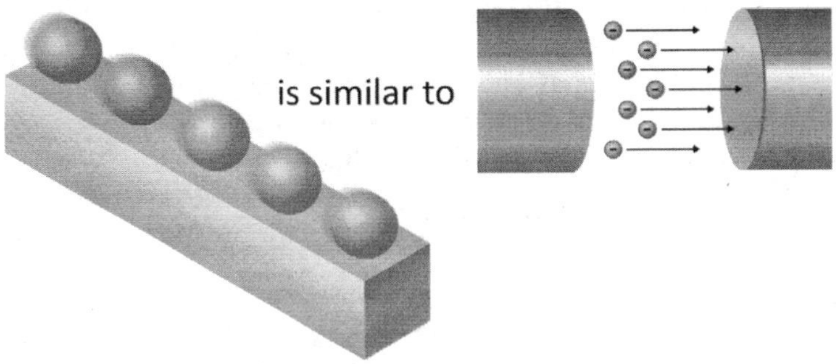

Electron flow theory states that electrons (e^-) flow from the negative terminal to the positive terminal. **Electricity** is the form of energy that exists statically (potential energy) with an accumulation of protons or electrons or dynamically with their movement (current).

Review Video: Electric Charge
Visit mometrix.com/academy and enter code: 323587

Alternating and Direct Current

For circuits with **direct current** (DC), when current flows in only one direction, the voltage and current are constant. Direct current is supplied by batteries and is used in cell phones, ships, and planes. **Alternating current** (AC), in which current periodically reverses direction, can be produced using generators and is used for land-based applications (including in homes) because less power is lost when electricity travels long distances. In the United States, AC electricity is supplied most commonly at 120 V and 240 V.

Electric Potential

Electric potential energy is the energy stored in a charge by virtue of its proximity to other charged regions. It can be calculated in the same way as calculating the amount of work required to move it to that location from an infinite distance away. The work required to move a charge of magnitude q from infinity to a distance r from another charge of magnitude Q is calculated to be $PE_e = W = \frac{kQq}{r}$, where k is the **electrostatic constant**.

Electric potential, V, is closely related to electric potential energy. The potential due to a charge Q can be found by dividing the electric potential energy of another charge q by its magnitude, $V = \frac{PE_e}{q}$, or by the equation $V = \frac{kQ}{r}$.

The difference between the electric potential of two points is known as **voltage**. It is measured in volts, or joules per coulomb. Since it is impractical to find a point of zero absolute electric potential, for each system a reference point or ground is defined, to which all other points in the system may be related. Voltage is similar to gravitational potential energy.

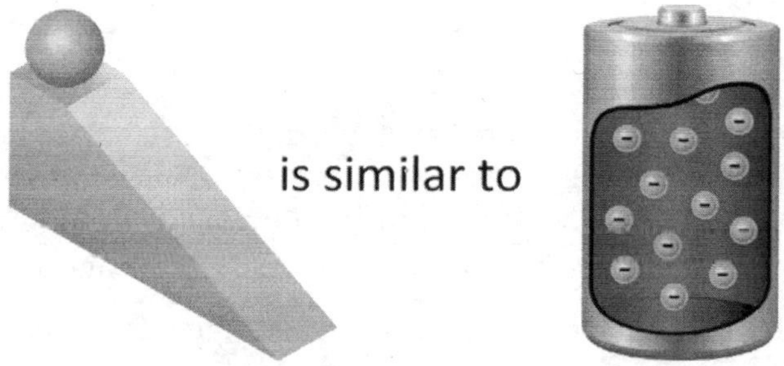

Electromotive Force and Common EMF Devices

A force that maintains a potential difference between two locations in a circuit is known as an **electromotive force (emf).** A device that creates this force is referred to as an **emf device**. The most common emf device is the battery. **Batteries** operate by converting chemical energy stored in the electrolyte, the internal chemical material, into electrical energy. The reaction causes a lack of electrons on the cathode, and when the circuit is connected, they flow from the anode, creating a flow of current. The electrolyte's composition also determines whether the battery is classified as acidic or alkaline, and wet or dry. Another emf device is the **photocell**, also commonly called the solar cell, since most photocells are powered by the sun. These operate by absorbing photons, which cause the electrons to be excited and flow in a current, a process of converting light energy into electrical energy. A third type of emf device is the **generator**. This device converts mechanical energy to electrical energy. A generator may be powered by such diverse sources as gasoline engines, flowing water, or even manually powered cranks. These devices utilize a rotating shaft to spin a coil within a magnetic field, creating a potential difference by induction.

Ohm's Law

If we were to apply the exact same potential difference between the ends of two geometrically similar rods, one made of copper and one made of glass, we would create vastly different currents. This is because these two substances have different **resistances**. **Ohm's Law** describes the relation between applied voltage and induced current, $V = IR$. This is one of the most important tools of circuit analysis. Resistance, then, can be calculated as $R = \frac{V}{I}$. The SI unit for resistance is the **ohm** (Ω), equal to a volt per ampere. When a component is placed into a circuit to provide a specific resistance, it is known as a **resistor**. For a given potential difference, the greater the resistance is to the current, the smaller the current will be. Electrical resistance is much like friction, resisting flow and dissipating energy.

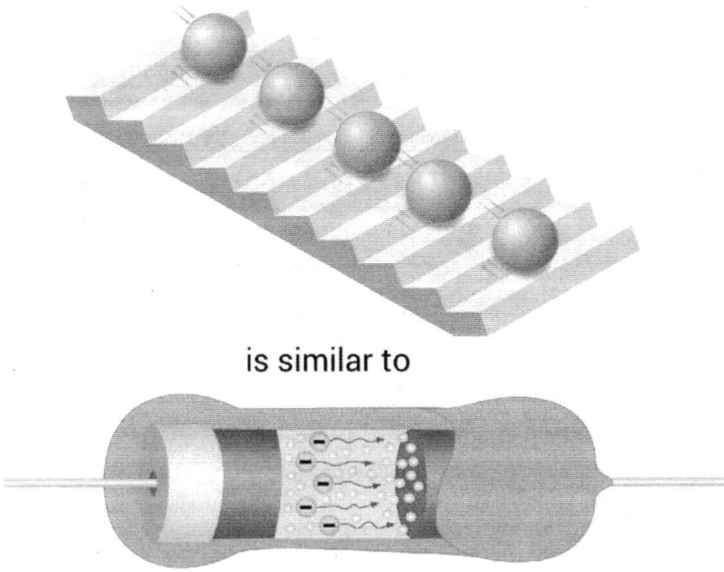

If we wish to look instead at the quality of the material of which the resistor is made, then we must consider resistivity. **Resistivity**, ρ, is a physical property of every material, which, if known, can be used to size a resistor for a specific resistance. Resistance is dictated by both the material and the dimensions of the resistor, given by the relation $R = \frac{\rho L}{A}$, where L is the effective length of the resistor and A is the effective cross-section. Alternatively, an unknown resistivity may be calculated by rearranging the equation as $\rho = \frac{RA}{L}$.

Resistivity will often change with temperature. In these cases, the relevant resistivity may be calculated $\rho = p_{ref}\left(1 + \alpha\left(T - T_{ref}\right)\right)$, where α is the resistivity proportionality constant and T is the material temperature.

Review Video: Resistance of Electric Currents
Visit mometrix.com/academy and enter code: 668423

Ground

Grounding is the process of neutralizing the charge of an object by removal of excess electrons to or donation of additional electrons by a much larger object (example: the Earth). This ground or large object can seemingly infinitely donate or accept electrons without mathematically significant changes to its net voltage. Examples of grounds include lighting rods and the round component of a three-pronged plug, as used for home appliances. Current does not usually flow through air, but lightning is the visible current that results when charge builds up in clouds; lightning rods provide a safe, low-resistance ground so the high-voltage current is less likely to be destructive. The round component of three-pronged plugs serves as one of the residential applications of this concept.

ENERGY AND POWER

Electric circuits operate by **transferring** electrical energy from one location in the circuit to another. Some devices in a circuit can store and release energy while other devices, like resistors, dissipate energy. **Power** is a measure of the rate at which energy is stored, released, transferred, or dissipated. It is measured in watts (W), or joules per second. Power is calculated by $P = VI$. The amount of power being released by a 9-V battery producing a current of 5 A is 45 W. When calculating the amount of power dissipated by a resistor, Ohm's Law can be combined with the power equation to form two other equations for power, $P = I^2R$ and $P = \frac{V^2}{R}$.

When power consumption over long periods of time needs to be measured, it will often be measured in units of kilowatt-hours, which is the amount of energy consumed at a rate of 1 kW over the course of an hour. One kilowatt-hour is equal to 3,600 kJ.

CAPACITORS AND DIELECTRICS

Capacitors are devices used in circuits to store energy in the form of electric fields. They are most often composed of two oppositely charged parallel plates separated by a medium, generally air. This medium is referred to as the capacitor's **dielectric**.

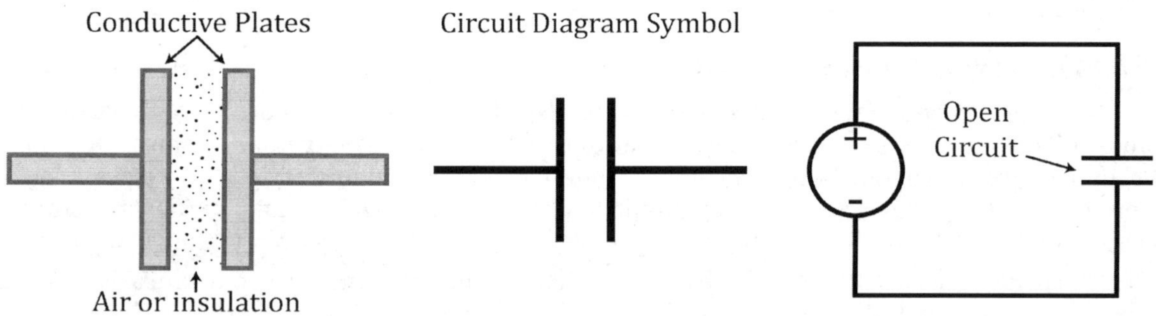

The dielectric material dictates the amount of energy in the electric field and, consequently, the amount of energy that can be stored by the capacitor. The measurable quality of a capacitor is known as its **capacitance**, which is defined as the amount of charge that it can store per volt of potential difference. This is given by the equation $C = \frac{Q}{V}$, with capacitance having units of farads or coulombs per volt. Physically, the capacitance depends on three things: the **area** of the parallel plates, the **separation distance** between them, and the **dielectric** material. For cases in which the separation distance is insignificant compared to the area, the capacitance can be found by the equation $C = \frac{\varepsilon A}{d}$, where ε is the permittivity of the dielectric material. Often, instead of being given the permittivity, we will be given the dielectric constant, κ, which is the ratio of the permittivities of the material and air, $\kappa = \frac{\varepsilon}{\varepsilon_{air}}$. This yields an obvious result of $\kappa_{air} = 1$.

The energy stored in a capacitor can be calculated in three different ways: $E = \frac{CV^2}{2} = \frac{Q^2}{2C} = \frac{VQ}{2}$. Another quantity associated with capacitors is the electric field energy density, η. This energy density is found by $\eta = \frac{\varepsilon E^2}{2}$.

INDUCTORS

When current passes through a wire coil, a magnetic field develops. An **inductor** is an electrical component made of a coil of wire that can store energy and opposes the rate of change of alternating current flowing through it; however, direct current passes through easily. They can be used as filters, sensors, motors, and transformers.

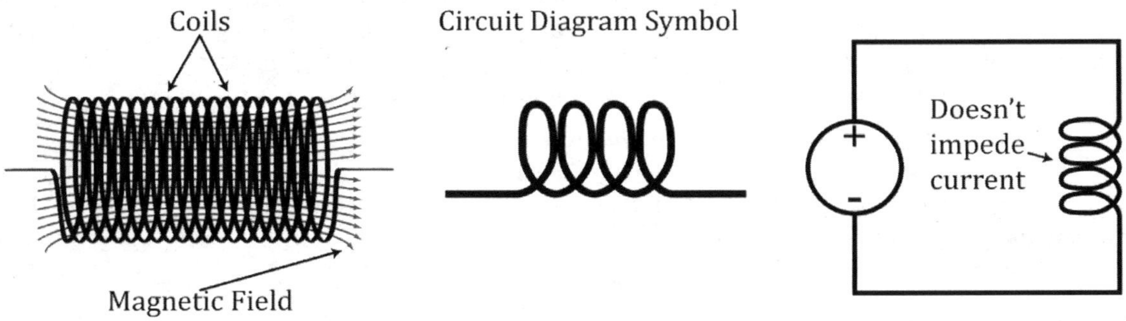

Inductance is the measure of ability of an inductor to resist changes in current. **Faraday's law of induction describes the ways voltage** or electromagnetic frequency can be generated by changing the magnetic environment in a coil of wire by moving a magnet within it, changing the external magnetic field of the magnet, or changing the area of the coil.

Capacitors and Inductors in AC Circuits

Capacitors and inductors both oppose immediate acceptance of the flow reversal of alternating current. This opposition is referred to as **impedance** and is similar to resistance, also having units of ohms, but unlike resistance, impedance is a complex value, meaning that it may have an **imaginary component** as well as a **real component**. For ideal capacitors and inductors, impedance is purely imaginary, and for ideal resistors, impedance is purely real. It is only when combining the effects of these devices that the full expression for impedance, Z, is necessary: $Z = R + X_i$, where $i = \sqrt{(-1)}$. X is a quantity known as reactance. For capacitors, $X_c = \frac{1}{\omega C}$, where ω is the angular frequency of the current, and for inductors, $X_L = \omega L$.

Other Electrical Components

Diodes

Diodes are a basic component of circuits, but they can't be described using Ohm's law; they operate as an electrical "valve", only allowing current to pass in one direction. This allows them to rectify alternating current by converting it to direct current, which is preferred or necessary for some applications. A common example is the light-emitting diode (LED) bulb, which emits light when powered more efficiently than regular light bulbs.

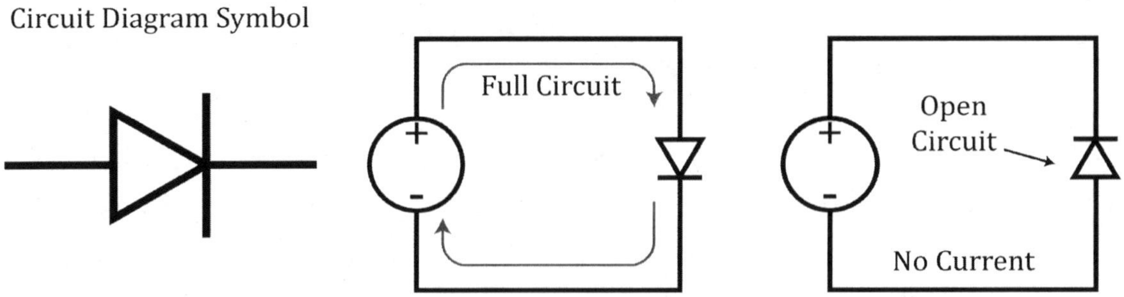

A p-n junction diode is formed by fusing a p-type semiconductor and an n-type semiconductor. It is considered a solid-state device because electricity flows through solid material rather than a vacuum tube. The p-region of the junction is positively charged and the n-region is negatively charged. Reverse bias occurs when the diode is connected such that the positive voltage is applied to the n-region; forward bias occurs when the positive voltage is applied to the p-region.

Transistors

A bipolar junction transistor, p-n-p or n-p-n, consists of two p-n junction diodes arranged back-to-back with three electrical leads or terminals: the emitter, the collector, and the base. Transistors are used to boost electrical signals or switch them on or off at high speeds. A large current flows from the emitter to the collector, and a smaller current entering through the base lead can be used to control the larger collector current.

Transformers

Transformers are devices made of two or more coils of wire that use induction to transfer electricity between circuits. A **step-up transformer**'s input (primary) voltage is lower than its output (secondary) voltage; and a **step-down transformer**'s input voltage is higher than its output voltage. This allows for electricity to be to be generated safely at a lower voltage (example: 12 kV), passed through a step-up transformer for transport through power lines at high voltage (example: 400 kV), and passed through step-down transformers for distribution and use (example: 240 V residential use).

Motors and Generators

Motors use electromagnetic induction to convert electrical energy (electricity) to mechanical energy (motion). In a **DC motor**, torque is produced by magnetic force, which results from current passing through coil located in a magnetic field. They have been around for more than 100 years and are simple, inexpensive, and easy to maintain. In **AC (synchronous) motors**, torque is produced the same way as in DC motors, but much higher current is required, and they are inefficient. **Induction (asynchronous) motors** are more common, and they rotate a magnetic field in order to induce alternating current.

Generators use electromagnetic induction to convert mechanical energy to electrical energy. **AC generators** mechanically turn a coil in a magnetic field to produce voltage output and induce alternating current.

Simple Circuits

The Use of Ohm's Law and Kirchhoff's Laws

Circuit analysis is the process of determining the **current** or **voltage drop** across devices of interest in a circuit. Ohm's Law is useful in doing this since it definitively relates the current to the voltage drop for resistors, $V = IR$. Kirchhoff's voltage law (KVL) states that if you sum the voltage drops across all devices in any closed loop of a circuit, the sum will always be zero, $V_1 + V_2 + \cdots + V_n = 0$. This law is particularly useful if there are multiple closed-loop pathways in a circuit. Kirchhoff's current law (KCL) states that the amount of current entering a point must equal the amount of current leaving, $I_{in} = I_{out}$. This law may also be expanded to apply to the current entering and leaving a larger region of a circuit. In any given circuit analysis, it may be necessary to use all three of these laws.

Another important principle to remember in an ideal circuit is that any two points connected by only wire are at equal voltage. Only devices on the circuit may change the voltage. In actual practice, however, all wire has some amount of resistance. A battery that provides an EMF of V_B is only able to deliver a voltage to the circuit of $V = V_B - IR_B$, where R_B is the internal resistance of the battery. To express this concept in an ideal circuit, we would need to add a small resistor in series after the battery.

Measuring Devices

There are several devices that allow various quantifiable properties of a circuit to be measured to a great degree of accuracy. An **ammeter** is a device placed in series with a circuit to measure the current through that location. Ideally, an ammeter has as little internal resistance as possible to prevent altering the current it is trying to measure. A **voltmeter** measures the voltage or potential difference between two locations in a circuit.

It has two leads that are connected in parallel with the circuit and consists of a very high resistance and an ammeter in series. This allows only a very small amount of current to be diverted through the voltmeter, but enough to determine the voltage by Ohm's Law. A **galvanometer** is the primary working component of an ammeter. It operates based on the idea that a wire in a magnetic field will experience a force proportional to the amount of current it is carrying. It converts the observed current into a dial reading. A **potentiometer** is a variable resistor, often controlled by a knob, that allows an operator to control the amount of voltage or current provided to a given circuit. They are commonly used in volume-control knobs. Potentiometers can also be called voltage dividers. Their use in circuit measurement is for finding voltages by comparing them to known voltages. A **multimeter** is a device that combines the functions of all the above devices into one. In addition to voltage, current, resistance and capacitance, they can typically measure inductance, frequency, and other quantities.

Resistance in Series Circuits

A **series circuit** is a loop through which charge can flow along only one path. Resistance of resistors (labeled R_n) lined up in series is additive, so $R_{total} = R_1 + R_2 + R_3 + \cdots$ for all resistors in that series. Current (I) is consistent in all locations throughout a closed series circuit, so $I_{battery} = I_{R_1} = I_{R_2} = I_{R_3} = \cdots$, regardless of the number of elements in the series. Charge at the positive terminal of the battery experiences a **voltage drop** (ΔV), or loss of potential energy, as it passes through each resistor, such that its voltage will be zero at the negative terminal of the battery. Therefore, $\Delta V_{battery} = \Delta V_1 + \Delta V_2 + \Delta V_3 + \cdots$, where each ΔV_n represents the voltage drop across each resistor in series.

Problem Solving with Series Circuits

Using the labeled diagram of a series circuit, solve the following problems:

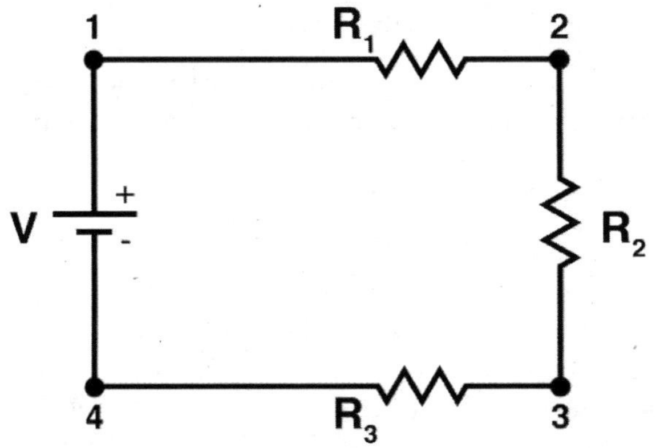

V = Voltage source (battery)

R = Resistor

Example 1: If each resistor is 3 Ω and the battery is 9 V, what is the current at each of the indicated corners?

Step 1:
Given: $R_1 = R_2 = R_3 = 3\ \Omega$
Equation: $R_{total} = R_1 + R_2 + R_3$
Solve: $\text{R}_{\text{total}} = 3\ \Omega + 3\ \Omega + 3\ \Omega = 9\ \Omega$

Step 2:
Given: $V_{battery} = 9\text{ V}$
Equation: $I = \frac{V}{R}$
Solve: $I_{battery} = \frac{9\text{ V}}{9\ \Omega} = 1\text{ A}$

Step 3:
Because current is the same throughout the circuit, current at each corner is the same:
$I_{total} = I_1 = I_2 = I_3 = I_4 = 1\ A$

Example 2: If the current at point 3 is 4 Amps, and each resistor is 1 Ω, what is the battery voltage?

Step 1:	Step 2:	Step 3:
Given: $I_3 = 4\text{ A}$ The circuit is in series so current is the same throughout: $I_{total} = 4\text{ A}$	Given: $R_1 = R_2 = R_3 = 1\ \Omega$ Equation: $R_{total} = R_1 + R_2 + R_3$ Solve: $R_{total} = 1\ \Omega + 1\ \Omega + 1\ \Omega = 3\ \Omega$	Equation: $V_{total} = I_{total}(R_{total})$ Solve: $V_{total} = (4\text{ A})(3\ \Omega) = 12\text{ V}$

Resistance in Parallel Circuits

Parallel circuits provide multiple pathways for current to follow, which adjusts the way that current, voltage, and resistance interact when compared to series circuits. Because current (I) can follow multiple pathways, it is divided among those pathways at each branch, so $I_{total} = I_1 + I_2 + I_3 + \cdots$, where 1, 2, and 3 represent each unique branch. In this example, there are 3.

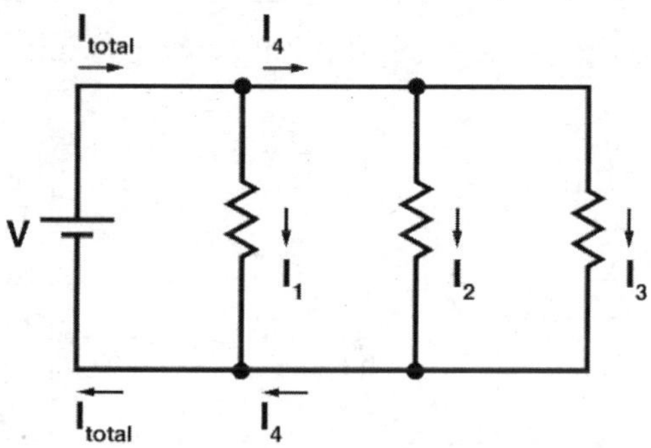

Equivalent resistance (R_{eq}) is the amount of resistance in a parallel circuit, represented as if there was only one resistor in series. All of the resistors in parallel can be simplified using the following equation:

$$\frac{1}{R_{eq}} = \frac{1}{R_1} + \frac{1}{R_2} + \frac{1}{R_3}$$

Because a charge will only pass through one resistor in the parallel circuit and not all three, the voltage drop across each resistor will be the same as that of the battery. Therefore, voltage drops for parallel circuits follow this rule:

$$\Delta V_{battery} = \Delta V_1 = \Delta V_2 = \Delta V_3 = \cdots$$

Note: If multiple resistors exist on a branch of a parallel circuit, they are in series and should be added together ($R_{total} = R_1 + R_2 + R_3 + \cdots$) before dealing with them as part of a parallel circuit.

PROBLEM SOLVING WITH PARALLEL CIRCUITS

Using the labeled diagram of a parallel circuit, solve the following problems:

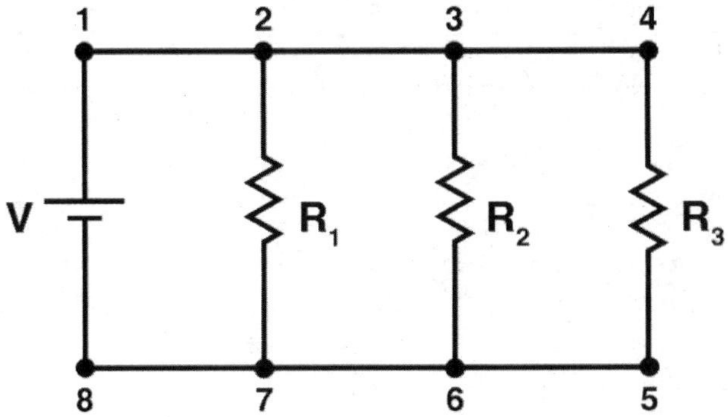

Example 1: If each resistor is 3 Ω and the battery is 9 V, what is the current at each of the indicated points (1-8) and each resistor?

Step 1:
Given: $R_1 = R_2 = R_3 = 3\ \Omega$
Equation: $\frac{1}{R_{eq}} = \frac{1}{R_1} + \frac{1}{R_2} + \frac{1}{R_3}$
Solve: $\frac{1}{R_{eq}} = \frac{1}{3\ \Omega} + \frac{1}{3\ \Omega} + \frac{1}{3\ \Omega}$
$\frac{1}{R_{eq}} = \frac{3}{3\ \Omega}$
$R_{eq} = 1\ \Omega$

Step 2:
Given: $V_{batt} = 9\text{ V}$
Equation: $I_{total} = \frac{V_{batt}}{R_{eq}}$
Solve: $I_{total} = \frac{9\text{ V}}{1\ \Omega} = 9\text{ A}$

Step 3:
Equation: $\Delta V_n = I_{R_n}(R_n)$
Solve: $I_{R_1} = \frac{9\text{ V}}{3\ \Omega} = 3\ A$
Current is the same for each branch in this example because $R_1 = R_2 = R_3 = 3\ \Omega$

Using this information and the additive properties of current in parallel circuits, the current through the following points and resistors is:

$$I_1 = I_2 = I_7 = I_8 = I_{total} = 9\text{ A}$$
$$I_3 = I_6 = 6\text{ A}$$
$$I_4 = I_5 = 3\text{ A}$$
$$I_{R_1} = I_{R_2} = I_{R_3} = 3\text{ A}$$

Example 2: If the current at point 4 is 4 Amps, and $R_1 = 3\ \Omega$; $R_2 = 2\ \Omega$; $R_3 = 6\ \Omega$, what is the total current?

Step 1:
Given: $R_3 = 6\ \Omega$; $I_4 = I_{R_3} = 4\ A$
Equation: $\Delta V_3 = I_{R_3}(R_3)$
Solve: $\Delta V_3 = (4\text{ A})(6\ \Omega) = 24\text{ V}$

Step 2:
Given: $R_1 = 3\ \Omega$; $R_2 = 2\ \Omega$
Equation: $I_n = \frac{V}{R_n}$
Solve: $I_1 = \frac{24\text{ V}}{3\ \Omega} = 8\text{ A}$
$I_2 = \frac{24\text{ V}}{2\ \Omega} = 12\text{ A}$

Step 3:
Equation: $I_{total} = I_1 + I_2 + I_3$
Solve: $I_{total} = 8\text{ A} + 12\text{ A} + 4\text{ A}$
$I_{total} = 24\text{ A}$

CAPACITORS AND INDUCTORS IN CIRCUITS

Capacitors have combination rules opposite to those of resistors. **Capacitors in series** have an equivalent value of:

$$C_{eq} = \left(\frac{1}{C_1} + \frac{1}{C_2} + \cdots + \frac{1}{C_n}\right)^{-1}$$

Capacitors in parallel have equivalence of:

$$C_{eq} = C_1 + C_2 + \cdots + C_n$$

Inductors follow the same combination rules as resistors. **Inductors in series** have an equivalent value of:

$$L_{eq} = L_1 + L_2 + \cdots + L_n$$

Inductors in parallel have equivalence of

$$L_{eq} = \left(\frac{1}{L_1} + \frac{1}{L_2} + \cdots + \frac{1}{L_n}\right)^{-1}$$

RC Circuits

An RC circuit consists of a battery wired in series with a **resistor** and a **capacitor**. Since a capacitor in steady state allows no current flow, it makes no sense to analyze a steady-state RC circuit. Instead, we will look at an RC circuit that has only just been connected, with the capacitor uncharged. The battery supplies voltage V_B to the circuit, and since the capacitor's voltage is initially zero, the voltage across the resistor is initially V_B, giving an initial current of $I = \frac{V_B}{R}$. As current flows, the charge on the capacitor increases, which in turn creates an opposing voltage that **lowers the voltage drop** across the resistor. Combining Ohm's Law with the KVL gives the voltage relation as $V_B = IR + \frac{Q}{C}$, where Q is the charge on the capacitor. Since the current is simply the transfer rate of the charge, this becomes a differential equation. Solving for charge and current yields the expressions $Q(t) = CV_B(1 - e^{-t/RC})$ and $I(t) = \left(\frac{V_B}{R}\right)e^{-t/RC}$. The factor RC in the exponent is referred to as the circuit's time constant. It is the amount of time required for the capacitor to charge up to 63.2% capacity.

If the battery is removed from the circuit after the capacitor is charged and the circuit is reconnected with just the resistor and capacitor, the capacitor will begin to drain at the same rate that it was charged. The current magnitude will follow the same equation as before, though it will be in the opposite direction. The new expression for the charge will be $Q(t) - CV_B e^{-t/RC}$.

Power in AC Circuits

Unlike DC circuits, the power provided by an AC voltage source is not constant over time. Generally, an AC source will provide voltage in a sinusoidal pattern, $V(t) = V_{max}\sin(\omega t)$. Similarly, the current will be given by $I(t) = I_{max}\sin(\omega t)$. From our known equations for power, this yields a power of $P(t) = RI_{max}{}^2\sin^2(\omega t)$. However, if we wish to find the average power or the amount of energy transmission after a given period of time, we need to find some way to average voltage and current. The root-mean-square (rms) method, as the name suggests, takes the square root of the time average of the squared value. For sinusoidal functions such as the voltage and current here, the rms value is the maximum value divided by the square root of 2. For voltage and current, $V_{rms} = \frac{V_{max}}{\sqrt{2}}$, and $I_{rms} = \frac{I_{max}}{\sqrt{2}}$. In this way, the average power can be found as $P_{avg} = V_{rms}I_{rms}$, which can also be stated $P_{avg} = \frac{V_{max}I_{max}}{2}$. A DC source with supplied voltage V_B will provide the same power over time as an AC source if $V_B = V_{rms}$.

Properties of Magnets

Magnets and Magnetism

A **magnet** is any object or material, such as iron, steel, or magnetite (lodestone), that can affect another substance within its **field of force** that has like characteristics. Magnets can either attract or repel other substances. Magnets have two **poles**: north and south. Like poles repel and opposite poles (pairs of north and south) attract. The magnetic field is a set of invisible lines representing the paths of attraction and repulsion.

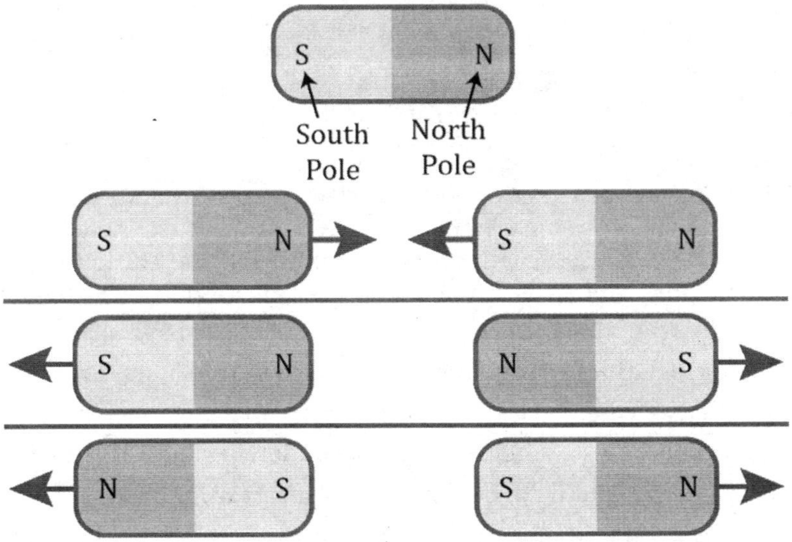

Magnetism can occur naturally, or ferromagnetic materials can be magnetized. Certain matter that is magnetized can retain its magnetic properties indefinitely and become a permanent magnet. Other matter can lose its magnetic properties. For example, an iron nail can be temporarily magnetized by stroking it repeatedly in the same direction using one pole of another magnet. Once magnetized, it can attract or repel other magnetically inclined materials, such as paper clips. Dropping the nail repeatedly will cause it to lose its magnetic properties.

Review Video: Magnets
Visit mometrix.com/academy and enter code: 570803

Magnetic Fields and Atomic Structure

Motion of a charge produces a **magnetic field**. Within an atom, the negatively-charged electrons moving around the nucleus each generate a magnetic field. In most materials, these fields all perfectly oppose and cancel each other, but in certain elements (e.g., iron, cobalt, nickel) the fields are not completely canceled, which makes each atom a tiny magnet. The strength and direction of a magnetic field is known as the magnetic moment.

Pairs of electrons moving in opposite directions cancel each other out, creating a **net magnetic field** of zero. Materials that have an unpaired electron are magnetic. Those with a weak attractive force are referred to as **paramagnetic materials**, while **ferromagnetic materials** have a strong attractive force. A **diamagnetic material** has electrons that are paired, and therefore does not typically have a magnetic moment. There are, however, some diamagnetic materials that have a weak magnetic field.

A magnetic field can be formed not only by a magnetic material, but also by electric current flowing through a wire. When a coiled wire is attached to the two ends of a battery, for example, an **electromagnet** can be formed by inserting a ferromagnetic material such as an iron bar within the coil. When electric current flows through the wire, the bar becomes a magnet. If there is no current, the magnetism is lost. A **magnetic domain** occurs when the magnetic fields of atoms are grouped and aligned. These groups form what can be thought of as miniature magnets within a material. This is what happens when an object like an iron nail is temporarily magnetized. Prior to magnetization, the organization of atoms and their various polarities are somewhat random with respect to where the north and south poles are pointing. After magnetization, a significant percentage of the poles are lined up in one direction, which is what causes the magnetic force exerted by the material.

Magnetic Fields

Magnetism and Magnetic Fields

Magnetism and magnetic attraction are similar in many ways to electrical charge and electrostatic force. Magnets have two distinct **polarities**, of which like polarities repel and opposite polarities attract. Just as an object that holds an electric charge will produce a vector field, so will a charged magnet. Like the electric field lines, magnetic field lines are drawn as **originating** from north poles and **terminating** on south poles. Magnetic field is typically represented with the letter $\boldsymbol{B}$, and has SI units of teslas (T), which are equivalent to newtons per Ampere-meter (N/A-m). Unlike electric charge, however, an isolated magnetic pole cannot exist. Magnets must exist as **dipoles**, meaning that if there is a north pole, the other end of the magnet, no matter how small, will be a south pole. Most common magnets can be demagnetized simply by heating the material or subjecting it to repeated impact. This is because magnets are composed of many tiny dipoles that, when aligned, create a large unified magnet. Some materials are permanently aligned in the manner and are known as permanent magnets. Ferromagnets are iron-based materials that can be magnetized if their dipoles are aligned by a sufficiently strong magnetic field.

Magnetic and **electric fields** are quite interrelated. It is believed that magnetic fields are set up by electric currents, and it has also been observed that magnetic fields can **induce electric current**. If we were to place a moving charge or a wire carrying current into a magnetic field, a magnetic force would act on it.

Forces Exerted by a Magnetic Field

We will define $\boldsymbol{B}$, the magnetic field, by measuring the magnetic force exerted on a moving electric charge within the field. This is generally done by firing a test charge into the area where $\boldsymbol{B}$ is to be defined. After a time, we will find that force $\boldsymbol{F}_{\text{B}}$ acting on a test charge of velocity $\boldsymbol{v}$ and charge q can be written $\boldsymbol{F}_{\text{B}} = q\boldsymbol{v} \times \boldsymbol{B}$, in which q can be either positive or negative. If q is negative, the direction of the force will be opposite to that shown by the right-hand rule from this cross product. From this equation, we will discover that the magnetic force always acts perpendicular to the velocity vector. This means a magnetic field can neither speed up nor slow down a charged particle; it can only deflect it. Also, a magnetic field will exert no force on a stationary charge or a charge that moves parallel to the field. We can see from this equation that the magnitude of the deflecting force will be $\boldsymbol{F}_{\text{B}} = q\boldsymbol{v}\boldsymbol{B}\sin(\varphi)$, where φ is the angle between the particle velocity vector and the magnetic field vector.

Cyclotrons and Mass Spectrometers

Cyclotrons are particle accelerators that operate by using a magnetic field to create a deflection force on a fast-moving charged particle. The field strength is designed to cause the particle to move in a **circular pattern**. An electric field provides a force for the particle to accelerate tangentially as well. Once the particle has achieved sufficient velocity, it will exit the magnetic field and continue on in a straight line. One big advantage of the cyclotron over other types of particle accelerators is its relatively small size. Particles can achieve incredible velocities without having to travel a great distance.

Mass spectrometers are used to find the charge-to-mass ratio of ionized materials. An ionized particle of known mass, but unknown charge, is sent at a known velocity into a perpendicular magnetic field of known magnitude. Since the magnetic field is perpendicular, the **tangential speed** of the particle is constant. The force on a particle with constant tangential speed is equal to $\frac{mv^2}{r}$, where r is the radius of curvature of the particle's path. The force exerted by the magnetic field can be calculated as $q\boldsymbol{vB}$, since it is perpendicular to the particle's direction of motion. Equating these two expressions gives us $\frac{q}{m} = \frac{v}{rB}$, allowing us to find the charge-to-mass ratio if we measure the radius of curvature.

Lorentz Force Law

The **Lorentz force law** describes the force exerted on a charged particle in an electromagnetic field. The force exerted on the particle with charge q can be found $\boldsymbol{F} = q(\boldsymbol{E} + \boldsymbol{v} \times \boldsymbol{B})$, where $\boldsymbol{v}$ is the particle's velocity vector and $\boldsymbol{E}$ and $\boldsymbol{B}$ are the electric and magnetic field vectors, respectively. Essentially, this law states that a positively charged particle will be accelerated in the same linear direction as the electric field, but will curve perpendicularly to the magnetic field according to the right-hand rule. The Lorentz force law is used in a number of devices currently employed by physicists, like the cyclotron, magnetron, mass spectrometer, motor, generator, and rail gun.

Gauss's Law for Magnetic Flux

Gauss's law for magnetism solidifies the assertion that **magnetic monopoles cannot exist**. It does so by making statements about magnetic flux, which is defined in much the same way as electric flux, $\Phi_m = \boldsymbol{B} \cdot \boldsymbol{A}$, where $\boldsymbol{A}$ is the surface's normal vector. Magnetic flux has SI units of webers (Wb). If the surface is taken to be an enclosing surface, or a Gaussian surface, Gauss's law states that the total flux through the surface will equal zero. Unlike the case with electric flux, which allows for contained net charge, there can be no net magnetic poles inside of a closed surface. For every north pole, there must be a south pole of equal magnitude. If, for instance, we envision our Gaussian surface as enclosing one end of a short solenoid (which will set up a magnetic field resembling that of a magnetic dipole), we will notice that the magnetic field $\boldsymbol{B}$ will enter the Gaussian surface inside the solenoid (at the north pole) and will leave it outside the solenoid. No lines will begin or end in the interior of the surface, so the total flux for the surface is zero.

Magnetic Force on a Current-Carrying Wire

A magnetic field will exert a **sideways force** on the conduction electrons in a wire. Since the conduction electrons cannot escape sideways out of the wire, we know that this force must be transmitted bodily to the wire itself. So, if we have a wire carrying current I, and we know that the longitudinal axis of the wire is perpendicular to a magnetic field $\boldsymbol{B}$, then we know that a force equal to $(-e)\boldsymbol{vB}$ will act on each conduction electron. Taken as a whole, the wire will experience a force of $IL\boldsymbol{B}$, where L is the length of wire in the field. If we were to reverse either the magnetic field or the direction of the current, then the force on the wire would reverse as well. If the magnetic field is not perpendicular to the wire, then we can find the magnetic force as $F_B = IL\boldsymbol{B}\sin(\varphi)$, where φ is the angle between the direction of current and the magnetic field vector. The torque on a current-carrying loop is a result of the same phenomenon, except that with a loop, the current travels in opposite directions on opposite sides of the loop. This causes a result of zero net force since all the current exits the field from the same direction that it entered. There is, however, a net torque since the current going in opposite directions is separated by a distance. The torque on the loop can be found by $\boldsymbol{\tau} = IA\boldsymbol{n} \times \boldsymbol{B}$, where A is the area enclosed by the loop and $\boldsymbol{n}$ is the unit vector perpendicular to the plane of the loop. The loop may be any shape so long as it does not cross itself and is a closed shape.

Relationship Between Magnetism and Electricity

AMPERE'S LAW

Ampere's law is a mathematical equation that relates current flowing to the magnetic field it generates. It is expressed by the closed-loop line integral:

$$\oint_c \boldsymbol{B} \cdot d\boldsymbol{L} = \mu_0 I$$

For a straight length of wire, the magnetic field encircles the wire in the direction indicated by the right-hand rule (with the thumb pointed in the direction of current and the fingers curling to indicate the magnetic field). For a very long wire where end effects may be ignored, the magnetic field is given as $\boldsymbol{B} = \frac{\mu_0 I}{2\pi r}$, where r is the distance from the wire.

For a loop of current-carrying wire, the magnetic field direction can still be determined from the right-hand rule. However, the field magnitude at most points around and inside the loop is difficult to determine. The field magnitude at the center of the loop is found to be $\boldsymbol{B} = \frac{\mu_0 I}{2r}$.

For a solenoid, a long coil of current-carrying wire that is sometimes wrapped around a metal core, the magnetic field direction may again be determined by the right-hand rule. At all points inside the solenoid, the field has magnitude $\boldsymbol{B} = \frac{\mu_0 n I}{h}$, where n is the number of loops in the solenoid and h is its height. For a long solenoid, it can be shown that the field magnitude outside the solenoid is negligible.

BIOT-SAVART LAW

Any current-carrying wire will produce a magnetic field that circles the wire in the direction indicated by the right-hand rule (with the thumb pointing in the direction of the current). The **Biot-Savart law** gives the **magnitude** and **direction** of the magnetic field created by each infinitesimal element of current. The equation form of this law is given as $d\boldsymbol{B} = \left(\frac{\mu_0 I}{4r^3\pi}\right) \times d\boldsymbol{L} \times \boldsymbol{r}$, where μ_0 is a physical constant called the permeability of free space, $d\boldsymbol{L}$ is an infinitesimal vector pointing along the length of the wire in the direction of current, and $\boldsymbol{r}$ is the vector pointing from the wire element to the location where the field is to be calculated. Integrating this expression along the full length of wire gives the total resultant field.

The primary shortcoming of Ampere's law is that it is only applicable for a **constant steady-state current**. For transient cases, such as RC circuits, it is necessary to take into account what is known as the displacement current. **Displacement current** is found by the equation $I_d = \varepsilon_0 \left(\frac{\partial \Phi_e}{\partial t}\right)$, where ε_0 is the permittivity of free space and $\left(\frac{\partial \Phi_e}{\partial t}\right)$ is the instantaneous rate of change of electric flux. It is not actually a current, but for use in Ampere's law, it is treated like one. Thus, for transient cases, the I in Ampere's law is calculated as $I = I_{actual} + I_d$.

TRANSFORMERS, GENERATORS, AND ELECTRIC MOTORS

Transformers are devices that allow power to be exchanged between two circuits through electromagnetic induction. They generally consist of a pair of coils wrapped around a single metal core. The magnetic field induced by the current in one coil in turn induces a current in the second coil. The amount of current induced in the second coil is dependent on the inducing current and the number of loops in each coil: $\frac{I_2}{I_1} = \frac{N_1}{N_2}$, where N is the number of loops in the given coil. Since the power given up by the one circuit is the same as that received by the second circuit, we may also say that $V_1 I_1 = V_2 I_2$, or equivalently $\frac{I_2}{I_1} = \frac{V_1}{V_2}$.

Generators operate by using mechanical energy to turn a coil in a magnetic field, thus converting it to electrical energy. Often, large generators will require gasoline combustion engines to provide the necessary power to operate, though some are able to tap natural power sources such as flowing water. Smaller generators may be powered by hand cranks or stationary bicycles.

Electric motors are basically the reverse of generators. They operate by using an alternating current source connected to an electromagnet to create an oscilating magnetic field that causes a current-carrying coil to rotate, thus generating a torque. DC motors require additional parts to direct the flow of current in such a way that the coil will be continuously rotating.

Faraday's Law and Lenz's Law

Electromagnetic induction is the process by which current is induced due to a change in magnetic flux. The magnetic flux through one or more loops of wire in a magnetic is $\Phi_m = \boldsymbol{B}A\cos(\theta)$, where A is the area enclosed by the loop and θ is the angle between a vector normal to the plane of the loop and the magnetic field vector. The produced electromotive force (emf) can be found by **Faraday's law**, stated in equation form as $V_{emf} = -N\left(\frac{\Delta\Phi_m}{\Delta t}\right)$, where N is the number of loops in the coil. So, this induced voltage will exist only as long as Φ_m is changing. A change in any of the variables ($\boldsymbol{B}$, A, or θ) can cause a change in magnetic flux. Generators operate by rotating a coil in a constant magnetic field.

The contribution to this concept by Lenz's law is the negative sign in the equation of Faraday's law. **Lenz's law** states that the induced emf will try to counter the changing magnetic flux by creating a current to produce a magnetic field that opposes the change in magnetic flux.

Chapter Quiz

Ready to see how well you retained what you just read? Scan the QR code to go directly to the chapter quiz interface for this study guide. If you're using a computer, simply visit the online resources page at **mometrix.com/resources719/ftcephysics** and click the Chapter Quizzes link.

Modern Physics

Modern Physics and Additional Topics

Wave-Particle Duality and Heisenberg Uncertainty Principle

Wave-particle duality is the insight of quantum mechanics that states that energy will behave with the characteristics of both a **particle** and a **wave**. For most of the history of physics, it was believed that light was composed of electromagnetic waves and electrons were tiny particles of matter. However, experiments with light have created situations in which light will behave as if it were a particle (called a *photon*), and other experiments have suggested that photons will often behave as if they were waves. Essentially, quantum mechanics was created to resolve this conundrum. The result has been a series of theories, including the de Broglie hypothesis, that try to unify these seemingly contradictory attributes of matter.

One important measurement issue that arises from this dual nature is the **Heisenberg uncertainty principle**. This principle states that the position and linear momentum cannot be accurately measured beyond a certain level. Specifically, the minimum uncertainty in measuring the position, x, and linear momentum, p, in a given dimension is dictated by the relation $(\Delta x)(\Delta p) \geq \frac{h}{4\pi}$, where h is Planck's constant.

Photoelectric Effect

The **photoelectric effect** is the emission of electrons by substances when light falls on their surfaces. One of the main inspirations for the development of quantum theory was the inability of the standard theory of electromagnetic radiation to fully explain the photoelectric effect. Einstein declared that the incident light is composed of discrete particles of energy, known as **quanta**. The quanta of energy in light are known as **photons**. The energy of each photon is proportional to its frequency according to the equation $E = hf$, where E is energy, h is Planck's constant, and f is the frequency. When light is incident on a portion of an electric circuit, a current may be induced in the circuit. One property associated with this effect is stopping potential. This value is dependent on both the surface metal and the frequency of the incident light. Light of a given frequency will induce a current only if it does not have to overcome more potential in the circuit than the stopping potential. The stopping potential, V_0, is calculated by the equation $eV_0 = hf - \varphi$, where e is the elementary charge and φ is the work function of the metal. If $hf - \varphi$ is calculated in electron volts, V_0 is simply the equivalent number of volts.

De Broglie's Hypothesis

The de Broglie hypothesis is the assertion that all matter has a **wave-like nature**. According to the hypothesis, it is not just subatomic particles that exhibit wave properties; all objects do. This insight of de Broglie was confirmed by experiments that fired electrons at a very high speed at a crystalline nickel target. The diffraction of the electrons upon impacting the target was consistent with the diffraction exhibited by waves when passing through a slit with a width approximately the same as the wavelength of the wave. From these experiments, he produced two relations for an electron's frequency, f, and wavelength, λ, similar to those for photons: $f = \frac{E}{h}$ and $\lambda = \frac{h}{p}$, where E is the electron's energy, p is its linear momentum, and h is Planck's constant.

Michelson-Morley Experiment

The Michelson-Morley experiment proved that there is no substance like **ether** in outer space. It involved the use of a Michelson interferometer, a device that measures length to a great degree of precision by means of interference fringes. Basically, an interferometer sends two beams of light out, splits them at right angles to one another, and then brings them back to a central location with a mirror. Any very minor shift in the position of the beams will be seen as a shift in the interference fringes. Michelson and Morley wanted to use this device to determine the characteristics of the "luminiferous aether" wind that blew through outer space and affected the transmission of light, but instead they ended up disproving the existence of the ether altogether. They were also able to conclude from this experiment that the measured velocity of light is independent of the observer's reference-frame velocity.

Einstein's Theory of Relativity

Relativity is composed of special relativity and general relativity. **Special relativity** relates that those observers in inertial reference frames, in uniform motion relative to each other, cannot perform experiments to find out which is stationary. This is the principle of relativity, which says that regardless of an observer's velocity or position in the universe, all physical laws will appear constant. It was in this context that Einstein found that the speed of light in a vacuum had to be the same for all the observers despite their motion or the motion of the light source. **General relativity** is a geometrical theory that reasons that the presence of mass and energy will curve space-time, a model that combines mass and energy to form the space-time continuum, and that the curvature will affect the path of free particles. This includes the path of light. It uses differential geometry and the generalized quantity of tensors to describe gravitation without using the force of gravity. The theory postulates that all observers should be equivalent, not only those that move with uniform speed.

Lorentz Transformations and Equations

Because of the phenomena associated with Einstein's theory of relativity, measurements taken from **reference frames** traveling at high velocities may noticeably differ from those taken in a **stationary reference frame**. These differences in observation may be reconciled using Lorentz transformations. In the equations that follow, all quantities with a subscript zero represent those quantities as measured in a stationary frame. The primary conversion factor in these equations is the Lorentz factor (γ):

$$\gamma = \frac{1}{\sqrt{1 - \frac{v^2}{c^2}}}$$

The equations for length contraction and time dilation both use this factor. $L = \frac{L_0}{\gamma}$, where L is the observed length of an object in the direction of the frame's velocity. When observed from a high-velocity frame, objects will appear shorter. Also, $\Delta t = \Delta t_0 \gamma$, where Δt is elapsed time in a stationary frame as observed from a high-velocity frame. This means that from the high-velocity frame, time will seem to pass more quickly in the stationary frame.

One further equation relating high-velocity and stationary-frame measurements is velocity addition. For those velocities encountered in everyday life, an observer traveling at velocity, v, who measures an object's velocity as u', traveling in the same direction, will reasonably assume that the object's velocity in a stationary frame is $u = v + u'$. For velocities significant relative to the speed of light, c, the equation becomes $u = \frac{(v+u')}{(1+vu'/c^2)}$.

Simultaneous Events

Let us imagine a situation in which one **stationary observer** records two events that happen at the same time. If another observer moving at a **constant velocity** also records these two events, it is unlikely that the moving observer will record these two events as having happened simultaneously. In other words, two observers who are in relative motion will not generally agree as to whether two events are simultaneous. Neither observer is objectively right or wrong. We may therefore conclude that simultaneity is not an absolute concept but a relative one. It depends on the state of motion of the observer. Of course, since in most cases the speed of the observers will be a great deal less than the speed of light, this lack of simultaneity will be too small to notice.

Nuclear Binding Energy

The **nuclear binding energy** of an atom is the energy that would be required to **disassemble** the nucleus into its constituent nucleons. They are held together by a strong nuclear force in the nucleus. Nuclear binding energy may be calculated by determining the difference in mass between the nucleus and the sum of the masses of its constituent particles. This mass, m, is converted to energy by the equation $E = mc^2$, where c is the speed of light in a vacuum.

Nuclei may be transformed by a **rearrangement of nucleons**. These nuclear transformations may occur by many different means, including radioactive decay, nuclear fusion, and nuclear fission. In nuclear fusion, two light nuclei merge into a single nucleus that is heavier. In nuclear fission, a single large nucleus divides into two or more smaller nuclei. In either case, if the mass of the nuclei before transformation is greater than the mass after transformation, then it is an exothermic process. Conversely, if the mass is greater after transformation, the process is endothermic. Nickel and iron have the most stable nuclei of any elements, having the largest binding energies.

Blackbody Radiation

A **black body** is an ideal black substance that will absorb all radiation and reflect none of the radiation energy that falls on it. Powdered carbon is the closest real approximation of a black body. Because a black body is a perfect absorber of radiation, it is also a perfect emitter of radiation. The distribution of radiant energy in a black body according to wavelength will depend on the absolute temperature of the body: the higher the temperature, the lower the wavelength at which energy is distributed as a maximum. Blackbody radiation was used by Max Planck to develop the quantum theory of mechanics in 1901.

Elementary Particles

The two basic types of **elementary particles** are bosons, which have integer spin, and fermions, which have half-integer spin. There are a few different types of bosons, but the type most commonly encountered are photons, which make up the full spectrum of light.

There are only two types of fermions: leptons and quarks. Both leptons and quarks have antiparticles as well, with opposite charge.

- **Leptons** may be one of three different flavors: muon, tauon, or electron. Each of these is accompanied by a small electrically neutral particle called a neutrino, also differentiated by the same three flavors. Each lepton has a charge of -1, while its antiparticle has a charge of $+1$. The electron's antiparticle is the positron.
- **Quarks** are most commonly encountered as the constituent particles of nucleons. There are six different flavors of quark; the two most common are *up*, having a charge of $+\frac{2}{3}$, and *down*, having a charge of $-\frac{1}{3}$. Neutrons consist of one up quark and two down quarks, while protons have two up quarks and one down quark.

Historical Models of the Atom

Atomic Models and Theories

There have been many theories regarding the **structure** of atoms and their particles. Part of the challenge in developing an understanding of matter is that atoms and their particles are too small to be seen. It is believed that the first conceptualization of the atom was developed by **Democritus** in 400 B.C. Some of the more notable models are the solid sphere or billiard ball model postulated by **John Dalton**, the plum pudding or raisin bun model by **J.J. Thomson**, the planetary or nuclear model by **Ernest Rutherford**, the Bohr or orbit model by **Niels Bohr**, and the electron cloud or quantum mechanical model by **Louis de Broglie** and **Erwin Schrödinger**. Rutherford directed the alpha scattering experiment that discounted the plum pudding model. The shortcoming of the Bohr model was the belief that electrons orbited in fixed rather than changing elliptical orbits.

Review Video: Atomic Models
Visit mometrix.com/academy and enter code: 434851

Review Video: John Dalton
Visit mometrix.com/academy and enter code: 565627

Thomson "Plum Pudding" Model

J.J. Thomson, the discoverer of the electron, suggested that the arrangement of protons and electrons within an atom could be approximated by dried fruit in a **plum pudding**. Thomson, whose discovery of the electron preceded that of the proton or neutron, hypothesized that an atom's electrons, the dried plums, were **positioned uniformly** inside the atom within a cloud of positive charge, the pudding. This model was later disproved.

Rutherford Scattering

Ernest Rutherford concluded from the work of Geiger and Marsden that the majority of the atom's mass was concentrated in a minute, positively charged region, the **nucleus**, which was surrounded by **electrons**. When a positive alpha particle approached close enough to the nucleus, it was strongly repelled, enough so that it had the ability to rebound at high angles. The small nucleus size explained the small number of alpha particles that were repelled in this fashion. The scattering led to development of the **planetary model of the atom**, which was further developed by Niels Bohr into what is now known as the Bohr model.

Bohr Model

Niels Bohr postulated that the electrons orbiting the nucleus must occupy **discrete orbits**. These discrete orbits also corresponded to discrete levels of energy and angular momentum. Consequently, the only way that electrons could move between orbits was by making nearly instantaneous jumps between them. These jumps, known as **quantum leaps**, are associated with the absorption or emission of a quantum of energy, known as a

photon. If the electron is jumping to a higher energy state, a photon must be absorbed. Similarly, if the electron is dropping to a lower energy state, a photon must be emitted.

> **Review Video: Structure of Atoms**
> Visit mometrix.com/academy and enter code: 905932

Atomic and Subatomic Structure

Basic Organization of Matter

An **element** is the most basic type of matter. It has unique properties and cannot be broken down into other elements. The smallest unit of an element is the **atom**. Most elements are found somewhere in nature in single-atom form, but a few elements only exist naturally in pairs. These are called diatomic elements, and some of the most common of these are hydrogen, nitrogen, and oxygen. A chemical combination of two or more types of elements is called a compound. **Compounds** often have properties that are very different from those of their constituent elements. The smallest independent unit of an element or compound of two or more atoms is known as a **molecule**. Elements and compounds are represented by chemical symbols, one or two letters, most often the first in the element name. More than one atom of the same element in a compound is represented with a subscript number designating how many atoms of that element are present. Water, for instance, contains two hydrogens and one oxygen. Thus, the chemical formula is H_2O. Methane contains one carbon and four hydrogens, so its formula is CH_4.

> **Review Video: Molecules**
> Visit mometrix.com/academy and enter code: 349910

Protons, Neutrons, and Electrons

The three major subatomic particles are the proton, neutron, and electron. The **proton**, which is located in the nucleus, has a relative charge of +1. The **neutron**, which is located in the nucleus, has a relative charge of 0. The **electron**, which is located outside the nucleus, has a relative charge of –1. The proton and neutron, which are essentially the same mass, are much more massive than the electron and make up the mass of the atom. The electron's mass is insignificant compared to the mass of the proton and neutron.

Orbits and Orbitals

An orbit is a definite path, but an orbital is a region in space. The Bohr model described electrons as orbiting or following a definite path in space around the nucleus of an atom. But, according to **Heisenberg's uncertainty principle**, it is impossible to determine the location and the momentum of an electron simultaneously. Therefore, it is impossible to draw a definite path or orbit of an electron. An **orbital**, as described by the quantum-mechanical model or the electron-cloud model, is a region in space that is drawn in such a way as to indicate the probability of finding an electron at a specific location. The distance an orbital is located from the nucleus corresponds to the principal quantum number. The orbital shape corresponds to the subshell or azimuthal quantum number. The orbital orientation corresponds to the magnetic quantum number.

Quantum Numbers

The **principal quantum number** (n) describes an electron's shell or energy level and actually describes the size of the orbital. Electrons farther from the nucleus are at higher energy levels. The **subshell** or azimuthal quantum number (l) describes the electron's sublevel or subshell (s, p, d, or f) and specifies the shape of the orbital. Typical shapes include spherical, dumbbell, and clover leaf. The **magnetic quantum number** (m_l) describes the orientation of the orbital in space. The spin or magnetic moment quantum number (m_s) describes the direction of the spin of the electron in the orbital.

Atomic Number and Mass Number

The **atomic number** of an element is the number of protons in the nucleus of an atom of that element. This is the number that identifies the type of an atom. For example, all oxygen atoms have eight protons, and all carbon atoms have six protons. Each element is identified by its specific atomic number.

The **mass number** is the number of protons and neutrons in the nucleus of an atom. Although the atomic number is the same for all atoms of a specific element, the mass number can vary due to the varying numbers of neutrons in various isotopes of the atom.

Isotopes

Isotopes are atoms of the same element that vary in their number of neutrons. Isotopes of the same element have the same number of protons and thus the same atomic number. Because isotopes vary in the number of neutrons, they are identified by their mass numbers. For example, two naturally occurring carbon isotopes are carbon-12 and carbon-13, which have mass numbers 12 and 13, respectively. The symbols $^{12}_{6}C$ and $^{13}_{6}C$ also represent the carbon isotopes. The general form of the symbol is $^{M}_{A}X$, where X is the element symbol, M is the mass number, and A is the atomic number.

Average Atomic Mass

The **average atomic mass** is the weighted average of the masses of all the naturally occurring isotopes of an atom in comparison to the carbon-12 isotope. The unit for average atomic mass is the atomic mass unit (u). Atomic masses of isotopes are measured using a mass spectrometer by bombarding a gaseous sample of the isotope and measuring its relative deflections. Atomic masses can be calculated if the percent abundances and the atomic masses of the naturally occurring isotopes are known.

Cathode Ray Tube (CRT)

Electrons were discovered by Joseph John Thomson through scientific work with cathode ray tubes (CRTs). **Cathode rays** had been studied for many years, but it was Thomson who showed that cathode rays were **negatively charged particles**. Although Thomson could not determine an electron's charge or mass, he was able to determine the ratio of the charge to the mass. Thomson discovered that this ratio was constant regardless of the gas in the CRT. He was able to show that the cathode rays were actually streams of negatively charged particles by deflecting them with a positively charged plate.

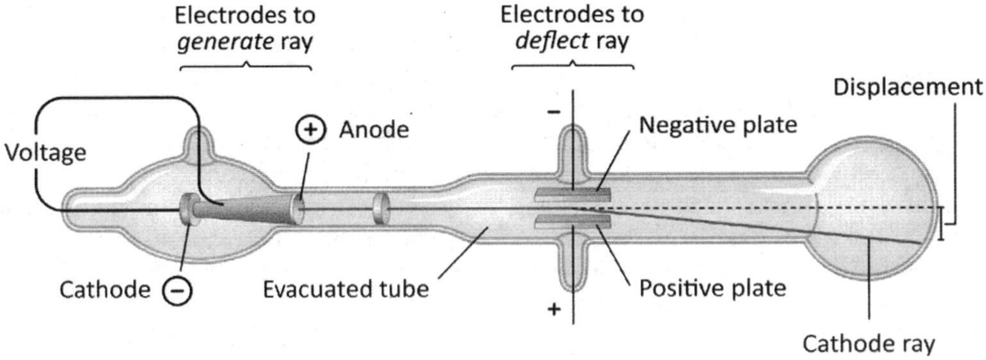

Gold Foil Experiment

After Thomson determined the ratio of the charge to the mass of an electron from studying cathode rays, he proposed the plum pudding model, in which he compared electrons to the raisins embedded in plum pudding. This model of the atom was disproved by the gold foil experiment. The gold foil experiment led to the discovery of the nucleus of an atom. Scientists at Rutherford's laboratory bombarded a thin gold foil with high-speed helium ions. Much to their surprise, some of the ions were reflected by the foil. The scientists concluded that the atom has a **hard central core**, which we now know to be the **nucleus**.

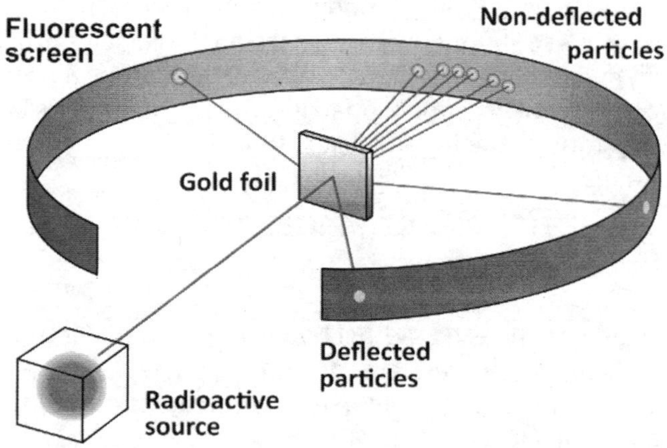

Problems that Rutherford's Model Had with Spectral Lines

Rutherford's model allowed for the electrons of an atom to be in an **infinite number of orbits** based on Newton's laws of motion. Rutherford believed that electrons could orbit the nucleus at any distance from the nucleus and that electrons could change velocity and direction at any moment. But, according to Rutherford's model, the electrons would lose energy and spiral into the nucleus. Unfortunately, if this was in fact true, then every atom would be **unstable**. Rutherford's model also does not correspond to the spectral lines emitted from gases at low pressure. The **spectral lines** are discrete bands of light at specific energy levels. These spectral lines indicate that electrons must be at specific distances from the nucleus. If electrons could be located at any distance from the nucleus, then these gases should emit continuous spectra instead of spectral lines.

Pure Substances and Mixtures

Pure Substances

Pure substances are substances that cannot be further broken down into simpler components or pieces and still retain their characteristics. Pure substances are categorized as either **elements** or **compounds.** Elements consist of only one type of atom may be monatomic, diatomic, or polyatomic. For example, helium (He) and copper (Cu) are monatomic elements, and hydrogen (H_2) and oxygen (O_2) are diatomic elements. Phosphorus (P_4) and sulfur (S_8) are polyatomic elements. Compounds consist of molecules of more than one type of atom. For example, pure water (H_2O) is made up of molecules consisting of two atoms of hydrogen bonded to one atom of oxygen, and glucose ($C_6H_{12}O_6$) is made up of molecules of six carbon atoms and twelve hydrogen atoms bonded together with six oxygen atoms.

Mixtures

Mixtures can be classified as either homogeneous or heterogeneous. The molecules of a **homogeneous mixture** are distributed uniformly throughout the mixture, whereas the molecules of a **heterogeneous mixture** are not. Air is an example of a homogeneous mixture, and a pile of sand and rock is an example of a heterogeneous mixture. Solutions are homogeneous mixtures consisting of a **solute** (the substance that is dissolved) and a **solvent** (the substance doing the dissolving).

Suspensions

Suspensions are heterogeneous mixtures in which the particle size of the substance **suspended** is too large to be kept in suspension by Brownian motion. Once left undisturbed, suspensions will settle out to form layers. An example of a suspension is sand stirred into water. Left undisturbed, the sand will fall out of suspension and the water will form a layer on top of the sand.

MIXTURES WITH COMPOUNDS

Mixtures are similar to compounds in that they are produced when two or more substances are combined. However, there are some key differences as well. Compounds require a chemical combination of the constituent particles, while mixtures are simply the interspersion of particles. Unlike compounds, mixtures may be **separated** without a chemical change. A mixture retains the chemical properties of its constitutent particles, while a compound acquires a new set of properties. Given compounds can exist only in specific ratios, while mixtures may be any ratio of the involved substances.

Basics of Radioactivity

RADIOACTIVITY

Radioisotopes: Also known as radionuclides or radioactive isotopes, radioisotopes are atoms that have an unstable nucleus. This is a nucleus that has excess energy and the potential to undergo radioactive decay, which most often results in the emission of alpha, beta, or gamma radiation. Many radionuclides occur naturally but others have only been produced artificially.

Radioactive decay: This occurs when an unstable atomic nucleus spontaneously loses energy by emitting ionizing particles and radiation. Decay is a form of energy transfer, as the energy lost by the nucleus is given to the particles or radiation emitted. It also results in products that are different from the initial atoms. Before decay there is one type of atom, called the **parent nuclide**. After decay there are one or more different products, called the **daughter nuclide(s)**.

Radioactivity: This refers to particles or energy that are emitted from nuclei as a result of nuclear instability.

Review Video: Radioactivity
Visit mometrix.com/academy and enter code: 537142

Radiation is the term for energy emitted or transmitted as waves or particles. Radiation is classified as either ionizing (able to detach an electron from an atom) or non-ionizing. Nuclear weapons, nuclear reactors, and radioactive substances are all examples of things that involve ionizing radiation. Acoustic radiation and electromagnetic radiation (with wavelength greater than 125 nm) are types of non-ionizing radiation.

Radioactive half-life is the time it takes for half of the radioactive nuclei in a sample to undergo radioactive decay. Radioactive decay rates are usually expressed in terms of half-lives. The different types of radioactivity lead to different decay paths, which transmute the nuclei into other chemical elements. **Decay products** (or daughter nuclides) make radioactive dating possible. **Decay chains** are a series of decays that result in different products. For example, uranium-238 is often found in granite. Its decay chain includes 14 daughter products. It eventually becomes a stable isotope of lead, which is why lead is often found with deposits of uranium ore. Its first half-life is equivalent to the approximate age of the earth, about 4.5 billion years. One of its products is radon, a radioactive gas.

Isotopes that have not been observed to decay are **stable**, or non-radioactive, isotopes. It is not known whether some stable isotopes may have such long decay times that observing decay is not possible. Currently, 80 elements have one or more stable isotopes. There are 256 known stable isotopes in total. Carbon, for example, has three isotopes. Two (carbon-12 and carbon-13) are stable and one (carbon-14) is radioactive.

Ionizing radiation comes in three types: alpha (α), beta (β), and gamma (γ). Alpha particles are positive, beta particles are negative, and gamma rays are neutral. **Alpha particles** are larger than beta particles and can cause severe damage if a source of alpha particles is ingested. Because of their large mass, however, they can be easily stopped. Even paper can protect against this type of radiation. **Beta particles** can be beta-minus or beta-plus. Beta-minus particles contain an energetic electron, while beta-plus particles are emitted by positrons. Beta particles can be stopped with a thin sheet of metal. **Gamma rays** are a type of high energy electromagnetic radiation. Gamma radiation is one of the ways a decaying nucleus emits excess energy after it has emitted either alpha or beta radiation. Gamma rays can cause serious damage when absorbed by living tissue, and it takes a lot of shielding (typically lead) to stop them. Alpha, beta, and gamma radiation can also have positive applications.

Nuclear fission and nuclear fusion are similar in that they occur in the nucleus of an atom, can release great amounts of energy, and result in the formation of different elements (nuclear transmutation). They are different in that **nuclear fission** is the splitting of a nucleus into smaller particles, and **nuclear fusion** is the joining of nuclei to form a heavier nucleus. It requires immense pressures and temperatures, but when fusion occurs, energy can either be absorbed or released, depending on the resultant nucleus. Fusion occurs naturally in stars, and is thought to be the process responsible for the generation of all naturally occurring elements (stellar nucleosynthesis).

Radioactive waste is a waste product that is considered dangerous because of either low levels or high levels of radioactivity. Radioactive waste could include discarded clothing that was used as protection against radiation, or decay products of substances used to create electricity through nuclear fission. Small amounts of radioactive material can be ingested as a method of tracing how the body distributes certain elements. Other radioactive materials are used as light sources because they glow when heated. Uncontrolled radiation or even small amounts of radioactive material can cause sickness and cancer in humans. **Gamma wave radiation** is fast-moving radiation that can cause cancer and damage genetic information by crashing into DNA molecules or other cells. Low-level radiation also occurs naturally. When related to everyday occurrences, radiation is measured in millirems per hour (mrem/hr). Humans can be exposed to radiation from stone used to build houses, cosmic rays from space, x-rays and other medical devices, and nuclear energy products.

Nuclear Chemistry and Radioactivity

Alpha Particles

Alpha particles are the products of **alpha decay**. They are identical to helium nuclei. An alpha particle consists of two protons and two neutrons. Because they have two protons but zero electrons, alpha particles have a net +2 charge. They are represented by the Greek letter alpha as α, α^{2+}, or ${}^{4}_{2}\alpha^{2+}$. Because they are identical to helium nuclei, they may also be written as He^{2+}, ${}^{4}_{2}He$, or ${}^{4}_{2}He^{2+}$. Because alpha particles have a strong charge and travel slowly, they interact significantly with matter that they pass through and may therefore be stopped by a sheet of paper or a few inches of air. Alpha particles cannot penetrate the skin.

Beta Particles

Beta particles are the products of **beta decay**. Beta particles may be high-speed electrons or high-speed positrons. These two forms of beta decay are designated by the Greek letter beta as β^- and β^+ or ${}^{0}_{-1}e$ and ${}^{0}_{+1}e$, respectively. Negative beta particles are created during radioactive decay when a neutron changes into a proton and an electron. Positive beta particles are created when a proton changes into a neutron and a positron. Beta particles have a greater penetrating ability than alpha particles. Beta particles can be stopped by thin plywood or metal or several feet of air.

Gamma Radiation

Gamma radiation (represented by the Greek letter gamma γ) is released during **gamma decay**. Often, atoms that have just undergone alpha or beta decay then undergo gamma decay. An atom produced during alpha or beta decay may still be in an excited state. The atom then releases this energy in a burst of gamma rays as high-energy photons. Gamma radiation is part of the electromagnetic spectrum and consists of electromagnetic waves that travel at the speed of light with frequencies higher than x-rays. Because gamma radiation has no charge, it easily penetrates solid substances. Gamma decay is useful in medical procedures, including cancer treatment.

Energy, Frequency, and Wavelength

The properties of energy, frequency, and wavelength can be used to describe electromagnetic waves. These properties also have a mathematical relationship with each other. Energy (E) is directly related to frequency (f) as given by $E = hf$, where h represents Planck's constant (6.626×10^{-34} J-s). As the frequency increases, the energy increases. For example, gamma rays, which have the highest frequency of the electromagnetic spectrum, also have the highest energy. The speed (v) of the wave is equal to the product of wavelength (λ) and frequency (f). Because the speed of light (c) is constant in a vacuum at 3.00×10^8 m/s, wavelength and frequency are inversely related. As wavelength decreases, frequency increases. For example, gamma rays have the shortest wavelength of the electromagnetic spectrum and the highest frequency.

Radioactive Decay and Half-Life

Radioactivity or **radioactive decay** occurs when an unstable atom splits to form a new atom and emits some type of radiation. An atom's nucleus contains protons and neutrons. The protons have positive charges and repel each other, but with the help of neutrons the repulsive force between protons is overcome by the strong nuclear force, which holds the nucleus together. With elements of greater atomic number, the repulsive force is increasingly a match for the strong force. All atoms with atomic number greater than 83 are unstable. The three basic types of **radioactive decay** are alpha decay, beta decay, and gamma decay. The **half-life** of an isotope is the length of time it takes for one-half of the atoms of a radioactive substance to decay into a new type of atom.

Typical Fission Reaction

A typical fission reaction is the fission of uranium-235 from neutron bombardment:

$$^{235}_{92}\text{U} + ^{1}_{0}\text{n} \rightarrow ^{139}_{56}\text{Ba} + ^{94}_{36}\text{Kr} + 3[^{1}_{0}\text{n}]$$

The uranium-235 atom $\left(^{235}_{92}\text{U}\right)$ is bombarded by a neutron ($^{1}_{0}\text{n}$). This neutron is absorbed, forcing the uranium-235 atom into an excited, unstable state. This excited, unstable uranium-235 atom splits into smaller more stable pieces, which consist of a barium-139 atom ($^{139}_{56}\text{Ba}$), a krypton-94 atom ($^{94}_{36}\text{Kr}$), and three neutrons ($^{1}_{0}\text{n}$). These neutrons in turn may bombard other uranium-235 atoms causing the nuclear fission to continue.

Review Video: Reading Nuclear Equations
Visit mometrix.com/academy and enter code: 688890

Nuclear Fusion

Nuclear fusion is the process in which the nuclei of atoms that are light and unstable will unite or fuse to form a heavier, more stable atom. Fusion requires extremely high temperatures and often pressures that force the atoms into a plasma state. In this high-energy state, the atoms collide frequently and are able to fuse together. In this process, some mass is lost and released as large quantities of energy. The Sun's heat and light are produced by a fusion reaction in the Sun's core, in which four hydrogen atoms fuse into a helium nucleus.

Review Video: Nuclear Fusion
Visit mometrix.com/academy and enter code: 381782

Alpha Emission

In alpha emission, the parent nuclide splits into **two parts** consisting of the daughter nuclide and an alpha particle. The alpha particle is identical to a helium nucleus and consists of two protons and two neutrons, represented by $^{4}_{2}\text{He}$ or $^{4}_{2}\text{He}^{2+}$. The daughter nuclide has a mass number that is four less than the parent nuclide and an atomic number that is two less than the parent nuclide. An example of alpha emission is the decay of a uranium-238 atom into a thorium-234 atom and an alpha particle, as shown below:

$$^{238}_{92}\text{U} \rightarrow ^{234}_{90}\text{Th} + ^{4}_{2}\text{He}$$

Positive and Negative Beta Decay

In **positive beta decay**, also known as **positron emission**, the parent nuclide splits into two parts consisting of the daughter nuclide and a positron. The positron is represented by ${}_{+1}^{0}e$ because its mass is negligible compared to a neutron or proton, and its charge is +1. The daughter nuclide has the same mass number as the parent nuclide and an atomic number of one less than the parent nuclide. An example of positive beta decay is when a carbon-11 atom splits into a boron-11 atom and a positron, as given by the equation shown here:

In **negative beta decay**, also simply called **beta decay**, the parent nuclide splits into two parts consisting of the daughter nuclide and an electron. The electron is represented by ${}_{-1}^{0}e$ because its mass is negligible compared to a neutron or proton, and its charge is −1. An example of negative beta decay is when a carbon-14 atom splits into a nitrogen-14 atom and an electron, as given by the following equation:

$${}_{6}^{14}C \rightarrow {}_{7}^{14}N + {}_{-1}^{0}e$$

Electron Capture

In electron capture, an electron from an atom's own electron cloud impacts the atom's nucleus and causes a **decay reaction**. The parent nuclide absorbs the electron, and a proton is converted to a neutron. A neutrino is emitted from the nucleus. Gamma radiation is also emitted. The daughter nuclide has the same mass number as the parent nuclide, and the atomic number of the daughter nuclide is one lower than the atomic number of the parent nuclide. An example of electron capture is when a nitrogen-13 atom absorbs an electron and converts to a carbon-13 atom while emitting a neutrino (${}_{0}^{0}\nu$) and gamma radiation (γ), as shown by the following equation:

$${}_{7}^{13}N + {}_{-1}^{0}e \rightarrow {}_{6}^{13}C + {}_{0}^{0}\nu + \gamma$$

Transmutation

Transmutation is a type of nuclear decay in which an atom is bombarded by **high-speed particles** to cause it to convert from one type of atom to another type of atom. Ernest Rutherford was the first to accomplish this, with the transmutation of the nitrogen-14 atom into an oxygen-17 atom by bombardment with a beam of high-speed helium ions. In this transmutation, the helium-4 ion is also converted to a hydrogen-1 ion:

$${}_{7}^{14}N + {}_{2}^{4}He \rightarrow {}_{8}^{17}O + {}_{1}^{1}H$$

Neutron Radiation

Neutron radiation is a type of **transmutation** that is used to create many isotopes that do not occur naturally. In neutron radiation, an atom is bombarded by high-speed neutrons (${}_{0}^{1}n$) to cause nuclear decay. In neutron radiation, the daughter nuclide has a mass number one higher than the parent nuclide, but the atomic number remains the same. The daughter is an atom of the same element as the parent nuclide, but it has one more neutron, which makes it a different isotope of that element. An example of neutron radiation is when a cobalt-59 atom is bombarded by a high-speed neutron and converts to a cobalt-60 atom, as shown in the following equation:

$${}_{27}^{59}Co + {}_{0}^{1}n \rightarrow {}_{27}^{60}Co$$

Balancing a Nuclear Reaction

When balancing a nuclear reaction, two key principles must be applied. First, the **mass number must be conserved**. Second, the **atomic number must be conserved.** To determine the products formed, the mass numbers and atomic numbers of the particles emitted or absorbed must be known. Alpha decay emits alpha particles (${}_{2}^{4}He$). Beta decay emits electrons (${}_{-1}^{0}e$). Positron decay emits positrons (${}_{+1}^{0}e$). Neutron radiation absorbs neutrons (${}_{0}^{1}n$). In alpha decay, the mass number decreases by four, and the atomic number decreases by two. In negative beta decay, the mass number stays the same, and the atomic number increases by one. In positive beta decay, the mass number stays the same, and the atomic number decreases by one. In neutron radiation, the mass number increases by one, and the atomic number stays the same.

Complete or Balance the Following Nuclear Reactions:

The key principles to completing or balancing nuclear reactions are that the mass number is conserved and the atomic number is conserved.

$$^{230}_{90}\text{Th} \leftrightarrow {}^{4}_{2}\text{He} + \_\_\_$$

In this reaction, thorium-230 under goes alpha decay and emits an alpha particle with a mass number of 4 and an atomic number of 2. Balancing the atomic numbers (90 − 2) yields an atomic number of 88, which corresponds to radium. Balancing the mass numbers (230 − 4) yields 226. Therefore, the missing product is $^{226}_{88}\text{Ra}$.

$$^{40}_{19}\text{K} \leftrightarrow {}^{0}_{-1}\text{e} + \_\_\_$$

In this reaction, potassium-40 undergoes beta decay and emits an electron with an assigned mass number of 0 and an assigned atomic number of −1. Balancing the atomic numbers $(19 - (-1))$ yields an atomic number of 20, which indicates calcium. Balancing the mass numbers (40 − 0) yields a mass number of 40. Therefore, the missing product is $^{40}_{20}\text{Ca}$.

Electronic Absorption and Emission Spectra

Electronic Energy Transition (Emission/Absorption of Energy) in Atoms

An electron must gain or absorb energy to **transition** to a higher or excited state, and the electron will emit that energy when it transitions back to the ground state. The **ground state** of an electron is the electron's lowest state of energy or when the electron is in the energy level that it normally occupies. An electron can gain energy if it absorbs a photon or collides with another particle. When an electron occupies an energy level higher that its normal level or ground state, it is in an excited state. The excited state is an unstable state, and the electron will return to the ground state as quickly as possible.

Absorption Spectroscopy and Emission Spectroscopy

When an electron makes a **quantum leap** from one electron shell to another, a **photon** is either **absorbed** or **emitted**. Because the energy levels of these shells are discrete, the energy of an absorbed or emitted photon is unique to a particular pair of shells. Thus, any element can be positively identified by the energy levels of the photons it emits.

Absorption Spectroscopy

Spectroscopy is most commonly used to determine the **composition of unknown compounds**. In absorption spectroscopy, a compound is bombarded with a full spectrum of photons, causing the compound to absorb those photons corresponding to its constituent elements' electron shell energy levels. By capturing and measuring the wavelengths of the photons **not absorbed**, it can be determined which wavelengths, and thus which energy levels, were absorbed, giving the identity of the elements contained in the compound. The resulting visible spectrum consists of color from red to violet with black bands at the wavelength of the absorbed photons.

Emission Spectroscopy

Emission spectroscopy works in a similar fashion. The compound's electrons are excited by an application of energy and allowed to decay back down to lower energy levels. This decay is necessarily accompanied by an emission of photons, whose wavelengths are measured to determine the identity of the elements. The resulting visible spectrum consists of colored bands at the wavelengths of the emitted photons.

Chapter Quiz

Ready to see how well you retained what you just read? Scan the QR code to go directly to the chapter quiz interface for this study guide. If you're using a computer, simply visit the online resources page at **mometrix.com/resources719/ftcephysics** and click the Chapter Quizzes link.

FTCE Practice Test

Want to take this practice test in an online interactive format?
Check out the online resources page, which includes interactive practice questions and much more: **mometrix.com/resources719/ftcephysics**

1. Which of the following measurements has the most significant digits?

a. 0.2990
b. 2.9900
c. 2.997
d. 0.00209

2. The masses of four different objects, taken with different scales, were 23.04 g, 7.12 g, 0.0088 g, and 5.423 g. What is the total mass of all four objects to the proper number of decimal places?

a. 35.59180 g
b. 35.5918 g
c. 35.60 g
d. 35.59 g

3. Which of the following is a vector quantity?

a. Distance
b. Speed
c. Velocity
d. Time

4. A person walks 4 meters in a single direction. He then changes directions and walks an additional 9 meters. What is the total magnitude of the displacement of the person?

a. It is 13 meters.
b. It is always larger than 9 meters but less than 13 meters.
c. It is less than 13 meters and as small as 5 meters.
d. It is less than 5 meters.

5. Consider the two vectors below:

Vector A: 

Vector B: 

Which vector best represents the vector obtained by subtracting *A* from *B* $(\vec{B} - \vec{A})$?

a.

b.

c.

d.

6. A perfectly circular track has a circumference of 400 meters. A runner goes around the track in 100 seconds instead of her usual time of 80 seconds because a leg cramp causes her to stop running for 20 seconds. What is her average speed?

a. 0 m/s
b. 5 m/s
c. 4 m/s
d. 20 m/s

7. An automobile increased its speed uniformly from 20 m/s to 30 m/s at a rate of 5 m/s². During this time, it traveled 50 meters. How long did it take the automobile to make this change?

a. 5 seconds
b. 2 seconds
c. 10 seconds
d. 20 seconds

8. You throw a baseball straight up near the surface of Earth and it falls back to the ground. Which statement is true about the acceleration of the baseball at the top of its path? (Ignore air resistance.)

a. The acceleration is zero.
b. The acceleration changes sign.
c. The acceleration is $-9.8\ \text{m/s}^2$.
d. The acceleration continues to increase.

9. A space station is revolving in a circular orbit around Earth. Consider the following three statements:

I. The center of mass of the space station is necessarily located at its geometric center.
II. The center of mass is moving at a constant velocity.
III. The center of mass of the space station is moving at a constant speed.

Which of the following statements is true?

a. I is true.
b. II is true.
c. III is true.
d. I, II, and III are not true.

10. Which of the following demonstrations best illustrates Newton's first law?

a. Giving a small push to a billiard ball that was at rest on a smooth, level table and letting it roll on the table
b. Dragging a box on a table at a constant speed by exerting just enough force to overcome the force of friction
c. Trying without success to move a heavy bureau or filing cabinet on the floor
d. Running a current through two parallel wires

11. Consider the following statements about Newton's law:

I. A newton is a fundamental unit.
II. Mass and acceleration are inversely related when the force is constant.
III. Newton's first law can be derived from Newton's second law.
IV. Newton's second law can be derived from the universal law of gravity.

Which of the statements are true?

a. I, II, and III.
b. II and III only.
c. III only.
d. None of them

12. A box with a weight of 10 newtons is resting on a table, which is resting on the ground. In the context of Newton's third law, if we consider the force of the box on the table to be the action force, which of the following statements is true?

a. The force of the table on the box is the reaction force.
b. The force of the table on the ground is the reaction force.
c. The force of the ground on the table is the reaction force.
d. There is no reaction force because the system is in equilibrium.

13. A lead sphere 10 centimeters in diameter is attached to a 10-meter wire and suspended from a beam in a large warehouse. A lead sphere 1 meter in diameter is hung next to the smaller sphere, almost touching. Ignoring friction, which statement is true?

a. The small sphere will move slightly toward the big sphere, but the big sphere will not move.
b. The big sphere will move slightly toward the small sphere, but the small sphere will not move.
c. Neither sphere will move.
d. Both spheres will move slightly toward each other.

14. In an amusement park ride, you stand on the floor of a cylindrical ring with your back touching the wall. The ring begins to rotate, slowly at first, but then faster and faster. When the ring is rotating fast enough, the floor is removed. You do not slide down but remain pressed against the wall of the ring. Which is the best explanation for why you don't fall down?

a. The centripetal force pushes you towards the wall.
b. The centripetal force changes the direction of your motion.
c. The force of friction between the wall and your body is greater than the force of gravity.
d. The rotating ring creates a weightless environment.

15. Bobsled tracks are flat when they are going straight, but when there is a turn, the track is angled (banked) to create a centripetal force. Assuming no friction, the banking angle is θ, the radius of curvature is r, and the maximum speed the bobsled can have without moving off the track is v. If the radius of curvature is doubled and the banking angle remains the same, which of the following statements is true?

a. The maximum speed is $2v$.
b. The maximum speed is $4v$.
c. The maximum speed is $1.4v$.
d. The maximum speed depends on the banking angle.

16. Two spring scales having negligible mass are connected together and used to weigh a 10 kg object, as shown below.

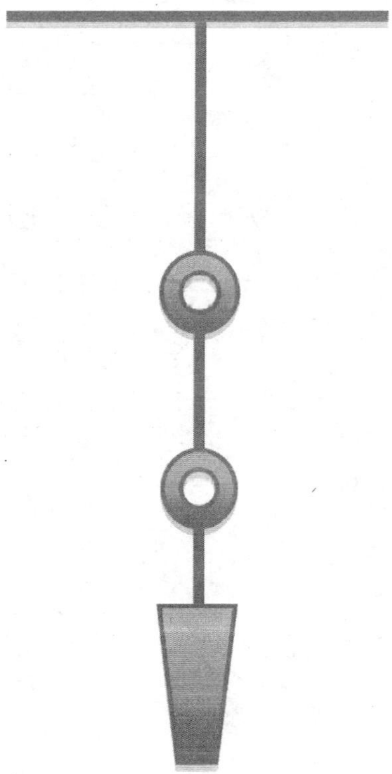

What will be the reading on the scales?

a. Both scales will read 10 pounds.
b. Each scale will read 49 newtons.
c. The sum of the two readings will be 196 newtons.
d. The bottom scale will read 98 newtons and the top scale will read 0 newtons.

17. A 10-kg plastic block is at rest on a flat wooden surface. The coefficient of static friction between wood and plastic is 0.6, and the coefficient of kinetic friction is 0.5. How much horizontal force is needed to start the plastic box moving?

a. 5 N
b. 49 N
c. 59 N
d. 98 N

18. The diagram below shows a force *F* pulling a box up a ramp against the force of friction and the force of gravity. Which of the following diagrams correctly includes vectors representing the normal force, the force of gravity and the force of friction?

a. 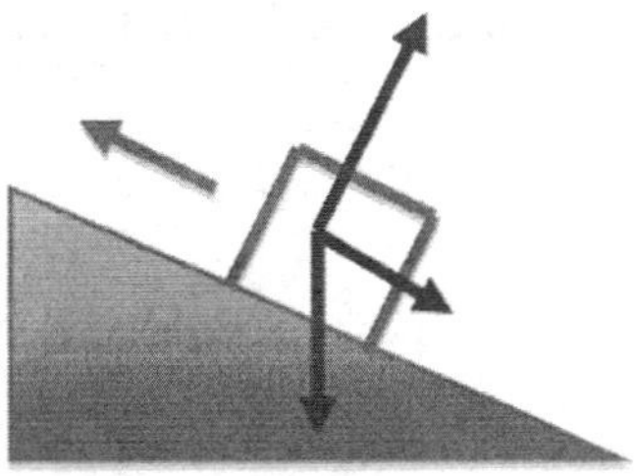

b. 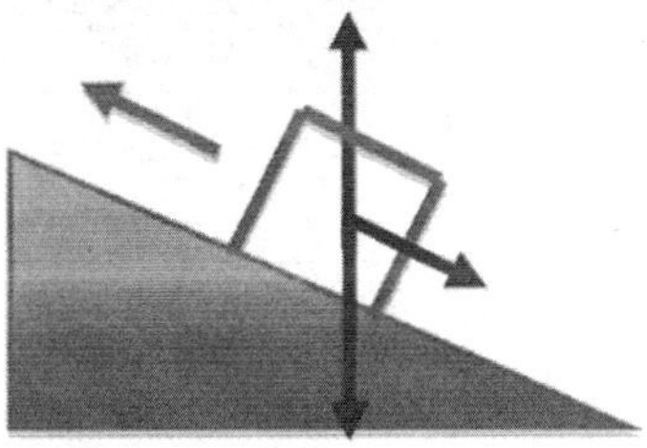

c. 

d. 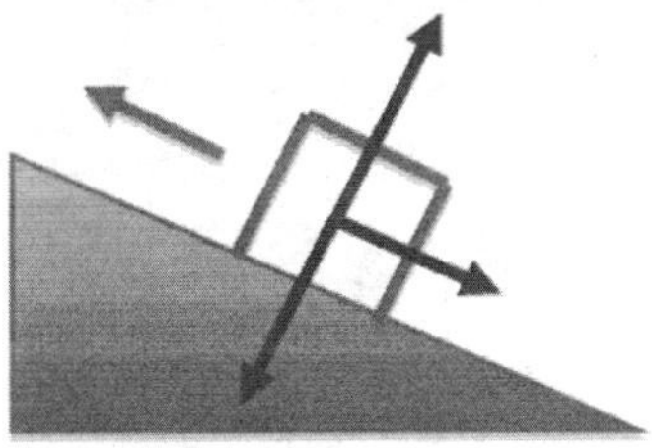

19. The ideal mechanical advantage (IMA) of a pulley system indicates how much force is required to lift a mass. A fixed pulley has an IMA of 1 because all it only changes the direction of the force. A floating pulley has an IMA of 2. The total IMA is the product of the individual pulleys' IMAs. What is the ideal mechanical advantage of the pulley system below?

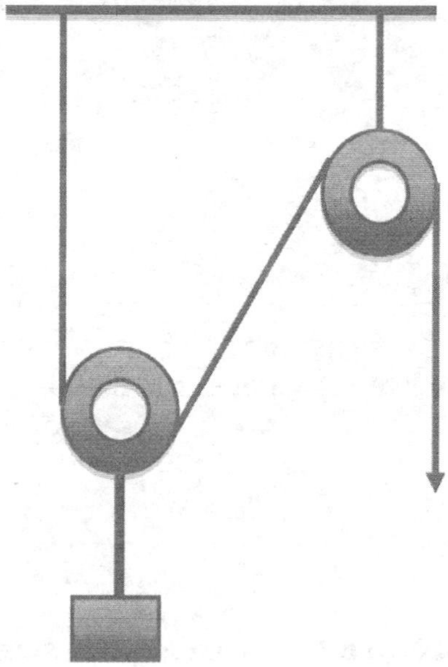

a. 1
b. 2
c. 3
d. 4

20. The pulley in the device below has no mass and is frictionless. The larger mass is 30 kg, and the smaller mass is 20 kg. What is the acceleration of the masses?

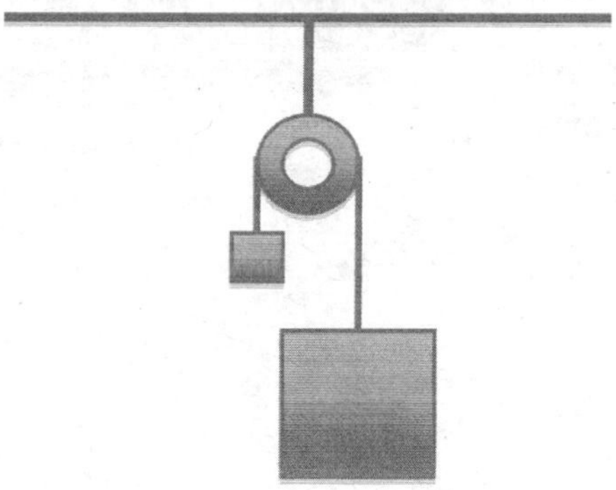

a. 0.5 m/s^2
b. 2.0 m/s^2
c. 9.8 m/s^2
d. 98 m/s^2

21. A force of 25.0 N pulls three blocks connected by a string on a frictionless surface. What is the tension in the rope between the 4.0-kg block and the 2.0-kg block?

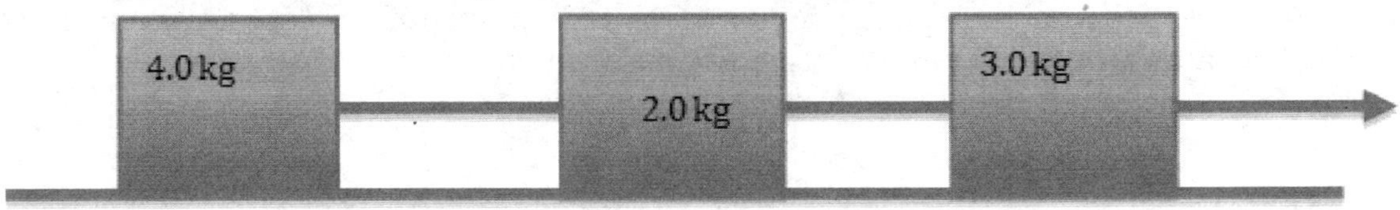

a. 0 N
b. 11.1 N
c. 16.7 N
d. 25 N

22. A piece of art with a mass of 200 kg is suspended from two nails so that the angle the hanging wires make is 40° with the horizontal. What is the tension in the hanging wires? (Note: $\sin 40° = 0.6428$ and $\cos 40° = 0.7660$).

a. 1,279 N
b. 1,525 N
c. 1,960 N
d. 3,049 N

23. Two unequal masses are balanced on a fulcrum using a massless bar, as shown below. If both masses are shifted towards the fulcrum so that their distances from the fulcrum are one-half the original distance, what happens to the masses?

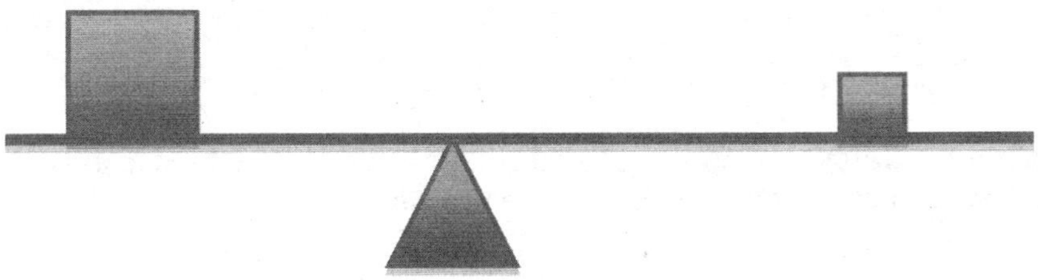

a. The heavier mass will tilt downward.
b. The masses will remain balanced.
c. Cannot be determined from the information given.
d. The lighter mass will tilt downward.

24. Which of the forces depicted below produces a counter-clockwise torque around the pivot point?

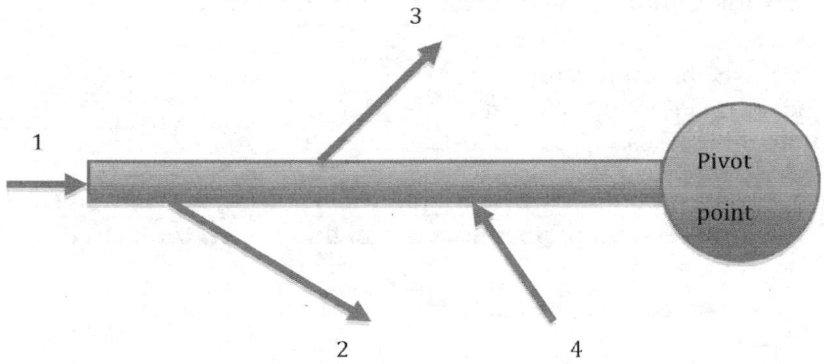

a. 1
b. 2
c. 3
d. 4

25. You blow up a rubber balloon and hold the opening tight with your fingers. You then release your fingers, causing air to blow out of the balloon. This pushes the balloon forward, causing the balloon to shoot across the room. Which of Newton's laws best explains the cause of this motion?

a. Newton's First Law
b. Newton's Second Law
c. Newton's Third Law
d. Newton's Fourth Law

26. Which has a greater moment of inertia about an axis through its center: a solid cylinder or a hollow cylinder? Both cylinders have the same mass and radius.

a. Solid cylinder
b. Hollow cylinder
c. Both have the same moment of inertia.
d. It depends on how quickly the cylinders are rolling.

27. Astronauts in orbit are sometimes considered to be "weightless." Consider the three propositions about *weightlessness* and determine which ones are true.

I. Weightlessness occurs in outer space because the force of gravity becomes negligible.
II. Weightlessness occurs when a ski jumper makes a jump.
III. Weightlessness occurs when you roll a baseball on the ground.

a. I only.
b. II only.
c. I and II.
d. I, II and III.

28. Two cars driving in opposite directions collide. If you ignore friction and any other outside interactions, which of the following statements is always true?

a. The total momentum is conserved.
b. The sum of the potential and kinetic energy is conserved.
c. The total velocity of the cars is conserved.
d. The total impulse is conserved.

29. Impulse is measured as the change in an object's momentum. Which statement is correct about the impulse on a ball rolling down a hill? Ignore air resistance and friction.

a. The impulse is constant.
b. The impulse only exists for a short time.
c. The units of impulse are joules per second.
d. The object's impulse increases.

30. Suppose a moving railroad car collides with an identical stationary car and the two cars latch together. Ignoring friction, and assuming no deformation on impact, which of the following statements is true?

a. The speed of the first car decreases by half.
b. The collision is elastic.
c. The speed of the first car is doubled.
d. There is no determining the final speed because the collision was inelastic.

31. A 4-kilogram bowling ball moving at 10 meters per second hits a stationary 1-kilogram bowling ball in a head-on elastic collision. What is the speed of the stationary ball after the collision?

a. 0 m/s
b. 10 m/s
c. Less than 10 m/s, but not 0 m/s
d. More than 10 m/s

32. A 75-kg ice skater moving eastward at 5 m/s collides with a 100-kg skater moving northward at 4 m/s. Anticipating the collision, they hug each other and produce an inelastic collision. What is their final speed?

a. It cannot be determined from the information given.
b. 3.1 m/s
c. 4.1 m/s
d. 2.1 m/s

33. A teacher pulls a box across the floor at a uniform speed. He pulls it with a spring scale showing that the force of kinetic friction is 2 newtons. How much total work is done in moving the box 5 meters?

a. 0 joules
b. 0.4 joules
c. 10 joules
d. 20 joules

34. Which statement best explains why the work done by a gravitational force on an object does not depend on the path the object takes?

a. Work depends on the path when there is friction. The longer the path, the more energy is required to overcome friction.
b. Gravitational fields that arise from the interaction between point masses always produce elliptical paths of motion.
c. Because gravitational force is conservative, the work it does depends only on the change in gravitational potential energy, which depends only on the initial and final heights
d. When an object falls down, the work done by gravity is positive, and when an object is thrown up, the work done by gravity is negative.

35. Which statement correctly states the work-energy theorem?

a. The change in kinetic energy of an object is equal to the work done by the object.
b. The change in kinetic energy of an object is equal to the work done on an object.
c. The change in potential energy of an object is equal to the work done by the object.
d. The change in potential energy of an object is equal to the work done on an object.

36. An athlete's foot is in contact with a kicked football for 100 milliseconds and exerts a force on the football over a distance of 20 centimeters. The force starts at 0 N and increases linearly to 2,000 N for 50 milliseconds through a distance of 10 centimeters and then decreases linearly for 50 milliseconds through a distance of 10 centimeters. What is the average power of the athlete's foot while it is in contact with the ball?

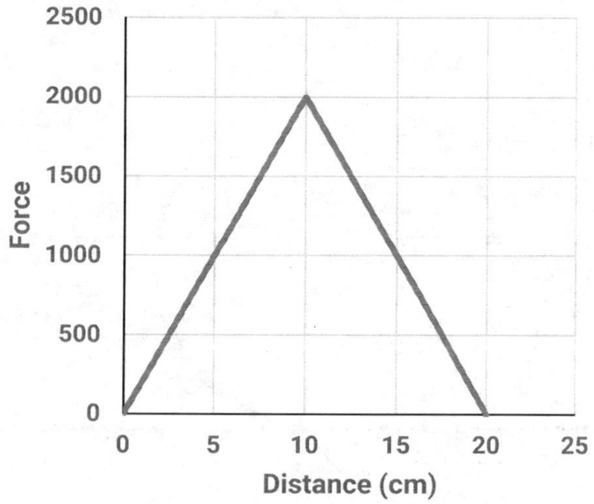

a. 2 kilowatts
b. 4 kilowatts
c. 2,000 kilowatts
d. 4,000 kilowatts

37. A motorcycle weighs twice as much as a bicycle and is moving twice as fast. Which of the following statements is true?

a. The motorcycle has four times as much kinetic energy as the bicycle.
b. The motorcycle has eight times as much kinetic energy as the bicycle.
c. The bicycle and the motorcycle have the same kinetic energy.
d. The bicycle has four times as much kinetic energy as the motorcycle.

38. A ball is released from a certain height along a frictionless track that does a loop-the-loop. The loop-the-loop part of the track is a perfect circle of radius *R*. At what height above the ground must the ball be released from in order to not fall off the track when it gets to the top of the loop-the-loop?

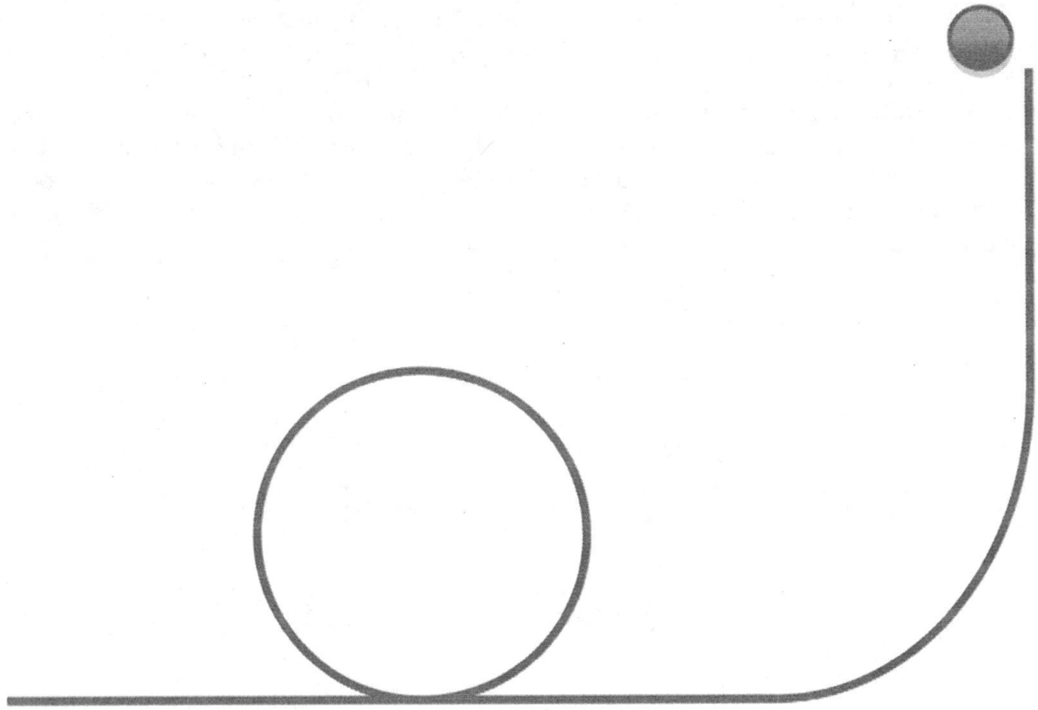

a. R
b. $2R$
c. $\frac{5R}{2}$
d. $3R$

39. The potential energy of a spring is represented as $\frac{1}{2}kx^2$, where k represents the spring constant and x is the displacement of the spring from its position when it is not stretched. A massless spring is suspended from a support and a 100-g mass is attached, stretching it 2 centimeters. If another 100-g mass is attached, what is the new potential energy of the spring?

a. Half as much as with one 100-g mass attached.
b. One-fourth as much as with one 100-g mass attached.
c. Twice as much as with one 100-g mass attached.
d. Four times as much as with one 100-g mass attached.

40. Two objects of masses m and M are a distance R apart. The force of their gravitational attraction is given by $\frac{GmM}{R^2}$. Their gravitational potential energy is given by $\frac{-GmM}{R}$. If the distance between these two objects doubles from 100 km to 200 km, what happens to the ratio of the gravitational force to the gravitational potential energy?

a. Doubled
b. Quadrupled
c. Halved
d. Quartered

41. Which of the following statements about energy is false?

a. Mechanical energy is always conserved in an isolated system.

b. Total energy is always conserved in an isolated system.
c. Energy is never created or destroyed.
d. Matter can be transformed into energy

42. Conservative forces are forces that do not lose energy to processes like friction and radiation and where the total mechanical energy is conserved. Which statement best explains why the work done by a conservative force on an object does not depend on the path the object takes?

a. This is the definition of a conservative force.
b. The work done by the force of friction on an object depends on the distance the object moves.
c. Work can be positive, negative, or zero.
d. If a force is conservative, any component of the force is equal to the change in potential energy divided by the change in position.

43. How much does it cost to operate a 5-kilowatt electric motor for 12 hours if electricity is 6 cents per kilowatt-hour?

a. $0.025
b. $3.60
c. $14.40
d. $360

44. What is the wavelength in the diagram?

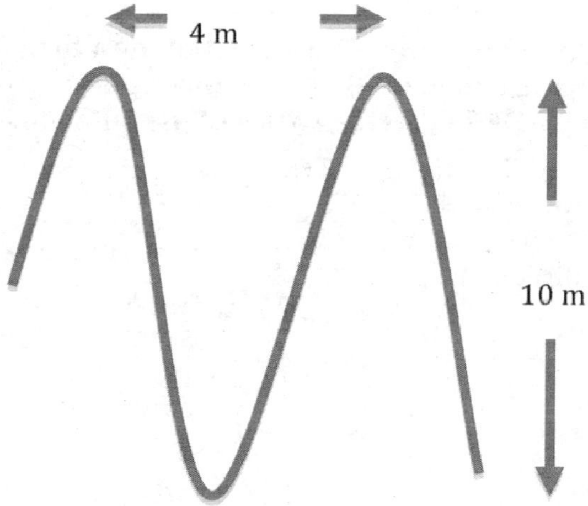

a. 2 meters
b. 4 meters
c. 5 meters
d. 10 meters

45. Which of the following statements best explains what is meant by the phase of a wave?

a. The height of a wave in 2π radians.
b. The length of a wave in 2π radians.
c. The period of oscillation of a wave.
d. An angle indicating the wave cycle's instantaneous location.

46. A 100-kg bungee jumper jumps off a bridge, attached to a 20-meter bungee cord. After bouncing around for a minute he finally comes to rest. The stretched cord is now 25 meters long. What is the spring constant of the bungee cord?

a. 20 newtons per meter
b. 39 newtons per meter
c. 49 newtons per meter
d. 196 newtons per meter

47. The equation for the position of an object undergoing simple harmonic motion as a function of time is $A\sin[(5.0\text{ Hz})t]$. Assuming the wave's phase is measured in radians, what is the period of the motion?

a. $\sin[(5.0\text{ Hz})t]$
b. 2.5 seconds
c. 1.26 seconds
d. A

48. Which of the following statements is true about the acceleration of a simple pendulum?

a. The acceleration is constant.
b. The magnitude of the acceleration is at a maximum when the bob is at the bottom of the path.
c. The magnitude of the acceleration is at a maximum when the bob is changing directions.
d. None of the above.

49. A RADAR gun sends out a pulsed beam of microwave radiation to measure the speed of cars using the Doppler effect. The pulsed beam bounces off the moving car and returns to the RADAR gun. For a car that's moving away from the RADAR detector, which of the following statements about the pulsed beam are true?

I. It returns with a longer wavelength.
II. It returns with a shorter wavelength.
III. It returns with a higher frequency.

a. I only.
b. II only.
c. I and III.
d. II and III.

50. What is the speed of a wave with a frequency of 12 Hz and a wavelength of 3 meters?

a. 12 meters per second
b. 36 meters per second
c. 4 meters per second
d. 0.25 meters per second

51. Two waves, each of which has an amplitude of A, cross paths. At the point where they cross, the peak of one wave meets the trough of another wave. What is the resulting displacement of the medium at the point where the waves cross?

a. 0
b. A
c. $2A$
d. $-A$

52. In resonance, small vibrations can produce a larger standing wave that becomes stronger than the original vibrations, assuming the vibrations are at the right frequency to generate resonance. If a pendulum is vibrated at a resonance frequency, what would you expect to happen?

a. The period of the pendulum will increase.
b. The time between swings will decrease.
c. The pendulum will swing higher.
d. The length of the pendulum will decrease.

53. Transverse traveling waves propagate through a taut string of length 20 meters at a speed of 4 m/s. Standing waves are set up in this string which is fixed at both ends. What is the smallest frequency possible for the standing waves?

a. 0.1 Hz
b. 0.05 Hz
c. 0.2 Hz
d. 0.4 Hz

54. Two tuning forks have a frequency of 500 Hz and 504 Hz and the same amplitude. How much time is there between beats?

a. 4 seconds
b. 15 seconds
c. 0.25 seconds
d. 2 seconds

55. Which of the following statements about refraction is true?

a. Refraction means a change in the direction of the wave.
b. The angle of reflection equals the angle of refraction.
c. The frequency in a refracted wave changes.
d. The phase of a refracted wave changes.

56. What corresponds to the amplitude of a sound wave?

a. Loudness
b. Pressure differential of fluctuations
c. Magnitude of motion of air molecules
d. Power

57. The density of helium is much lower than that of air. How does the speed of sound traveling through helium gas compare to the speed of sound in air?

a. It is faster.
b. It is slower.
c. It is the same speed.
d. It cannot be determined without knowing their atomic masses.

58. What property of a sound corresponds to the frequency of the sound wave in air?

a. Pitch
b. High and low
c. Timbre
d. Overtones

59. In musical instruments with two open ends, the first harmonic fits one-half wave inside the tube. The second harmonic fits 1 full wave in the tube. The third harmonic fits 1.5 full waves in the tube. Etc. An organ pipe, open at both ends, has a length of 1.2 meters. What is the frequency of the third harmonic? The speed of sound is 340 meters per second.

a. 142 Hz
b. 284 Hz
c. 425 Hz
d. 568 Hz

60. The speed of a travelling wave in a stretched string is given by $\sqrt{\frac{T}{\mu}}$, where T is the tension in the string and μ is the mass per unit length. A 2-meter-long stretched string with a mass of 0.010 kilograms is made to resonate with standing waves at 50 Hz. What tension in the string is needed to produce the fourth harmonic? (Note: the fourth harmonic fits 2 full waves into the length of the string).

a. 12. 5 newtons
b. 25 newtons
c. 50 newtons
d. 10,000 newtons

61. What will happen to light waves as they hit a convex lens?

a. They will be refracted and converge.
b. They will be refracted and diverge.
c. They will be reflected and converge.
d. They will be reflected and diverge.

62. Substance A has a density of $5.0\ kg/m^3$ and substance B has a density of $4.0\ kg/m^3$. What is the ratio of volume A to volume B when the masses of the two substances are equal?

a. 1.25
b. 0.80
c. 1.12
d. 0.89

63. A submarine sits underwater at a constant depth of 50 meters. Which of the following is true about the submarine's buoyant force?

a. It is 0 N.
b. It is greater than 0 N but less than the submarine's weight.
c. It is equal to the submarine's weight.
d. It is greater than the submarine's weight.

64. A hydraulic lift needs to raise a 3.5×10^3 newton truck. The input piston has a diameter of 2.0 cm, and the output piston has a diameter of 24 cm. What minimum force must be applied to the input piston?

a. 24 N
b. 292 N
c. 42,000 N
d. 504,000 N

65. The center of a circular aquarium window with a radius of 1 meter is 14 meters below the surface. What is the force of the water at this depth pushing on this window? The density of water is 1,000 kg/m³.

a. 1.37×10^5 newtons
b. 1.08×10^5 newtons
c. 4.3×10^5 newtons
d. 0 newtons

66. Suppose you have a pipe of length L and radius r, and a liquid with viscosity η. You also have a sensor to detect the liquid's flow rate, which measures the volume of liquid passing through the pipe per second. If you want to increase the flow rate of the pipe, what changes to L, r and η should you make? Assume that the pressure differential remains constant.

a. Increase L, increase r, and decreases η
b. Decrease L, increase r, and decreases η
c. Decrease L, increase r, and increase η
d. Increase L, decrease r, and decreases η

67. An incompressible ideal fluid is flowing through a pipe 5.0 cm in radius at a speed of 6.0 m/s. The pipe narrows to 3.0 cm. What is the speed of flow in the narrower section?

a. 10 m/s
b. 3.6 m/s
c. 16.7 m/s
d. Can't be determined from the given information.

68. The air passing over an airplane's wing is considered an irrotational fluid flow. Which of the following statements correctly describes the concept of irrotational fluid flow?

a. The fluid flows in a straight line.
b. All particles have the same velocity as they pass a particular point.
c. A tiny paddle wheel placed in the fluid will rotate.
d. The fluid does not have any rotating points, whirlpools, or eddies.

69. A cube of aluminum is placed at the bottom of a deep ocean where the pressure is over 20 atmospheres. What happens to the density of the cube?

a. It remains the same.
b. It decreases slightly.
c. It increases slightly.
d. It becomes zero.

70. Which statement correctly describes the elastic limit of a metal rod?

a. The elastic limit occurs when a deformed object will no longer return to its original shape.
b. The elastic limit occurs when the rod breaks.
c. The elastic limit occurs when the stress stops producing a strain.
d. The elastic limit assumes that the forces between molecules in a metal act like springs.

71. Which statement best explains why water expands when it freezes?

a. The coefficient of thermal expansion is negative.
b. The hydrogen bonding between water molecules affects how they crystallize.
c. The density of water increases linearly with temperature.
d. The internal energy of water decreases as it cools.

72. A cube of a substance is 5 centimeters on each side. It is placed in a pressure chamber where the pressure on each surface is 3.0×10^7 N/m^2, causing the density of the cube increases by 0.01 %. Which of the following theories is used to describe this?

a. Young's Modulus
b. Shear Modulus
c. Elastic modulus
d. Bulk Modulus

73. An object with a net charge is brought into the vicinity of an object with a net charge of zero coulombs. Which statement describes the electrostatic force between the two objects?

a. It is a repulsive force.
b. It is an attractive force.
c. There is no force.
d. It is a perpendicular force.

74. What does it mean when someone says that electric charge is conserved?

a. Like charges repel, and unlike charges attract.
b. The net charge of an isolated system remains constant.
c. Charges come from electrons and protons.
d. Charge can never be created or destroyed.

75. Which of the following is the correct definition of a conductor?

a. A metal wire in an electrical circuit.
b. A material that contains movable electric charges.
c. A material that is not a semiconductor or insulator.
d. Any device that allows electricity to flow.

76. A charge $+2q$ is placed at the origin of a coordinate system and a charge of $-q$ is placed at a distance d from the origin. How far from the origin must a third charge $+q$ be placed so that the net force on it is 0 newtons?

a. Less than $\frac{d}{2}$
b. Between $\frac{d}{2}$ and d
c. Between d and $2d$
d. Greater than $2d$

77. Which of the following statements best describes the electric field shown below.

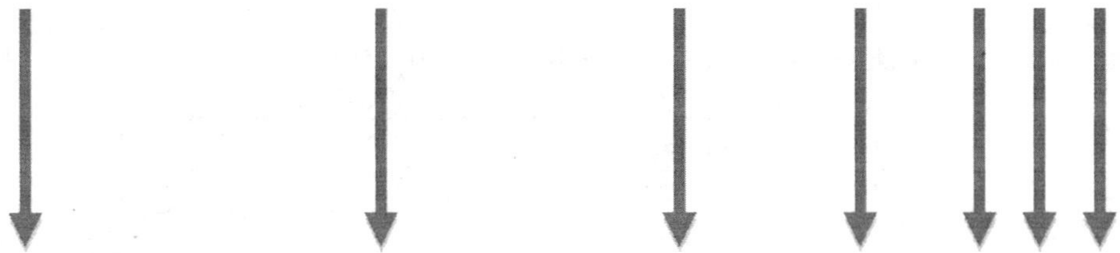

a. The field is decreasing down.
b. The field is decreasing to the right.
c. The field is increasing to the right.
d. The field is uniform.

78. Which of the following statements about a solid metal sphere with a net charge is true?

a. If the charge is positive, it will be distributed uniformly throughout the sphere.
b. The charge will be distributed uniformly at the surface of the sphere.
c. The charge will leave the sphere.
d. The electric field will be tangent to the surface of the sphere.

79. An electron moves in a uniform electric field in the same direction as the electric field from point A to point B. Which of the following statements is true?

a. The potential energy of the electron decreased
b. The potential energy of the electron increased
c. The potential energy of the electron remained constant
d. The potential energy of the electron was converted into kinetic energy

80. Which of the following is true of an electric dipole?

a. It doesn't exist in nature.
b. The charges are equal in magnitude and both are negative.
c. The charges have opposite signs and can be unequal in magnitude.
d. The charges are equal in magnitude and have opposite signs.

81. An electric field is pointing from south to north. If a dipole is placed in the field, how will the dipole's orientation change?

a. The positive charge will be on the northern side and the negative charge will be on the southern side.
b. The positive charge will be on the southern side and the negative charge will be on the northern side.
c. The positive charge will be on the eastern side and the negative charge will be on the western side.
d. There will be no change in the orientation.

82. When is the potential of a point charge with respect to a dipole equal to 0 volts per coulomb?

a. At the midpoint between the positive and negative charge.
b. At an infinite distance from the dipole.
c. At the negative charge.
d. At the positive charge.

83. A plastic comb is used to comb someone's dry hair and acquires a large positive charge. The comb is brought close to a small bit of uncharged paper lying on a table. Against the force of gravity, the bit of paper jumps up and sticks to the comb. What is likely to happen next?

a. The paper will stick to the comb indefinitely.
b. Air will eventually cause the comb to lose its charge and the paper will fall from the comb under the force of gravity.
c. The paper will acquire a positive charge and be repelled by the comb.
d. The paper will acquire a negative charge and be repelled by the comb.

84. Which law says the number of electric field lines passing through an imaginary surface is proportional to the net charge inside the surface?

a. Coulomb's law
b. Gauss's law
c. Faraday's law of induction
d. The Biot-Savart law

85. The charged particle moving through a magnetic field will be subject to a force of $F = qvB \sin \theta$, where q is the charge, v is the particle's velocity, B is the magnetic field strength, and θ is the particle's angle between the magnetic field vector and the velocity vector. Charged particles from space enter the earth's atmosphere all the time. For example, the Aurora Borealis or Northern Lights are created by positive and negative charges passing through the Earth's magnetic field. Assume a proton with a speed of 8.0×10^6 meters per second enters a magnetic field at an angle of $45°$, at a point where the magnetic field is 0.5 tesla. What is the magnetic force acting on the proton? Note: the proton has a charge of 1.6×10^{-19} coulombs.

a. 6.4×10^{-17} N
b. 4.5×10^{-17} N
c. 4.5×10^{-13} N
d. 5.5×10^{-17} N

86. A magnetic field is directed into this page and an electron is moving from left to right as indicated in the diagram below.

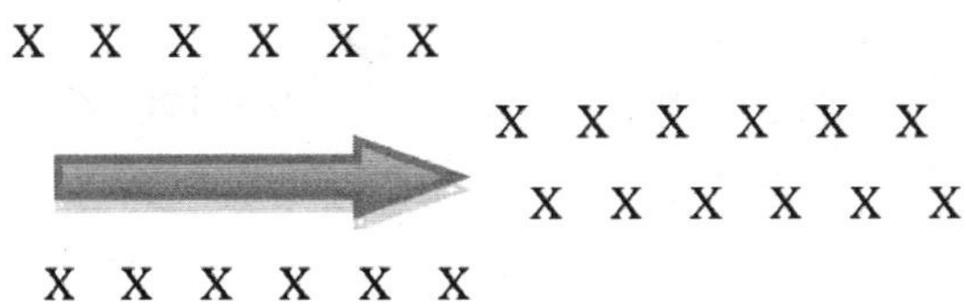

In which direction will the electron move when it enters the magnetic field?

a. It will curve upward.
b. It will curve downward.
c. It will curve in the direction of the magnetic field.
d. It will curve in the direction opposite the magnetic field.

87. An electron is moving in a straight line. Another particle is moving in a straight line parallel to the path of the electron but in the opposite direction. Initially the electron and particle are far apart, but get closer together. When the two particles are in the vicinity of one another, they experience an attractive magnetic force. Which of the following is a correct inference from this fact?

a. The particle has a north pole and a south pole.
b. The particle is positively charged.
c. The particle is negatively charged.
d. The particle has either a north pole or a south pole.

88. A solenoid is made of loops of wire, through which a current is run. What is the purpose of putting a lot of loops into a solenoid?

a. To increase the magnetic field inside the solenoid.
b. To increate the magnetic field outside the solenoid.
c. To decrease the magnetic field inside the solenoid.
d. To decrease the magnetic field outside the solenoid.

89. In the 19th century, James Clerk Maxwell calculated the speed of light in a vacuum from the proportionality constants used in electrostatics and magnetism. Which of the following relationships correctly identifies how light moves in a vacuum?

a. High frequencies of light travel faster than low frequencies.
b. Low frequencies of light travel faster than high frequencies.
c. All frequencies of light travel at the same speed in a vacuum.
d. Light moves at infinite speed through a vacuum.

90. Electromagnetic radiation — also known as light — consists of perpendicularly oscillating electric and magnetic fields. Which of the following statements about electromagnetic radiation is untrue?

a. The energy of the radiation is determined by the frequency and Plank's constant.
b. The "color" of light is determined by its wavelength.
c. Electromagnetic radiation sometimes obeys wave theory.
d. Electromagnetic radiation sometimes obeys particle theory.

91. Which of the following gives the correct order of electromagnetic radiation from the lowest frequency to the highest frequency?

a. Microwaves, UHF radio waves, x-rays, visible light
b. UHF radio waves, visible light, microwaves, x-rays
c. UHF radio waves, microwaves, visible light, x-rays
d. Microwaves, x-rays, visible light, UHF radio waves

92. The diagram below shows two batteries connected in series to a resistor. What is the direction of current flow?

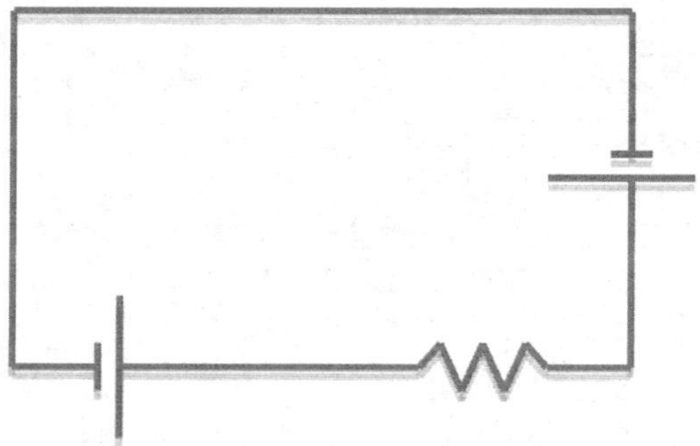

a. clockwise
b. counterclockwise
c. neither clockwise nor counterclockwise
d. Can't be determined from the information given.

93. Current in an electrical circuit is normally measured in amperes. Which of the following does NOT represent an alternative way of expressing current?

a. Coulombs per second
b. Volts per ohm
c. Electrons per second
d. Watt-volts

94. Which of the following devices changes chemical energy into electrical energy?

a. battery
b. closed electric circuit
c. generator
d. transformer

95. Which of the following statements about electricity flowing through a circuit can be correctly derived from Ohm's law?

a. Increasing the voltage decreases the current if the resistance remains unchanged.
b. Increasing the current and the resistance decreases the voltage.
c. Increasing the current increases the voltage if the resistance is unchanged.
d. Increasing the resistance increases the current if the voltage remains unchanged.

96. A circuit consists of a battery and a resistor. An real ammeter is used to measure the current in the circuit and is connected in series to the circuit. Which of the following is true?

a. The current flowing in the resistor increases.
b. The current flowing in the resistor decreases.
c. The voltage drop across the resistor increases.
d. The current flowing in the resistor remains the same.

97. What is the total resistance between points X and Y in the circuit diagram below?

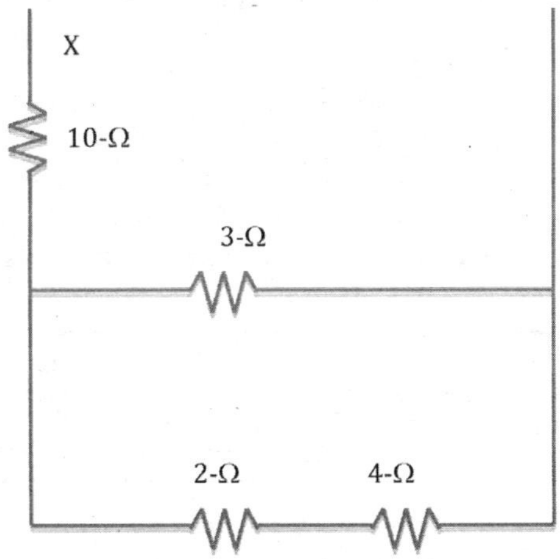

a. 0 Ω
b. 12 Ω
c. 19 Ω
d. 16 Ω

98. Consider one tungsten wire of length *L* and cross-sectional area *A* and another tungsten wire of length 2*L* and area 2*A*. Assuming both wires are the same temperature, which of the following statements is true?

a. The resistance of the two wires is the same.
b. The resistance of the longer wire is twice the resistance of the shorter wire.
c. The resistance of the longer wire is half the resistance of the shorter wire.
d. The resistance of the longer wire is four times the resistance of the shorter wire.

99. A capacitor is connected in series to a battery and a resistor. After the capacitor is charged, the battery is disconnected and replaced by a battery with a greater electromotive force (emf), causing the capacitor to gain additional charge. After the capacitor has fully charged again, which of the following statements is true about the capacitance of the circuit?

a. It has increased.
b. It has decreased.
c. It has remained the same.
d. It has become zero.

100. Which is the correct formula for the energy stored in a fully-charged capacitor with capacitance *C* when it's attached to a battery of voltage *V*?

a. $\frac{C}{V}$
b. $\frac{1}{2}CV^2$
c. CV
d. 0 volts

101. Adding multiple capacitors to a circuit is much the opposite as adding multiple resistors. Adding resistors in series, for example, creates an effective resistance equal to their sum. To add resistors in parallel, you must add the reciprocals of their resistance. With capacitors, however, you use reciprocals when adding them in series and you sum the capacitance when adding in parallel. Given the following diagram, what is the total capacitance of the circuit?

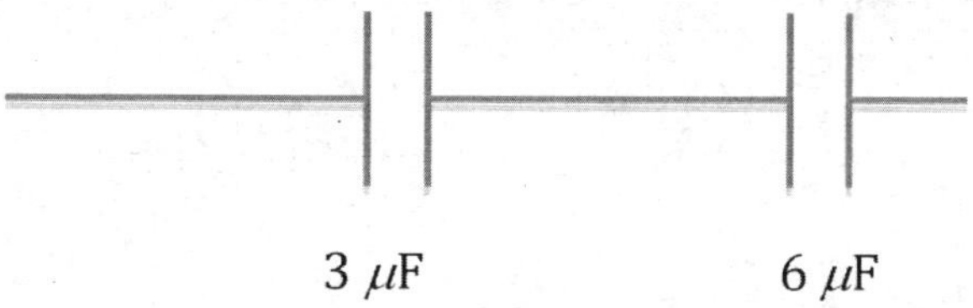

a. 2 microfarads
b. 9 microfarads
c. 0.5 microfarads
d. 4.5 microfarads

102. A 5-microfarad and a 15-microfarad capacitor are connected as shown in the diagram. What is the total capacitance of the circuit?

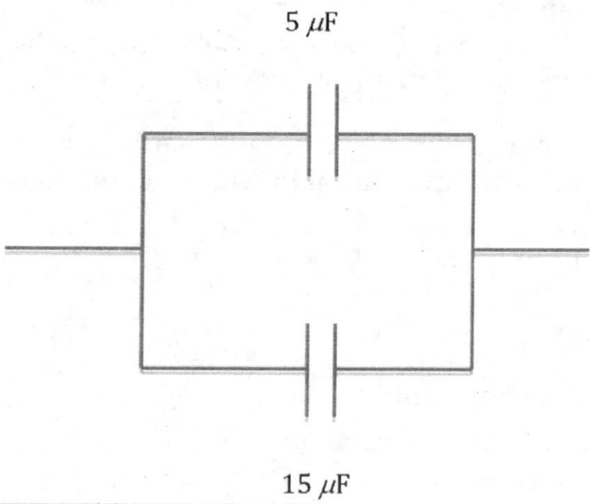

a. 3.8 μF
b. 3 μF
c. 20 μF
d. 75 μF

103. A 6.0-megaohm resistor is connected in series with a 5.0-microfarad capacitor and fully charged with a 3-volt battery. The battery is disconnected and the capacitor is connected directly to the resistor. How long will it take for the capacitor to fully discharge?

a. Infinite time
b. 30 seconds
c. 0.0333 second
d. 90 seconds

104. A miniature heater has a power rating of 50 watts and is connected to a battery with an electromotive force of 10 volts. What current flows through the heater?

a. 500 amperes
b. 5 amperes
c. 200 milliamperes
d. 3.1×10^{19} electrons per second

105. A homemade generator rotates at a constant frequency and produces an alternating current with a maximum voltage of 40 volts. It is connected to a resistor of 20 ohms. What is the average current that flows through the resistor?

a. 0 amperes.
b. 1.4 amperes
c. 2.0 amperes
d. 2.8 amperes

106. Two beams of light with the same phase and wavelength travel different paths and arrive at the same point. If maximum constructive interference occurs at this point, which of the following statements is true?

a. The two beams arrive 180° out of phase.
b. The two beans arrive 90° out of phase.
c. The lengths of the paths differ by an odd-number of half wavelengths.
d. The lengths of the paths differ by an integral number of wavelengths.

107. When light from a single source strikes two slits, alternating bright and dark lines appear on a screen on the far side. What is the best explanation for this phenomenon?

a. Doppler shift
b. Diffraction and interference
c. Chromatic aberration
d. Total internal reflection

108. Which of the following is true about a diffraction grating?

a. The more slits per inch, the greater the amount of destructive interference.
b. Blue light diffracts more than red light in a diffraction grating.
c. A diffraction grating produces maxima and minima only for monochromatic light.
d. Light passing through a diffraction grating produces a bull's-eye pattern.

109. Which of the following statements best explains how light can be polarized?

a. Light waves' electromagnetic fields can be oriented in a particular direction by a polarizer.
b. Photons of light can be pointed in the same direction by microscopic holes in a polarizer.
c. Light travels in a vacuum.
d. Light is a longitudinal wave.

110. Which of the following phenomena implies that light consists of specific quanta?

a. ultraviolet catastrophe
b. threshold frequency
c. emission of light
d. stability of atoms

111. Which of the following phenomena is most closely related to the phenomenon that produces the light from lasers?

a. radioactivity
b. phosphorescence
c. sunlight
d. blackbody radiation

112. Specular reflection might occur on a surface like a mirror, while diffuse reflection might occur on a wooden tabletop. Which of the following statements best describes the difference between specular and diffuse reflection?

a. For diffuse reflection, the angle of incidence is equal to the angle of reflection.
b. For diffuse reflection, surface irregularities are large compared to the wavelength of visible light.
c. One hundred percent of the light is reflected for specular reflection.
d. The conservation of momentum is followed in specular reflection.

113. A ray of light travelling in a vacuum ($n = 1$) is incident upon a glass plate ($n = 1.3$). It hits with an angle of incidence of 45°. If the angle of incidence increases to 50°, what is the new angle of refraction?

a. It is 45°
b. It is 50°
c. It is below 45°
d. It is above 50°

114. Which of the following statements explains what causes a rainbow?

a. The components of sunlight strike water droplets at different angles.
b. Water molecules produce an emission spectrum when sunlight strikes them.
c. The speed of light in water depends on its wavelength.
d. There is total internal reflection for certain wavelengths of sunlight.

115. Which of the following statements best explains the phenomenon of total internal reflection?

a. The speed of light is at a maximum in a vacuum.
b. Light consists of bundles of energy called photons.
c. Snell's law places a limit on the angle of refraction.
d. Light consists of transverse waves.

116. Two rays parallel to the optical axis of a concave mirror are incident upon the mirror. Where do the two rays intersect?

a. At a point behind the mirror
b. At infinity
c. At the center of curvature
d. At the focal point

117. An object is placed a certain distance away from a convex spherical mirror. Which of the following statements is true?

a. No image is formed.
b. The image will be larger or smaller, depending on the object's distance from the mirror.
c. The image will be smaller and right side up.
d. The image will be smaller and either right side up or upside down, depending on the object's distance from the mirror.

118. Which of the following statements about the image created by a magnifying glass is true?

a. The image is always upside down.
b. The image is always right side up.
c. The image may be right side up or upside down, depending on the location of the object.
d. The image may be right side up or upside down, depending on the thickness of the lens.

119. An object is 20 cm in front of a thin convex lens with a focal point of 10 cm. Where is the image located?

a. 10 cm in front of the lens
b. 20 cm in front of the lens
c. 10 cm behind the lens
d. 20 cm behind the lens

120. A lens forms an upright image 19 cm from a lens of an object 49 cm from the lens. The object and image are on the same side of the lens. What is the magnification of the image?

a. 0.39
b. 2.6
c. 13.7
d. 31.2

121. A thin convex lens has focal length of 30 cm. An identical lens is placed right behind it. What is the focal length of this combination of lenses?

a. 30 cm.
b. 60 cm
c. 15 cm
d. 0.067 cm

122. Which type of aberration does NOT occur with concave spherical mirrors?

a. Astigmatism
b. Chromatic aberration
c. Spherical aberration
d. Distortion

123. Which of the following statements is NOT a principle used in constructing ray diagrams to show the creation of images using a thin convex lens?

a. A ray parallel to the optical axis is refracted so that it goes through the focal point of the lens.
b. A ray that goes through the focal point of a lens and strikes the lens is refracted parallel to the optical axis.
c. A ray that goes through the center of a lens is not deflected.
d. A ray that strikes the surface of a lens follows Snell's law for refraction.

124. What is the magnification of a combination of three lenses with magnifications 3.0, –4.0, and 0.3?

a. – 0.7
b. 0.7
c. – 3.6
d. 3.6

125. A hydrogen atom makes a transition from the first excited state to the ground level. Which of the following statements is true?

a. A 10.2 eV photon is emitted.
b. A 13.6 eV photon is emitted.
c. A 1.9 eV photon is absorbed.
d. No photon is emitted.

126. A substance has a half-life of 2.4×10^4 years. How long does it take for 87.5% of the substance to decay?

a. 2.1×10^4 years
b. 4.5×10^4 years
c. 7.2×10^4 years
d. 9.6×10^4 years

127. A nucleus absorbs a neutron and undergoes a fission reaction. Which of the following statements explains why this happens?

a. The nucleus is more stable with the additional neutron.
b. The new nucleus is unstable.
c. Energy is released.
d. The binding energy per nucleon decreases.

128. How is light created in the core of the Sun?

a. Convection
b. Fission reactions
c. Fusion reactions
d. Chemical reactions

129. How is energy generated in a nuclear reaction?

a. Matter is converted into energy
b. Photon excitation and emission
c. Kinetic collision of highly energetic hydrogen atoms
d. Gravitational energy is converted into electromagnetic radiation

130. Which of the following statements about isotopes of an element is true?

a. They have the same number of nucleons.
b. They have the same number of neutrons, but different numbers of protons.
c. They have the same number of protons, but different numbers of neutrons.
d. They have a different number of electrons.

131. What happens to a nucleus when it emits an alpha particle?

a. Its atomic number decreases by one.
b. Its mass decreases by two atomic mass units.
c. Its nucleon number decreases by four.
d. Its charge increases by +2.

132. Cobalt-63 can be produced in a laboratory and is unstable. When it decays, a neutron in its core will likely decay into a proton, changing Cobalt-63 into Nickel-63. Which of the following products will be emitted from this transition?

I. alpha particles
II. beta particle
III. gamma rays

a. I only
b. III only
c. II and III
d. I, II and III

133. An inch is approximately equivalent to which of the following?

a. 25.4 mm
b. 25.4 cm
c. 2.54×10^{-4} km
d. 2.54×10^{2} m

134. Which of the following numbers has the most significant digits?

a. 1,500,000
b. 1.5000×10^{5}
c. 0.15000
d. 0.00150000

135. Suppose your actual weight is 150 pounds and you weigh yourself with an analog scale and get a reading of 152.1 pounds. You repeat the measurement twice more and get 152.1 pounds each time. Which of the following statements is true?

a. There is no random error.
b. There is no systematic error.
c. The systematic error is 2.1 pounds.
d. The random error is 2.1 pounds.

136. A school nurse measures the height of every boy in a school with 1,000 pupils and determines that the average height is 1.64 meters with a standard deviation of 0.05 meter. Which of the following statements is true?

a. Sixty-eight percent of the students have heights between 1.59 meters and 1.69 meters.
b. There are as many students with heights above 1.64 meters as below 1.64 meters.
c. More students are 1.64 meters tall than any other height.
d. None of these statements may be made conclusively.

Answer Key and Explanations

1. B: Significant digits indicate the precision of the measurement. Answer B has 5 significant figures. A and C each have 4. D has 3. The leading zeros in Answers A and D and are not counted as significant digits, but zeros at the end of the number (as in Answers A and B) do count. In answer D, the zero in between 2 and 9 is significant.

2. D: When adding, the answer should be rounded to the same number of decimal places as the measurement with the fewest decimal places. The total mass is obtained by adding up all four measurements. This yields 35.5918. Since the first and second masses are precise to only a hundredth of a gram, your answer can't be more precise than this. The number 35.5918, when rounded to two decimal places, is 35.59.

3. C: Vectors have a magnitude (e.g., 5 meters/second) and direction (e.g., towards north). Of the choices listed, only velocity is defined as a vector. Speed, distance, and time are all quantities that have a size but not a direction. That's why, for example, a car's speedometer reads 35 miles/hour, but does not indicate your direction of travel.

4. C: Displacement is a vector that indicates the change in the location of an object. Answer A would be correct if the question asked for the total distance the person walked or if the person didn't change direction. If the person turned around 180°, the displacement could be as small as 5 meters. If the person changed directions only a fraction of a degree, the displacement's magnitude would be *less* than 13 meters, not as *large* as 13 meters.

5. C: To add and subtract vectors algebraically, you add and subtract their components. To add vectors graphically, you shift the location of the vectors so that they are connected tip-to-tail. The resultant is a vector that starts at the tail of the first vector and ends at the tip of the second. To subtract vectors, connect the vectors tip to tail, starting with the vector that is not subtracted, and ending with the one that is. Think of this just like vector addition, except the vector that is subtracted (the one with the negative sign in front of it) switches directions.

6. C: The average speed is the total distance (400 m) divided by the total time spent travelling (100 s). Answer A would be correct if the question asked for the instantaneous velocity while the runner was stopped. Answer B is the runner's average speed when running at her usual time, finishing the race in 80 seconds. Answer D is the average speed if the runner had completed the race in 20 seconds, not 100.

7. B: The answer can be determined because the rate of acceleration is uniform. Since the acceleration is 5 m/s^2, the velocity increases by 5 m/s every second. If it starts at 20 m/s, it will be going 25 m/s after 1 second. After another second, it will be going 30 m/s, so the total time is 2 seconds. You can also calculate this time by using the average speed. Since the object undergoes uniform acceleration, the average speed is 25 m/s. Using the distance traveled, the same result is obtained. $t = \frac{d}{v} = \frac{50 \text{ meters}}{25 \text{ m/s}} = 2$ seconds.

8. C: This is a problem of free fall in two dimensions. A thrown ball without air resistance will only be subjected to one force, gravity. This causes a downward acceleration of exactly 9.8 m/s^2 on all objects, regardless of their size, speed or position. Note: since the ball was thrown directly upwards, the horizontal acceleration is 0 m/s^2 and the horizontal speed at all times is 0 m/s. Answer choice B is wrong because the force of gravity is always pointed downward and never changes direction.

9. C: In a uniform gravitational field, such as occurs near Earth's surface, an object will move like a point mass located at the center of mass. However, this does not necessarily mean that the geometrical center of an object is the same as its center of mass, depending on its shape, design and mass distribution. The center of mass of a sphere or cube is at its geometric center because you can imagine the sphere as consisting of a large number of point masses located at certain points in space. Multiplying the point masses by their location and dividing by the total mass gives the center of mass. Statement I is not true because the space station may not be completely symmetrical. Statement III is true because the space station is undergoing uniform circular motion around Earth. If the orbit had been elliptical, this would not be true because the speed would have changed depending on the station's position. However, even though the speed is constant in a circular orbit, the velocity is not. Since velocity has a direction associated with it, and the space station is moving in a circular path, its velocity is constantly changing.

10. A: Newton's first law (inertia) says an object in motion stays in motion, and an object at rest stays at rest, unless external forces act on them. Choice A is an excellent demonstration because it shows the ball at rest and in motion. At rest, the ball stays at rest until a force acts on it. When the ball is moving, there is no force acting on the ball in the direction of motion. Thus, the natural state of the ball is to be at rest or moving with a constant speed. Choice C is not a good demonstration because the force of friction is what makes it hard to move the heavy object. Choice B is a good demonstration of equilibrium and friction. Running a current through parallel wires (D) has nothing to do with Newton's first law.

11. B: The newton can be defined in terms of the fundamental units of meters, kilograms, and seconds as $\text{N} = \text{kg} \times \text{m/s}^2$, so it is not a fundamental unit. Statement II is a result of $F = ma$, Newton's second law, which is true. If $F = 0$ N, then the acceleration is $0\ \text{m/s}^2$. If the acceleration is $0\ \text{m/s}^2$, then the speed is $0\ \text{m/s}$ or a nonzero constant. This is a nonverbal statement of Newton's first law, meaning Newton's first law can be derived from his second law. Newton's second law cannot be derived from the universal law of gravity.

12. A: Newton's third law states that for every action there is an equal and opposite reaction. Put another way, if object A exerts a force on object B, then object B exerts a force of the same magnitude on object A in the opposite direction. Since we're considering the force of the box on the table to be the action force, the reaction force is then the force of the table on the box.

13. D: There will be a gravitational force of attraction between the two spheres determined by the universal constant of gravity, the distance between the spheres, and the mass of the spheres. Since both objects are affected by this force (remember, Newton's third law says the force needs to be equal and opposite), both objects will experience a slight acceleration and start moving towards each other a tiny amount (when we ignore friction). Using $\text{F} = \text{ma}$, you know that the less massive sphere will experience a larger acceleration than the more massive one.

14. C: As the ring spins, the wall of the ring exerts centripetal force on your body. This force also causes friction between your back and the wall, and that's why you don't fall when the floor is removed, assuming the frictional force is large enough to overcome gravity. As the speed of rotation increases, the force exerted by the wall on your body increases, so the frictional force between you and the wall increases. Answer B is factually correct, but it does not explain why you do not fall—centripetal force does cause you to change direction. Also note that "centrifugal force" is an illusion; because you feel the wall pushing against your back, you feel like you're being pushed outwards. In fact, you're being pulled inwards, but the wall is also being pulled inwards and is pushing against you. Finally, choice D is incorrect because you are not weightless on a ride like this.

15. C: Centripetal force can be expressed as $F = m\left(\frac{v^2}{r}\right)\cos\theta$. Increasing the radius effectively decreases the force unless you also increase the velocity. By assuming that the maximum centripetal force remains constant, you can increase the maximum speed v by as much as $\sqrt{2}$. Any higher and the v^2 term will be too high for the new radius.

16. C: The weight of an object near Earth's surface is given by $W = mg$, where $g = 9.8\ \text{m/s}^2$. The Earth exerts a force on the 10 kg object equal $10\ \text{kg} \times 9.8\ \text{m/s}^2 = 98\ \text{N}$. This weight pulls on the lower spring, stretching it until it reads 98 N. The lower spring then exerts a force of 98 N on the upper spring, causing it to read 98 N.

17. C: The question asks how much friction is needed to start the block moving, which means you need to calculate the force of static friction. If the question had asked about the force needed to keep the object moving at a constant speed, you would calculate the force of kinetic friction. Here, the force of static friction is equal to $\mu_{static} \times N$, where N is the Normal force. The normal force (N) on the plastic block is the weight of the block ($w = mg$) which is 10 kg × 9.8 m/s^2 = 98 newtons. The force of static friction is 0.6 × 98 N = 59 N. Answer B is the force of kinetic friction, once the block starts moving. (Note: molecular bonding and abrasion cause friction. When the surfaces are in motion, the bonding is less strong, so the coefficient of kinetic friction is less than the coefficient of static friction. Therefore, more force is required to start the box moving than to keep it moving.)

18. A: The force of gravity points straight down. The normal force is perpendicular to the surface of the block. The force of friction points down the slope. The only one of these diagrams with all three vectors pointing in those directions is Answer A.

19. B: The ideal mechanical advantage (IMA) of a simple machine ignores friction. It is the effort force divided into the resultant force. It is also the distance the effort force moves divided by the distance the resultant force moves. The IMA of a fixed pulley is 1 because all a fixed pulley does is change the direction of the effort force. A moveable pulley, however, doubles the force by increasing the distance by two. In this case, there is one fixed pulley and one floating pulley. Since the IMA of the fixed pulley is 1, and the floating pulley doubles this, the total IMA is 2.

20. B: The weight of the masses is determined from $W = mg$. In this case, there is a force to the left/down of 20 kg × 9.8 m/s^2 = 196 N, and a force to the right/down of 30 kg × 9.8 m/s^2 = 294 N. The net force is 98 N to the right/down. This force is moving both masses, however, which have a total mass of 50 kg. Using $F = ma$ and solving for acceleration gives $a = \frac{98\text{ N}}{50\text{ kg}} = 2\text{ m/s}^2$.

21. B: Using Newton's second law $F = ma$, the acceleration of all three blocks, which have a combined mass of 9 kg, is $a = \frac{25\text{ N}}{9\text{ kg}} = 2.78\text{ m/s}^2$. The force pulling the rear block is $F = ma = 4\text{ kg} \times 2.78\text{ m/s}^2 = 11.1\text{ N}$. Another way of thinking of this is the tension represents $\frac{4}{9}$ of the total force, since the total mass is 9 kg and the rear block has a mass of 4 kg. This must equal the tension on the rope pulling on that block. Answer C is the tension of the string connecting the 3 kg and 2 kg masses. Answer D is the tension on the rope pulling all 3 masses.

22. B: The weight of the art is 200 kg × 9.8 m/s^2 = 1,960 N. This is the total force pulling DOWN on the wires. However, the tension acts along a 40° angle, and the vertical force is $T \sin\theta$. Additionally, there are two ends to the wire, which splits the tension, meaning the weight is spread across $2T \sin\theta$. So $2T \sin\theta = w$. Therefore, $T = \frac{1}{2} \times \frac{1{,}960\text{ N}}{\sin(40°)} = 1{,}525\text{ N}$. Note: There's also a horizontal component to the tension forces, each expressed as $T \cos\theta$. The net force of the left and right tensions is zero. Answer A is calculated using the cos(40°) instead of sin(40°).

23. B: The torque acting on an object is the force acting on the object (in this case, its weight $= mg$) times its distance from the pivot point. Here, the masses and the bar are balanced, so the net torque is 0 N × m. This means the clockwise torque is equal and opposite to the counter clockwise torque ($m_1 g d_1 = m_2 g d_2$). Dividing the distance in half would only add a factor of $\frac{1}{2}$ to both sides of this equation. Since this affects both sides equally, the net torque is still zero when both distances are halved. C would be the correct answer if the mass of the bar was not zero.

24. B: Clockwise is the direction the hands of a clock rotate when looking at the clock, so a counterclockwise torque would require a force that pushes or pulls down on the lever. The pivot point is the axis of rotation. We don't care about the components of these forces that push either to the left or right, since these components do not produce any torque. Force 1 is directed into the axis, so it produces no torque. Forces 3 and 4 both push up on the lever. The only force producing a counter-clockwise rotation is Force 2.

25. C: All three laws of motion are operating, but the third law (forces come in equal and opposite pairs) best explains the motion. The first law (inertia) is shown from the fact that the balloon doesn't move until a force acts upon it. The second law (F = ma) is shown because you can see the force and the acceleration. The force comes from the contraction of the rubber balloon. The stretched rubber exerts a force on the air inside the balloon. This causes the air to accelerate in accordance with the second law. You can't see this acceleration because the air is invisible and because it is the air inside the balloon being pushed out through the opening that the balloon is exerting a force on. However, the air being pushed out of the balloon exerts an equal and opposite force on the balloon (this is Newton's third law), which causes the balloon to accelerate in the direction it did.

26. B: The moment of inertia of a point mass, m, about any axis is given by mR^2, where R is the distance from the axis of rotation. The moment of inertia of a solid object is calculated by imagining that the object is made up of point masses and adding the moments of inertia of the point masses. The average radius of the particles in a hollow cylinder will be R (all the mass is at radius R). For a solid cylinder, however, much of the mass lies at radii less than R, meaning the overall moment of inertia will be smaller. The moment of inertia of a cylinder of thickness $R_2 - R_1$, where R_1 and R_2 are the inner and outer radii, respectively, is calculated by $\frac{1}{2}m({R_1}^2 + {R_2}^2)$. For a solid cylinder, $R_1 = 0$ meters. For a thin hollow cylinder, $R_1 = R_2$.

27. B: The phenomenon known as weightlessness is caused by an object being in free fall. An object in space still experiences a gravitational force due to the earth, but if that object is in orbit, it's effectively free falling around the earth, which causes it to experience weightlessness. Here, proposition I is wrong because you have to be pretty far away from a star for gravity to become negligible. In fact, objects only stay in orbit because the earth's gravity pulls on them and causes them to change direction. This means the usual experience of weight is lost, as you can see by the floating objects and people inside an orbiting spaceship. The same thing happens to a ski jumper, who is in free fall after he or she jumps. If the jumper is carrying a rock, for example, that rock will feel weightless while the jumper is in the air. A rolled baseball is not in freefall and does not experience weightlessness.

28. A: In a closed system (when you ignore outside interactions), the total momentum is constant and conserved. The total energy would also be conserved, although not the sum of the potential and kinetic energy. Some of the energy from the collision would be turned into thermal energy (heat) for example. Nor is the total velocity conserved, even though the velocity is a component of the momentum, since the momentum also depends on the mass of the cars. The impulse is a force over time that causes the momentum of a body to change. It doesn't make sense to think of impulse as conserved, since it's not necessarily constant throughout a collision.

29. D: Impulse is the change in an object's momentum (mv), which is in units of kg × m/s. An object's impulse can change, depending on the forces acting upon it. For a ball rolling down a hill, gravity provides a constant force, which causes the ball to accelerate. This creates an impulse that increases as the ball gets faster and faster. This impulse does not exist for a short time, but will continue as long as the ball is accelerating.

30. A: A collision is considered elastic when neither object loses any kinetic energy. Since the cars latch together, this can't be the case. You could prove this by calculating the cars' kinetic energy: $KE = \frac{1}{2}mv^2$. If the railroad cars had bumpers instead of couplers, the moving car would stop and transfer all its momentum and kinetic energy to the stationary car, causing an elastic collision. In a closed system like this one, however, the conservation of momentum is an absolute law, where an object's momentum is its mass times its velocity. There are no external forces acting on the two cars. The only forces are between the two cars themselves. The momentum before the collision is the same as the momentum after the collision: $mv_{initial} + m\left(0\,\frac{\text{m}}{\text{s}}\right) =$

$mv_{final} + mv_{final}$. So $mv_{initial} = 2mv_{final}$, and $v_{initial} = 2v_{final}$. Thus, the final velocity is half the initial velocity.

31. D: Since this is a head-on elastic collision, you could use conservation of kinetic energy and momentum to actually solve this problem. However, in this case, you only need to think through the answers to arrive at a correct conclusion. After the ball is struck, it won't be going 0 m/s. And since this is an elastic collision, and it is hit by a much larger ball, it must be going faster than the larger ball was originally moving. Therefore, the ball will be moving at more than 10 m/s. If this were an inelastic collision where the balls stuck together, the balls' final velocity would be less than 10 m/s.

32. B: Because momentum is conserved in collisions, the combined initial momentums of the two skaters needs to equal the final momentum of the two skaters together.

$$p_1 = m_1 v_1 = 75 \text{ kg} \times 5 \text{ m/s} = 375 \text{ kg} \cdot \text{m/s}$$
$$p_2 = m_2 v_2 = 100 \text{ kg} \times 4 \frac{\text{m}}{\text{s}} = 400 \text{ kg} \cdot \text{m/s}$$

Remember, the first skater was moving eastward and the second skater was moving northward, which means that we need to find their combined momentum in the final direction they will be moving (northeast). This can be done by using the Pythagorean theorem.

$$p_i = \sqrt{375^2 + 400^2} \approx 548$$

Therefore, the initial momentum of the system is approximately 548 kg · m/s. This is equal to the final momentum of the system. Since the collision is inelastic, the two masses need to be added together before they are multiplied by the final velocity.

$$\begin{aligned} p_f &= (m_1 + m_2) v_f \\ 548 &= (75 + 100) v_f \\ 548 &- 175 v_f \\ v_f &\approx 3.1 \text{ m/s} \end{aligned}$$

Therefore, the final velocity, and speed since the velocity is positive, is approximately 3.1 m/s.

33. A: Since the box is moving at a uniform speed, the net force on the box is 0 newtons. Thus the work (W = Fd) is also 0 joules. Answer C incorrectly assumes that 2 newtons of force are used to move the box 5 meters, and while it's true that the teacher is pulling with 2 newtons, the frictional force counteracts this. Answer D incorrectly assumes the work performed by the teacher and the work due to friction add together for a net work of 20 newtons. Answer B incorrectly uses W = F/d. The vertical forces acting on the box—gravity and the normal force—also have a net force of 0 newtons and work of 0 joules.

34. C: To determine how much work is done by a gravitational force, you should calculate the change in that object's gravitational potential energy. Near Earth, gravitational potential energy is given by U = *mgh*. ΔU depends only on the change in height between initial and final positions, and the work done by gravity is W_{grav} = -ΔU, hence independent of path. Therefore, the work done only depends on the change in height and not on the path taken. In answer A, the work done by gravity doesn't have anything to do with friction, so this is not a good explanation. Friction is a separate force. Answer D, although true, doesn't explain why the work doesn't depend on the path.

35. B: The work-energy theorem can be written $W = \Delta KE$. It is derived from Newton's second law ($F = ma$) by multiplying both sides by the distance the object moves. This work is the work done by a force on an object, and not the work done by an object. Work is only done by an object if that object exerts a force on another object, causing a change in its kinetic energy or position. The work done on an object may equal its potential energy, but only if that potential energy is converted into kinetic energy. In real-life cases, some energy is converted to heat, for example, so the change in potential energy does not equal the change in kinetic energy.

36. A: In addition to understanding power, this problem requires you to understand unit conversions. Power is work done divided by time taken, and the work here is the average force times distance. Since the force increases evenly from 0 to 2,000 N and decreases at the same rate, the average force is 1,000 N. Keeping in mind that 20 cm = 0.2 m and 100 ms = 0.1 s, this means:

$$P = \frac{1{,}000 \text{ N} \times 0.2 \text{ m}}{0.1 \text{ s}} = 2{,}000 \text{ W} = 2 \text{ kW}$$

37. B: Kinetic energy is the energy of motion and is defined as $KE = \frac{1}{2}mv^2$. Using this equation, if you double the mass and the velocity of an object, you find $KE = \frac{1}{2}(2m')(2v')^2$, or 8 times the original KE; therefore, the motorcycle has 8 times as much kinetic energy as the bicycle.

38. C: The initial gravitational potential energy of the ball is mgh, where h is the height above the ground. At the top of the loop, some of this energy will be converted into kinetic energy $\left(\frac{1}{2}mv_{top}{}^2\right)$. Since its height is $2R$ at the top of the loop, it will have a potential energy here of $mg(2R)$. Using the conservation of energy: $mgh = \frac{1}{2}mv_{top}{}^2 + mg(2R)$. Additionally, in order to maintain a circular path, the centripetal force must equal the gravitational force at the top of the loop: $\frac{(mv_{top}{}^2)}{R} = mg$, which can be rewritten as $v_{top}{}^2 = gR$. Putting this into the energy equation, you find $mgh = \frac{1}{2}m(gR) + mg(2R)$. Dividing m and g from both sides of this equation shows that $h = \frac{1}{2}R + 2R = \frac{5}{2}R$. Answers A, B and C represent choices that testers are likely to find if they do the math incorrectly.

39. D: The formula for the potential energy of a spring comes from calculating how much work is required to stretch a spring an amount x. Hooke's law applies, so the force increases uniformly from 0 N to kx, where k is the spring constant. Hence, $PE = \frac{1}{2}kx^2$. There are two ways to solve this problem. If you recognize that doubling the mass will double how much the spring is stretched, you can easily see that $(2x)^2$ shows the potential energy of the spring quadruples. If you don't realize that the displacement doubles, you can easily prove it, since $F = ma = -kx$ for a spring. Doubling the mass would double the force, and thereby double the displacement x. The spring constant is just that, a constant, and will not change unless you use a different type of spring.

40. C: From the question, doubling distance would lower the gravitational force by a factor of $\frac{1}{4}$, since the force is proportional to $\frac{1}{R^2}$. The gravitational potential would be $\frac{1}{2}$ of the original because it is proportional to $\frac{1}{R}$. Therefore, the ratio of the new force to the new potential would be $\frac{1}{4} \div \frac{1}{2}$, or $\frac{1}{2}$ of the original ratio.

41. A: The total energy of an isolated system is always conserved. However, the mechanical energy may not be, since some mechanical energy could be converted into radiation (light) or heat (through friction). According to Einstein's famous equation $\text{E} = \text{mc}^2$, where E is energy, m is mass, and c is the speed of light, energy can be converted into mass, and vice versa (like in nuclear reactions). This does not affect the conservation of energy law, however, since the mass is considered to have an energy equivalent. This equation does not tell anything about the mechanical energy of a particle; it just shows how much energy would be generated if the mass was converted directly into energy.

42. D: Answers A, B, and C all shed light on what conservative forces are but do not answer the question of why the work on an object doesn't depend on its path. Friction is a force that causes kinetic energy to be lost and where the amount of loss depends on the path taken. Work can be expressed in multiple ways, including as the sum of potentials, and all that matters is the beginning and ending position. Think of this in terms of gravity, gravitational potential energy, and the work done by gravity. In this case, $W = \Delta PE = -mg\Delta h$, where Δh is the change in an object's height. Dividing work by the change in position shows $\Delta PE/\Delta h = -mg$. Since $-mg$ is a force, you can say $F = \Delta PE/\Delta h$, or the force equals the work, or change in potential energy, divided by its change in position; the path taken is not a factor.

43. B: Power is the amount of work done divided by the time it took to do the work. A kilowatt-hour is a unit of work. A 5 Kw engine running for 12 hours produces $5 \times 12 = 60$ kilowatt-hours of work. At \$0.06 per Kw-h, this is $60 \times 0.06 = \$3.60$. The other answers all arise from math mistakes.

44. B: The wavelength is the distance (often in meters) between two peaks or two troughs of a wave. In this case, that distance is labeled as 4 meters. The height of the wave from the center is the amplitude. This wave has an amplitude of 5 meters, which is half of the total vertical distance from the top of one peak to the bottom of a trough. 2 meters represents $\frac{1}{2}$ of the wavelength, which would be the horizontal distance across a single peak or trough, but not from peak to peak.

45. D: The phase of a wave changes as the wave moves. When measured in radians, the phase fluctuates between 0 and 2π radians. It is this fluctuating angle that allows two identical waves to be either in or out of phase, depending on whether their sinusoidal forms are matching or not when they cross. Answers A and B are meant to emulate the wave's amplitude and wavelength, both of which are measured in units of distance (meters, for example) and not radians.

46. D: The jumper's weight is $9.8 \text{ m/s}^2 \times 100 \text{ kg} = 980$ Newtons. Insert the weight—a force—into the equation $F = kx$, where k is the spring constant and x is the displacement from rest of the spring. The displacement here is 5 meters. 20 meters is unnecessary information, and just a measure of how long the spring is, not how far it was displaced. $k = F/x = 980 \text{ N}/5 \text{ meters} = 196 \text{ N/m}$.

47. C: The phase will cycle through 2π radians. Therefore, $(5.0 \text{ Hz})t = 2\pi$ and $t = \frac{2\pi}{5} = 1.26$ seconds.

48. C: Although the acceleration of a falling object is constant (9.8 m/s^2), this is not true for a pendulum. The total force on a simple pendulum is the resultant of the force of gravity on the bob acting downward and the tension in the string. When the pendulum is at the bottom of its swing, the net force is zero ($tension = weight$), although the bob does have a velocity. At the top of its swing, when it's changing direction, the tension is least. Therefore, the net force is greatest here, too. The bob is stationary momentarily at its highest level. Since $F = ma$, a large force means that the acceleration here is highest, too.

49. A: The Doppler effect shows that light/radiation from an object moving away has a longer wavelength. A car moving towards the RADAR gun would have a shorter wavelength. Since $c = vf$ (where c = speed of light, v = wavelength and f = frequency), increasing the wavelength would cause the frequency to become smaller.

50. B: The speed of a wave is the product of its wavelength and frequency. $V = \lambda f$. Here, $V = 3 \times 12 = 36 \text{ m/s}$.

51. A: The displacement of each wave is A and -A, so the net displacement is A + (-A) = 0; the amplitude of the resulting wave would be the maximum absolute displacement, which is 0 at this point. Had the waves both been peaking, the sum would be $A + A = 2A$. If they had both been at a minimum, the sum would be $-2A$.

52. C: As the amplitude of the pendulum increases due to resonance, it will swing higher. However, the period of a pendulum is not connected to how high it swings. Only the length of the pendulum affects its period. The length of a pendulum will not be affected by how high it's swinging or whether it's in resonance.

53. A: A standing wave remains stationary, and the fixed points at both ends are the wave's nodes. Nevertheless, a standing wave with nodes at both ends of the string can have several forms. It may have one anti-node (i.e., it will arc across), two anti-nodes (this looks like a sine wave), three anti-nodes (with 1.5 sine waves), etc. However, waves with just one anti-node will have the longest wavelength and thus the smallest frequency. For a wave with one anti-node, the string will have only one-half of a wave, so 20 m represents a half-wavelength, and the full wavelength is 40 m. Using the wave equation ($v = \lambda f$) gives the correct answer. $f = \frac{v}{\lambda} = \frac{4\text{ m/s}}{40\text{ m}} = 0.1$ Hz.

54. C: If the waves are 500 Hz and 504 Hz, they will have $504 - 500 = 4$ beats per second. By definition, this would have a frequency of 4 Hz. This would mean 0.25 seconds between beats.

55. A: Refraction occurs when a wave enters a new medium. The boundary between the old medium and the new medium produces a reflected wave and a refracted wave. Since the medium is different, the speed and direction of the refracted wave changes. This changes the wavelength, but the frequency remains the same. The angle of reflection depends on the angle of incidence of the wave that strikes the boundary. The angle of refraction depends partly on this angle of incidence, but also on the indices of refraction of the two substances. Although refraction is defined as a wave changing direction when it enters a new substance, a wave will not change direction if it enters this new medium exactly perpendicular to the surface.

56. B: When a tuning fork vibrates, it creates areas of condensation (higher pressure) and rarefaction (lower pressure) that propagate through the air because of the air's elasticity. The distance between the condensations or rarefactions is the wavelength of the sound. The amplitude of the sound is half the difference between the pressure of the condensation and the pressure of the rarefaction. Loudness and power are both logarithmic measures that depend on the amplitude, but are not directly proportional to it. For example, doubling the amplitude will not double the loudness or power; those quantities will increase just slightly.

57. A: Sound travels much faster through helium than through air. Generally, the speed of sound can be calculated by $v = \sqrt{k \times \frac{P}{\rho}}$, where k is the heat capacity ratio for the gas (the heat capacity at constant pressure divided by the heat capacity at constant volume), P is pressure, and ρ is density. Since helium has a much lower density, it would have a higher speed.

58. A: The frequency of a sound wave directly determines its pitch. We say the pitch of 480 Hz is higher than the pitch of 440 Hz. High and low are the words we use to describe pitch. Overtones refer to the frequencies above the fundamental frequency in a musical instrument. Two singers singing the same note at the same loudness will sound different because their voices have different timbres.

59. C: Three full waves fit into the pipe, according to the question description. The wavelength of the third harmonic in this pipe organ is $\frac{1.2\text{ m}}{1.5\text{ waves}} = 0.8$ m. Using the wave equation ($v = \lambda f$), $f = \frac{340\text{ m/s}}{0.8\text{ m}} = 425$ Hz.

60. A: For standing waves, the string must be fixed at both ends. The wavelength at the fundamental frequency is 4 meters and the wavelength when the string resonates at the fourth harmonic is 1 meter. Using the wave equation $v = \lambda f$, the frequency at the fourth harmonic is $\frac{v}{1\text{ m}} = 50$ Hz. Hence the necessary speed is 50 m/s. Furthermore, the mass per unit length is $\frac{0.01\text{ kg}}{2\text{ meters}} = 0.005$ kg/m. Thus, the tension is the string is $v^2 \times \mu = 50^2 \times 0.005 = 12.5$ newtons.

61. A: When light waves hit a convex lens, they are refracted and converge. A convex lens curves or bulges with the middle being thicker and the edges thinner. A magnifying glass is an example. Light rays are refracted by different amounts as they pass through the lens. After light rays pass through, they converge at a point called the focus. An object viewed with a magnifying glass looks bigger because the lens bends the rays inward. Choice B would indicate a concave lens as it would cause the light to be refracted and diverge. Light is not reflected in this case, so neither choice C nor D would be applicable.

62. B: The density of a homogeneous object, liquid, or gas is its mass divided by its volume, or the ratio of its mass to its volume. Density is inversely proportional to the volume and directly proportional to the mass. The ratio of the density of A to the density of B is 5 : 4 or $\frac{5}{4}$. Hence, the ratio of the volume of A to the volume of B is 4 : 5 or $\frac{4}{5}$. Alternatively, one could solve the equation $5V_A = 4V_B$.

63. C: If the sub stays at a constant depth, its buoyant force must be equal to its weight. If the buoyant force were larger, it would rise. If the buoyant force were lower, it would sink. All objects underwater experience a buoyant force, so it cannot be zero.

64. A: Pascal's law states that the pressure on the input piston is equal to the pressure on the output piston. (To move the truck, of course, the input piston moves a much greater distance than the output piston.) Since the pressure depends on the area of the pistons, and the area is πr^2, one needs only find the ratio of the two areas to find the necessary force. Since the diameter is twice the radius, one can simplify this step by taking the ratio of the square of the diameters. $\frac{2^2}{24^2} = 0.007$. Multiplying this by the weight of the car gets $0.007 \times 3{,}500\text{ N} = 24\text{ N}$. It is also important to note that the point of a hydraulic lift is to reduce the force, not increase it.

65. C: The pressure of water at a depth h is given by ρgh where ρ is the density of water. Here $P = (1{,}000\text{ kg/m}^3 \times 9.8\text{ m/s}^2 \times 14\text{ m}) = 1.37 \times 10^5\text{ N/m}^2$. To find the force of the water on the window, multiply this pressure by the window's area. $F = \pi(1\text{ m})^2 \times 1.37 \times 10^5\text{ N/m}^2 = 4.3 \times 10^5\text{ N}$.

66. B: To increase the flow rate, you'd want to: (1) reduce the length L of the pipe, (2) make the pipe wider, and (3) have a fluid with low viscosity (just think of how much slower a viscous fluid like molasses runs as compared to water). Answer B is the only answer that describes all of these changes.

67. C: In an ideal fluid, from the conservation of mass, ρvA is constant. Since the area (A) decreases by a factor $\frac{3^2}{5^2} = 0.36$, the speed increases by $\frac{5^2}{3^2}$. So $6\text{ m/s} \times \frac{5^2}{3^2} = 16.7\text{ m/s}$. Incompressible means the density (ρ) is a constant. An ideal fluid has no viscosity, there is no rotational flow, and the flow is the same throughout the liquid, so answer D is not correct.

68. D: Irrotational fluid flow consists of streamlines, which describe the paths taken by the fluid elements. The streamlines don't have to be straight lines because the pipe may be curved. Answer B describes the conditions for steady flow. The image of a paddle wheel may be used to explain irrotational flow, but the wheel will not turn about its own center due to vorticity. Rotational flow includes vortex motion, whirlpools, and eddies.

69. C: In a vacuum, the only forces acting on the molecules of aluminum are other aluminum molecules. Inside a fluid, the molecules of the fluid collide with the sides of the cube and exert a force on the surface causing the cube to shrink in size slightly. Also, the temperature of water deep in the ocean is very low. This causes the vibratory motion of the aluminum molecules to decrease, which decreases the dimensions of the cube.

70. A: When an external force deforms a solid material, it will return to its initial position when the force is removed. This is called elasticity and is exhibited by springs. If too much force is applied and the elastic limit is exceeded, the rod won't return to its original shape any longer. As with springs, the deformation is directly proportional to the stress. The elastic limit occurs in rods subjected to a tensile force when the strain stops being directly proportional to the stress. The typical pattern when the force increases is that the strain increases linearly, then it doesn't increase as much, and then it breaks.

71. B: Most substances contract when they freeze because the average distance between the atoms of the substance decreases. Water, on the other hand, forms a crystal lattice that is impacted by hydrogen bonding, and this creates gaps between the molecules when freezing. While the density of water is temperature dependent, it is not a linear relationship. While the internal energy does decrease as the water cools, this does not explain the expansion of freezing water.

72. D: The bulk modulus describes a substance's reaction to being squeezed and its change in volume, which directly affects its density. The elastic modulus is the ratio of stress to strain for an object. Young's modulus deals with the elasticity and length of an object. The shear modulus deals with the elasticity of a shape and the stress that's applied perpendicular to its surfaces.

73. B: If the charged object is negative, it will cause electrons in the neutral object to move away from the charged object. If the charged object is positive, it will attract electrons. In both cases, there will be an attractive force. There is also an induced repulsive force, but the repulsive force is less because the like charges are farther away. An object has a net charge because electrons have been added to a neutral object or electrons have been removed from the atoms, ions, or molecules in the object.

74. B: Although like charges do repel, and unlike charges do attract, the question is indirectly asking about the law of conservation of charge. In other words, when someone mentions electric charge being conserved, they are saying the net charge of system remains constant. Charge originates from electrons and protons is only partially true because there are other elementary particles with charge. Charge can be created or destroyed because a photon will produce an electron-positron pair. There is also the example of a proton and electron combining to form a neutron.

75. B: Answer B correctly states the definition of a conductor. Answer C is incorrect because a current will also flow in an insulator, for example, although that current will be very low. In metals, the current flow caused by an electric field is much greater than in an insulator or semiconductor because the electrons are not bound to any particular atom, but are free to move. Answer D is incorrect because a vacuum tube is a device that electrons can flow in, but a vacuum tube is not considered a conductor.

76. D: The third charge, which is positive, will be repelled by the charge of $+2q$ and attracted to the charge of $-q$. For this reason, the third charge can't be between the two other charges and have a net force of 0, since it would always jointly be pushed and pulled towards the negative charge. It must be past the more distant negative charge. If the charge were situated at a distance of $2d$ from the origin, which is distance d from the negative charge, it would have a repulsive force of $F = k(q)(2q)/(2d)^2$ and an attractive force of $F = k(q)(q)/(d)^2$, meaning the attractive force is still too small by half the repulsive force. Thus, the particle must be past the distance of $2d$, or (D). If you solve this distance quadratically, the particle is at $3.41d$.

77. C: The electric field at a point in space is the force acting on a small positive test charge divided by the magnitude of the test charge. Its units are newtons per coulomb and it is a vector pointing in the direction of the force. The electric field produced by a charge distribution refers to the electric fields at each point in space. All the electric field vectors are tangent to electric field lines or electric lines of force. The electric field produced by a charge distribution can be represented by all the electric field vectors. Or, it can be represented by electric field lines. In this case, the stronger the electric field the closer together the electric field lines are. Arrows on the lines indicate the direction of the electric field. Answer D is incorrect because the field is being represented by electric field lines, not electric field vectors.

78. B: In electrostatic equilibrium, excess charge on a conductor moves freely and redistributes itself so that it resides entirely on the outer surface. For a spherical conductor, symmetry causes the charge to spread uniformly over the surface, making B correct. Option A is incorrect because charge does not remain throughout the volume. Option C is incorrect because charge will not leave the sphere without a path such as grounding. Option D is incorrect because the electric field at the surface of a conductor is perpendicular, not tangent.

79. B: The direction of the electric field is the same as the direction of the force on a positive test charge. Moving a negative charge in the direction of the electric field requires an external force to oppose the electric field. This would increase the electron's potential energy.

80. D: A dipole—meaning two poles—can be either electric or magnetic and represents a pair of opposite charges with equal magnitude present in the same material. Dipoles are important in chemistry because many molecules, water for example, are polarized. The oxygen side of a water molecule has a concentration of negative charge, and the hydrogen side has a concentration of positive charge even though the molecule is neutral overall. The charges in nonpolar molecules are uniformly distributed throughout the molecule and thus they don't have any polarity.

81. A: Since like charges repel and opposite charges attract, putting a dipole in an electric field would cause the dipole to orient so that its negative side will point towards the electric field's positive side. Since electric fields flow from positive towards negative, an electric field pointing from south to north could be caused by positive charges in the south and negative charges in the north. Consequently, the dipole will line up opposite to this, with the positive charge on the north side. Answer B is not correct because such an orientation would be unstable. The least disturbance would cause the dipole to flip 180°.

82. B: The electric potential, which comes from the electrostatic potential energy, is the potential of a charged particle in an electrical field. The stronger the field or the higher the charge, the higher the potential. So putting a point charge near a dipole will create a potential, depending on how strong the dipole's field is. For a potential of 0, you would need to be far from the dipole, so its electric field strength was effectively 0. At an infinite distance from a dipole, the distance between the charges is approximately 0 meters, so the net charge is 0 coulombs.

83. C: This is a classroom demonstration of electrostatics. The paper is initially charged by induction and is attracted to the comb. When in contact with the comb, electrons migrate from the paper to the comb and the paper acquires a positive charge. Answer B might be true, but the transfer of electrons from the paper to the comb occurs before the transfer of electrons from the air to the comb.

84. B: This is Gauss's law, which concerns electric field lines. Electric field lines leave positive charges and enter negative charges. Electric field lines entering a surface are positive, and electric field lines leaving a surface are negative. If there is no charge inside the surface, the sum of the electric field lines is zero. Coulomb's law refers to attractive force between any two charged particles. Faraday's law regards the creation of electric fields from moving magnetic fields. The Biot-Savart law concerns the creation of magnetic fields from moving charges.

85. C: The force $F = qvB\sin\theta = (1.6 \times 10^{-19}\text{ coulombs})(8.0 \times 10^{6}\text{ m/s})(0.5\text{ T})\sin(45°) = 4.5 \times 10^{-13}\text{ N}$.

86. B: For a positively charged particle, you would use the right hand rule (RHR) to solve this. Since this is an electron, you can either use the left hand rule, or use the RHR and switch the direction of the inducted force. The RHR gives you the direction of a force exerted by a magnetic field on a magnetic field. Holding your right hand flat, the fingers point in the direction of the velocity of a positive charge, the palm points in the direction of the magnetic field, and the thumb points in the direction of the magnetic force. For a negative charge, the force is in the opposite direction, or downward in this case.

87. B: A moving electron produces a circular magnetic field that is perpendicular to the velocity of the particle. Since the magnetic field produced by the electron exerts a magnetic force towards the electron, the charge on the particle is positive. This conclusion requires the correct application of the right-hand rule for the creation of a magnetic field by a current (thumb in the direction of the velocity of a positive charge with fingers curling in the direction of the magnetic field) and the right-hand rule for the magnetic force on a moving charge (fingers in the direction of the positively charged particle's velocity, thumb in the direction of the magnetic force, and palm in the direction of the magnetic field). Answer D is wrong because there are no particles with only a north pole or a south pole. There may be a force between the electron and the particle if the particle is a tiny magnet, but the direction of the force would depend on the magnet's orientation, and hence answer A is wrong.

88. A: Solenoids create a magnetic field inside the coils. Outside the solenoid, the magnetic field is practically zero, so increasing the number of coils won't have much effect on the exterior field strength. Inside the coils, increasing the number and density of coils increases the field strength.

89. C: In a vacuum, the speed of light has nothing to do with its wavelength, frequency, or color. It's a constant 3×10^8 m/s. When light travels through a medium other than a vacuum, such as glass or a prism, it slows down, and different colors of light travel at slightly different speeds in different media. However, in most physics problems, you should treat all light as traveling at the same speed.

90. B: Although the wavelength of light is related to its color, the frequency really determines light's color. For example, light slows down when it enters water. This doesn't change the frequency or the color of light, but it does change its wavelength. The fact that light sometimes acts like a wave and sometimes acts like particles is called "duality." The energy of light can be expressed as $E = \text{h}\nu$, where h is the Plank's constant and ν is the frequency.

91. C: Radio waves have the lowest frequency and the longest wavelength. Microwaves also have low frequencies and long wavelengths compared to visible light. X-rays are highly energetic and have higher frequencies and smaller wavelengths than visible light.

92. D: "Conventional current" -- as is typically used in physics and elsewhere -- is the flow of positive charges from the positive to negative sides of a battery. In reality, protons don't actually move through a wire. Negatively charged electrons move, so conventional current really reflects the effective positive charge that's created by electrons moving in the opposite direction. Normally, the wide side of the battery represents the positive side, so conventional current would start from the wide side and move around until it reached the narrow side of the battery. Here, the batteries aren't labeled with positive or negative. However, that doesn't matter, since the batteries are oriented in opposite directions. If they had the same exact voltage, no current would flow. However, if one battery has a higher voltage than the other, the higher voltage battery would dominate the direction of current flow. Since you don't know the voltage of the batteries, you cannot determine the direction of current flow.

93. D: Current can be expressed as the flow of charge per time, which Answer A expresses. Answer B follows from the units in Ohm's law, V = IR. Answer C represents the number of electrons flowing per second and this corresponds to a charge flow because each electron carries the same elementary charge (so current = electrons per second × electron charge). Answer D is the only incorrect way of expressing current, although watts per volts would be an acceptable way to express amperes, which follows from the Power equation P = IV.

94. A: In a Zn-Cu battery, the zinc terminal has a higher concentration of electrons than the copper terminal, so there is a potential difference between the locations of the two terminals. This is a form of electrical energy brought about by the chemical interactions between the metals and the electrolyte the battery uses. Creating a circuit and causing a current to flow will transform the electrical energy into heat energy, mechanical energy, or another form of electrical energy, depending on the devices in the circuit. A generator transforms mechanical energy into electrical energy, and a transformer changes the electrical properties of a form of electrical energy.

95. C: Ohm's law is that V = IR. Answer C is the only relation that holds true using this equation. If the resistance doesn't change, increasing the current on the right side must cause the voltage to also increase on the left side.

96. B: Since the ammeter is connected in series, it will slightly increase the total circuit resistance, and the current in the resistor will be decreased. However, ammeters have a very small resistance so as to draw as little current as possible. That way, measuring the current doesn't significantly affect the amount of current traveling through a circuit. Voltmeters, on the other hand, are connected in parallel and have a high resistance.

97. B: For resistors in series, the total resistance is the sum of their individual resistances. For resistors in parallel, the total resistance is given by $\frac{1}{R} = \frac{1}{R_1} + \frac{1}{R_2} + \cdots$. First, the bottom two resistors have a total resistance of $2\ \Omega + 4\ \Omega = 6\ \Omega$. Then add this in parallel with the 3 Ohm resistor. $\frac{1}{R} = \frac{1}{3} + \frac{1}{6} = \frac{1}{2}$. So $R = 2\ \Omega$ for the bottom three elements. To find the total resistance, add this in series to the top resistor, for a total $R = 10\,\Omega + 2\Omega = 12\Omega$.

98. A: Wires have the least resistance when they are short and fat. This is expressed as $R = \frac{\rho L}{A}$, where ρ is the resistivity of the substance, L is the length and A is the area. Since both wires are tungsten, they must have the same resistivity. So doubling the length and area adds a factor of 2 to both the top and bottom of the equation, giving no change in overall resistance.

99. C: A capacitor connected to a battery with a small internal resistance will charge up very quickly because of the high current flow. Once the potential difference on the two plates becomes equal to the emf of the battery, the electrons will stop flowing from the positive plate to the negative plate and the capacitor will be fully charged up. Connecting the capacitor to a battery with a greater emf will cause the plates to acquire a greater charge. However, the charge is directly proportional to the voltage. The capacitance is the ratio of charge to voltage and depends only on the physical characteristics of the capacitor.

100. B: Answers A and C are wrong because they don't have the units of energy (joules). To make things easier, the correct answer follows the same form as other kinds of energy ($KE = \frac{1}{2}mv^2$, a spring's potential energy is $\frac{1}{2}kx^2$, etc.) The capacitance is defined as $\frac{Q}{V}$, so the energy is proportional to QV. The potential at a point in space is determined by the concentration of charge at that point, but the potential difference $\left(V = \frac{\text{work}}{\text{charge}}\right)$ is defined in terms of the motion of a small test charge. At the very beginning of the process of charging up a capacitor, the work needed to move a test charge from the positive plate to the negative plate is 0 volts. As the capacitor charges up, more energy is required to move the charge because the charge is repelled by the negative plate. The total energy stored is $Q \times$ average voltage. Since the voltage increases linearly, the average voltage is $\frac{1}{2}\ V$.

101. A: Since these capacitors are connected in series you must add the reciprocals of their capacitance. $\frac{1}{C_{\text{total}}} = \frac{1}{C_1} + \frac{1}{C_2}$. So $\frac{1}{C_{total}} = \frac{1}{3} + \frac{1}{6} = \frac{1}{2}$. Thus $C_{\text{total}} = 2\ \mu\text{F}$.

102. C: When capacitors are connected in parallel the voltage drop across each capacitor is equal to the electromotive force of the battery ($V = V_1 = V_2$). Because these capacitors are in parallel, you can simply add their capacitances to find the total capacitance.

103. A: The current that flows in the resistor connected to the battery without the capacitor is 5×10^{-5} ampere. When the battery is disconnected this is the initial current as the electrons flow from the negative plate through the resistor to the positive plate. As electrons build up on the positive plate, the current decreases. The decrease is exponential, so the capacitor never fully loses its charge. Answer B is the time constant for the RC circuit (resistance × capacitance). After 30 seconds, the current is 37% of its initial value. When the time lapsed is three times RC, the current will be reduced to 95%. Within a short time, the current will be so small it will not be measurable with an ammeter, although it will technically never fully discharge.

104. B: Power is the rate at which work is done. It can be expressed as $P = VI$ or $P = IR^2$. With 10 volts and 50 watts, the current is $I = \frac{P}{V} = \frac{50\text{ w}}{10\text{ v}} = 5$ amps. Current is measured in coulombs/second, watts in joules/second, and volts in joules/coulomb. Answer D is equivalent to 5 amps since the charge on an electron is 1.6×10^{-19} coulombs.

105. A: The maximum current is derived from Ohm's law. $I = \frac{V}{R} = \frac{40\text{ V}}{20\text{ ohms}} = 2$ amps. However, because this is an alternating current, the instantaneous current actually fluctuates between +2 amps and –2 amps. Electrons effectively move back and forth. This means the average current is 0 amps.

106. D: For constructive interference, the waves must arrive having the same phase. Therefore, neither Answers A or B can be correct. Constructive interference occurs when the waveforms add together, producing a maximum that is twice as intense as either of the individual waves. Answer C would cause the waves to be out of phase by 1, 3, 5 or 7 (etc.) half-wavelengths, meaning the waves would be out of phase by a half-wavelength. Only Answer D assures that the two waves arrive in phase.

107. B: The two slits cause the light beams to diffract, that is, spread out instead of traveling in a straight line. As a result, there are two light beams superimposed on one another. When the two light beams constructively interfere, there are bright lines, and when the two light beams destructively interfere, there are dark lines. A chromatic aberration has to do with blurring through a lens due to different colors of light. Doppler shift affects the wavelength of light from moving sources. Total internal reflection is 100% reflection of light at the boundary between certain materials.

108. A: Diffraction gratings produce so much destructive interference that large distances separate the bright lines due to interference. This means diffraction gratings can be used to separate light consisting of different wavelengths. Answer B is wrong because blue light, which has a shorter wavelength than red light, refracts and diffracts less than red light. The greater the wavelength of light, the more it changes direction when it hits an edge.

109. A: Polarization is a property of transverse waves when the medium vibrates in the direction perpendicular to the direction of propagation of energy. A polarizer orients these waves so they're all oscillating in the same direction. Polarization is a property of waves, not particles, so the particle nature of light cannot be used to polarize light. Nor are there tiny holes in a polarizer, although there are thin lines. The fact that light travels in a vacuum means that light does not need a medium, but does not affect polarization. Also, light travels in transverse, not longitudinal waves.

110. C: The emission of light is caused by photons of a specific frequency striking gas molecules, which excites their electrons and eventually causes them to emit light. Since this light comes in very specific colors, it implies that light comes is specific quanta. The ultraviolet catastrophe refers to the frequency distribution of light emitted by a blackbody. A black body is, basically, a hot object that emits radiation in a predictable pattern. The threshold frequency refers to the photoelectric effect. The stability of atoms is a quantum phenomenon; however, it is only indirectly connected to the existence of light quanta.

111. B: Laser is an acronym for "light amplification by stimulated emission of radiation." Lasers produce light because the substance used goes into a relatively stable excited state before emitting light. In phosphorescence, a substance absorbs light and goes into a relatively stable excited state. Light is re-emitted at a later point in time. Radioactivity produces different types of radiation from unstable nuclei. Sunlight comes from nuclear reactions in the Sun. Blackbody radiation comes from hot materials and not from the transition of atoms from a higher energy state to a lower energy state.

112. B: Specular reflection occurs with smooth surfaces such as mirrors or a water puddle. All of the light is not necessarily reflected because there can be refraction and absorption. Answer A is wrong because a rough surface consists of many smooth surfaces oriented in different directions, so the light will not necessarily reflect at the same angle as incidence. Note, however, that for each small surface on a rough tabletop, for example, the angle of incidence is equal to the angle of reflection.

113. C: The angles of incidence and refraction are defined as the angle made by the rays with a line perpendicular to the surface. The angles of incidence and refraction are given by Snell's law: $n_1 \sin \theta_1 = n_2 \sin \theta_2$. In this case, because glass has a higher index of refraction (n) than air, the angle of refraction will be smaller than the angle of incidence. Increasing the angle of incidence by 5 degrees will increase the angle of refraction, but it will still be below the original 45°. Proving this with Snell's law: $1.0 \times \sin(50) = 1.3 \sin(\theta)$, so $\sin \theta = 0.59$ and $\theta = 36°$.

114. C: A ray of sunlight consists of many different colors of light. The speed of red light in water is slightly greater than the speed of violet light, so the angle of refraction of violet light is greater than that of red light. This causes the light to separate and creates a spectrum of colors, like in a prism. Raindrops do exhibit total internal reflection for all the wavelengths inside the droplet, although this is not what causes the rainbow. Instead, this causes a second refraction as the sunlight emerges from the water droplet, which can sometimes be seen in nature as a "double rainbow."

115. C: Snell's law is $n_1 \sin\theta_1 = n_2 \sin\theta_2$. This means the angle of refraction is greater than or less than the angle of incidence depending on which index of refraction is bigger. It also gives the critical angle at which there is no refracted beam. This only happens when light is in a substance with a high index of refraction and strikes a substance with a lower index of refraction at a large angle of incidence. The fact that light slows down when leaving a vacuum, coupled with the wave nature of light, leads to Snell's law. It is not relevant to understanding total internal reflection, that light is made of quanta, or that light consists of transverse electric and magnetic fields.

116. D: Parallel rays striking a concave mirror intersect at the focal point. If the rays weren't parallel—say they were both coming from an object near the mirror—then they would intersect elsewhere, depending on the focal length and their distance from the mirror. For example, intersecting at infinity be correct if the rays both started at the focal point. For an object between the focal point and the mirror, the virtual image is created by extending the rays geometrically behind the mirror. The center of curvature is at the center of the sphere that defines the spherical mirror and is equal to twice the focal length.

117. C: Convex is the opposite of concave. A convex mirror bulges outward like the outside of a sphere. They always produce a small image that is right side up. These images are always virtual, also, meaning the image appears to lie behind the mirror. A convex mirror with an infinite radius of curvature is essentially a plane mirror.

118. C: A magnifying glass is a convex lens, just like the lens used in a telescope or microscope. For objects located beyond the focal point of the lens, the image is inverted (upside down) and real. For objects located between the focal point and the lens, the image is virtual and erect (right side up). The focal length is determined by the radii of curvature of the two lens surfaces and the index of refraction of the lens material.

119. D: Since the lens is convex, the focal length is positive and the image will appear behind the lens. You can use the lens equation to solve this. $\frac{1}{f} = \frac{1}{o} + \frac{1}{i}$, where f is the focal length, i is the image location and o is the object location. Since the object is in front it has a positive sign. $\frac{1}{10}\text{ cm} = \frac{1}{20}\text{ cm} + \frac{1}{i}$, so $\frac{1}{i} = \frac{1}{20}$ and $i = 20$ cm. The positive sign for the image means that it is behind the lens.

120. A: The magnification of a lens can be calculated from its image distance, i, and its object distance, o. $M = \frac{i}{o}$. Here $M = \frac{19}{49} = 0.39$.

121. C: Adding a second convex lens will shorten the focal length, thereby eliminating answers A and B. To find this total, you need to add their reciprocals: $\frac{1}{f} = \frac{1}{30} + \frac{1}{30} = \frac{2}{30}$. So $f = \frac{30}{2} = 15$ cm. You would follow this same procedure if the second lens had been concave, except the focal length would then have been a negative number.

122. B: This question is asking about a concave mirror, not a lens. Since light does not pass through a mirror—it only reflects off of it—the different colors of light all bend the same amount. If light was passing through a lens, the different colors would bend slightly different amounts, causing chromatic aberration. That's not the case here. Spherical aberration occurs because the focal point of the mirror changes slightly as you move away from the center (optical axis). Astigmatism occurs when incident rays are not parallel to the optical axis. A circular beam, striking a lens or mirror at an angle to the optical axis, will become a parabola. Distortion concerns magnification and occurs in both mirrors and lenses.

123. D: All of these principles are true except Snell's Law. Snell's law is $1.0 \times \sin(\theta_{\text{incident}}) = n \times \sin(\theta_{\text{refraction}})$ for a ray striking a transparent substance from a vacuum. It is true for all rays striking a lens. However, this is not a principle used in ray diagrams. Although light is bent when it enters the lens, as Snell's Law describes, it returns to its original direction when it leaves the lens. To simplify this process, it's often best to assume that a lens is infinitely thin when solving many physics problems.

124. C: To find the total magnification, multiply the magnification of the three lenses. The magnification of a lens is the ratio of the object size to the image size and is the negative of the ratio of the object distance to the image distance. The sign is positive if the image is upright and negative if the image is inverted. Answer A comes from adding the magnifications instead of multiplying the magnifications. Answer D has the wrong the sign.

125. A: When electrons drop to the ground level, they emit energy. In the same way, they can absorb energy and jump from the ground state to an excited state, or from an excited state to a more excited state. To completely ionize a Hydrogen atom — for an electron to jump from the ground level and completely escape— takes 13.2 eV. However, it takes less energy to simply jump from the ground level to the first excited state. However, most of the energy needed to escape is used for that first jump. Answer C would be correct if the transition was from $n = 3$ to $n = 2$. Answer B would be correct if the hydrogen atom in the ground state was ionized by the absorption of a photon. Answer D would be correct if the hydrogen atom absorbed a photon and became more excited.

126. C: In 2.4×10^4 years, 50% of the substance will have decayed. In another half-life, half of this will be gone, or 75%. 87.5% represents 3 half-lives, or a total of $3 \times 2.4 \times 10^4$ years $= 7.2 \times 10^4$ years.

127. B: Fission occurs when the nucleus breaks up into two smaller nuclei. When certain nuclear isotopes absorb a neutron, they become unstable and split, starting the process of fission. The average binding energy per nucleon increases with a fission reaction, and the two new nuclei are more stable than the initial nucleus. The increase in binding energy comes from the changes in mass of the protons and neutrons (note: both protons and neutrons are nucleons). The release of energy is part of the fission reaction, but this does not explain why the fission reaction occurs.

128. C: Sunlight consists of electromagnetic radiation in the form of photons. Sunlight is produced when hydrogen nuclei fuse to form helium. This nuclear reaction is called fusion. Fission occurs when a nucleus disintegrates into two smaller nuclei. In both fission and fusion, energy is released because the binding energy per nucleon increases. This decreases the mass of the nuclei.

129. A: In a nuclear reaction, be it fission or fusion, matter is converted into energy. Einstein first postulated the law of energy-mass conservation using the equation $E = mc^2$, where m is mass, E is energy and c is the speed of light. Looking closely at this equation shows that a tiny amount of matter can produce a large amount of energy, which is why nuclear reactions are so energetic.

130. C: Protons and neutrons are both considered nucleons. The number of nucleons in a nucleus is called the mass number. Isotopes of the same element have different mass numbers. But since they are the same element, they must have the same atomic number, which is equal to the number of protons. Thus, only the number of neutrons changes, since electron's mass is so low that it doesn't have much effect on the mass number of an element. Unless they are also ionized, they would have the same number of protons and electrons.

131. C: When a nucleus emits an alpha particle, its nucleon number decreases by four. An alpha particle is two protons bound together with two neutrons. Since it doesn't have any electrons, it has a charge of +2. Emitting an alpha particle causes the atomic number of the nucleus to decrease by two, and its mass to decrease by approximately four atomic mass units. Exactly how much the mass decreases depends on the binding energies of the two nuclei. Its charge decreases by two.

132. C: Cobalt-63 has too many neutrons to be stable. By emitting a beta particle (aka an electron, one of the neutrons in the cobalt is converted to a proton, thereby maintaining the mass number but changing the atomic number from 27 (cobalt) to 28 (nickel). In addition, some energy is radiated away in the form of gamma radiation. Electron emission is usually associated with the emission of gamma rays because the daughter nucleus is not likely to be in a ground state. The daughter nucleus, in other words, is likely to be unstable and emit a gamma ray.

133. A: An inch is about 2.54 cm = 25.4 mm = 2.54×10^{-5} km = 2.54×10^{-2} m.

134. D: There are only 2 significant digits in A. Answers B and C have 5 significant digits. Answer D has 6 significant digits. Trailing zeroes after a decimal point are considered significant because it implies a certain level of specificity. Trailing zeroes in a whole number that does not contain a decimal are not significant.

135. C: In physics, a systematic error is a consistent difference between the measured value and the true (or accepted) value. Here, all three measurements are 2.1 lb above the true weight of 150 lb, so the systematic error is +2.1 lb. Because all readings are the same to the scale's resolution, the random error is negligible, so it cannot be 2.1 lb and choice A is not correct.

136. D: Because you do not know the exact distribution of heights, answer D is correct. The deviation of a measurement is the difference between the mean (average measurement) and the measurement. The standard deviation is the square root of the mean of the deviations squared. On average, about 68% of a sample will fall within one standard deviation. So if the standard deviation is 0.05 meters, ABOUT 68% of the students will stand between 1.64 ± 0.05 meters. But this is only true if you have a fairly normal distribution of values. Similarly, this does not mean that half of the students are necessarily taller or shorter than the average. Since it is an average, you could have a class with a 20-foot giant and seven 5-foot-tall students and have an average that is a fairly large 6.857 feet. Answer C refers to the Mode, which looks for the most popular value.

Online Resources

Due to our efforts to try to keep this book to a manageable length, we've created a link that will give you access to all of your online resources:

mometrix.com/resources719/ftcephysics

It's Your Moment, Let's Celebrate It!

Share your story @mometrixtestpreparation